Sair Linux and GNU Certification®
Level I: Installation and Configuration

Tobin Maginnis

Wiley Computer Publishing

John Wiley & Sons, Inc.

NEW YORK · CHICHESTER · WEINHEIM · BRISBANE · SINGAPORE · TORONTO

Publisher: Robert Ipsen
Editor: Cary Sullivan
Managing Editor: Micheline Frederick
Text Design & Composition: Benchmark Productions, Inc.

Designations used by companies to distinguish their products are often claimed as trademarks. In all instances where John Wiley & Sons, Inc., is aware of a claim, the product names appear in initial capital or all capital letters. Readers, however, should contact the appropriate companies for more complete information regarding trademarks and registration.

This book is printed on acid-free paper. ∞

Published by John Wiley & Sons, Inc.

Published simultaneously in Canada.

This publication is designed to provide accurate and authoritative information in regard to the subject matter covered. It is sold with the understanding that the publisher is not engaged in professional services. If professional advice or other expert assistance is required, the services of a competent professional person should be sought.

Library of Congress Cataloging-in-Publication Data:

Maginnis, Tobin.
    Sair Linux and GNU certification level I: Installation and configuration/Tobin Maginnis.
      p. cm.
    "Wiley computer publishing."
    ISBN 0-471-36978-0 (pbk.)
    1. Electronic data processing personnel--Certification. 2. Operating systems
(Computers)--Certification. 3. Linux.

QA76.3 .M3235 2000
005.4'469--dc21   99-049095
                                                            CIP

Printed in the United States of America.

10 9 8 7 6 5 4 3 2 1

Contents

Preface

At first glance, this may appear to be a "regular book," instead, it is a different kind of computer text that has evolved over the last few years called a "study guide." In the same way that *Cliff Notes* help students study for a college test, these study guides prepare computer professionals (candidates) to take a test. Upon passing a number of tests, these candidates earn a certificate which assists with job placement, promotions, and merit pay increases.

Compared to many other study guides, this book is also unusual. Other study guides focus on one computer vendor where as this book covers many distributions of Linux. Other study guides usually focus upon one product where we cover free, open source software packages (products). Finally, other study guides usually cover point-by-point user interaction with a vendor's product where as this one presents the common elements that describe all Linux distributions and the key differences among the more popular distributions.

Is this too much broad information for a candidate to absorb? Our experience says "no." People do not want to be told by a vendor that their particular Linux distribution is the best. They want to see the "big picture" and how each Linux distribution fits into the open source software landscape. They see the benefits of free, open source software and they want to maximize its use in their companies.

Therefore, this study guide contains a compendium of theory, principles and facts that relate to installation and configuration of Linux on the PC platform. The information is organized around a "knowledge array" that contains just the essential concepts and facts for installation and configuration. Information is presented in a no-frills fashion concept by concept. Chapters 1–6 traverse the first row of the knowledge array. Appendix A provides step by step installation instructions for four Linux distributions. Appendix B provides sample questions as a review of the material and self-assessment guide. And finally, there is a glossary of key terms and phrases that reviews concepts described in the text.

Acknowledgments

I am but a microscopic component in the mitochondria of one cell of the cooperative body of knowledge referred to as Linux. Therefore, it is a great honor for me to assist with the establishment of criteria for professional competency in free and open source software through these study guides and tests. Although responsibility for any mistakes rests on my shoulders, I would like to thank the following for their support in our endeavor: advisory board members: Jon "maddog" Hall, Bill Patton, Bruce Perens, Eric Raymond, and Richard Stallman. I also want to thank industry representatives: Graeme Newey, EXCOM Education; Evan Blomquist, Viking Systems; Adam Goodman, Linux Magazine; The Linux International Technical Board; Robert McMillan, Linux Magazine; and Stuart Trusty, Linux Labs.

Shaping mountains of trivia into some semblance of organization and working with the information so that it can be communicated quickly and effectively is the task of the Sair team and I am deeply indebted to them for all of their effort. They are Elizabeth Dillon, Lenny Sawyer, Kevin Seddon, John Weathersby, Jason McAfee, Andrew Neel, Sudharshan Vazhkudai, Nileshwar Dosooye, Billy Patton, Angus Tong, Carlos Pruitt, Stephen Goertzen, Allison Mull Howard, Flossie Pruitt, Julie Seay, Albert Phillips, and Tian Jin. Also, thanks to John Wiley and Sons Computer Publishing, especially Cary Sullivan, for their foresight, effort, and belief in the future of free, open source software.

Thanks must also go out the thousands of individuals that have participated in creating a free and open software system. But special thanks must go to key system architects: Ken Thompson and Dennis Ritchie, who co-developed many of the basic ideas now called Linux. To Robert Scheifler and James Gettys, who co-developed the X Window System. To Richard Stallman, who invented the GNU general public license. To Linus Trovalds, who forged an Internet community to build the kernel. And to the Linux distributions, who developed packages to distribute the software system called Linux.

Finally, thanks to my family (Lindsay, Meredith, Jordan, & Anneal) for enduring an absentee husband and father during this process.

Introduction

Welcome to the Level I Installation and Configuration study guide for Sair Linux and GNU certification. This is the first of four study guides for the Sair Linux and GNU Certified Administrator (LCA) certificate. The other three study guides are System Administration, Networking, and Security. The four tests may be taken in any order, but the study guide material is organized with the assumption that Installation is the first test taken, followed by the System Administration, Network, and Security tests.

Testing is done through Sylvan Prometric at any one of their 2400 testing sites. To take a test in the United States, simply call the Sylvan Prometric registration line at 1-888-895-6717. For test registration outside of the United States please visit www.linuxcertification.com/sylvanphone.php3 on the Web. The customer service representative will answer any test-taking questions, describe available testing centers in your area, and if requested, schedule an exam.

Passing either the 3X0-101 or the 3X0-102 exams will earn the Sair Linux and GNU Certified Professional (LCP) certificate. Completion of all four exams (the 3X0-101, the 3X0-102, the 3X0-103, and the 3X0-104) will earn the Sair Linux and GNU Certified Administrator (LCA) certificate.

Although the LCA will attest to a certificate-holder's knowledge and capability to administer a Linux system, there are two more certificates, the LCE and MLCE, that will confirm knowledge and skills in increasingly difficult Linux topic areas.

Minimum Candidate Requirements

The Sair Linux and GNU tests were not designed for the novice computer user. We assume that the candidate has approximately two years of computer experience and has experience in the configuration of one or more operating systems. For example, the candidate should be familiar with basic hardware concepts, such as CPU, cache, memory, interface adapters, hard disks, and network. The candidate should also be familiar with basic operating system concepts such as booting, file access, and device drivers. Finally, the candidate should know basic commands and the use of a Unix-type editor such as joe, pico, vi, or emacs.

Knowledge Matrix

The test is based upon the first row of the first array in the knowledge matrix described at www.linuxcertification.com. Examination topics are as follows:

Installation and Configuration vs. Theory of Operation

1.1.10   History of Open Source and Free Software
1. Historical trends in free software
2. Definition and cost of free software
3. Advantages and disadvantages of free software

1.1.20   The GNU General Public License (GPL)
1. A brief history of the GNU GPL
2. The use of copyright to enforce copyleft

1.1.30   Third Party Analysis of Open Source Software
1. The Microsoft Halloween memos and conclusions

1.1.40   Living with Free Software
1. The nature of free software development
2. The business of selling free software
3. Using software without warranty

1.1.50   Linux System Concepts
1. Modular structure of Linux
   a. Kernel
   b. Network
   c. Init
   d. Daemons
   e. User level system process (login, shells, utilities)
   f. The X Windows System
2. Preemptive multitasking software
3. Single user vs. multi-user software
4. Switching among virtual terminals and page scrolling
6. Command line administration vs. GUI system administration

1.1.60   Hardware Configuration Issues
1. IBM-PC system architecture
   a. System busses
   b. IO addresses
   c. IRQs
   d. DMA
   e. Shared memory
3. RAM requirements and configuration issues
4. The PC BIOS and the Linux kernel
5. Hard disk partitioning strategies

Installation and Configuration vs. Base System

Installation and Configuration vs. Shells and Commands

Installation and Configuration vs. System Utilities and Services

Installation and Configuration vs. Troubleshooting

Objectives

The Sair Linux and GNU installation and configuration test is design to assess the following objectives.

Theory of Operation

State the definition, origins, cost, and tradeoff of free software.
Compare proprietary versus open source software licenses.
List the GNU public license (GPL) principles.
Describe how to sell free software.

Describe the structural components of Linux.

Contrast multi-user, multitasking versus single-sequential user, multi-tasking.

Contrast command-line interpreters versus graphical user interfaces with tradeoffs.

List PC system architecture configuration issues.

Describe hard disk partitioning strategies.

Contrast video adapter versus monitor capabilities.

List the network configuration parameters.

Base System

List and give the tradeoff of installation media.

Explain the Linux device driver lag and give examples.

List the installation steps common to all distributions.

Contrast high volume Linux distributions and give tradeoffs.

Install four Linux distributions.

Describe the configuration tools COAS, Linuxconf, and Yast.

List the boot up sequence, log-in, and shut-down sequence.

Define "package" and describe how to use it.

Describe basic file system principles.

Explain the use of mounting versus the use of mtools for removable media.

List and describe the role of common directories.

List and describe the use of basic system navigation programs ps, kill, w, etc.

Describe the use and misuse of the superuser account.

List the steps in creating a user account.

Install, configure, and navigate two X11 window managers.

Shells and Commands

Describe shell configuration files.

Compare and contrast environmental versus shell variables.

Use commands that pass special characters among programs.

Use commands that allow programs to communicate.

Manipulate files and directories.

Use the shell for multitasking.

Describe common shell editing commands.

Use the following commands in isolation or in combination with each other: ls, cd, more, less, cp, mv, mkdir, rm, rmdir, ln, head, tail, file, grep, du, df, and zcat.

Use the following vi commands i, ZZ, :w, :w! :q!, dd, x, D, J.

System Utilities and Services

List and describe seven tools that provide information on other tools.
Describe and use LILO.
Install runtime device drivers.
Configure a printer capabilities file.
Configure a printer filter.
Use lpr, lpq, lprm, and lpc to control file printing.
List the sections of the X server configuration file.
Configure the X server video hardware.
Contrast xf86config, XF86Setup, Xconfiguator, and SaX.
Describe five components of the X Window system architecture.
List and give the tradeoffs of Afterstep, KDE, Window Maker, FVWM95, Enlightenment, and Blackbox.

Applications

Describe the general control of X11 desktops.
Describe Netscape functions, FTP functions, Telnet functions, and mail functions.
Contrast WYSIWYG versus mark-up word processing.
Contrast ApplixWare, WordPerfect, and StarOffice.
Contrast GIMP, X-Fig, and ImageMagick.

Troubleshooting

Describe the cause and solution to read errors.
Explain why FTP keeps missing certain files in group transfers.
Explain the problem and solution when LILO says LI.
Define rescue disk and describe three reasons for using it.
Explain how to get around a locked-up program.
List eight steps to resolve an unresponsive printer.
Explain why Linux may report the wrong time and describe how to fix the problem.
Describe how to reset the console screen, the keyboard repeat rate, and the num lock key.
Describe the role of system logging and how to use it for troubleshooting.

CHAPTER

1

Theory of Operation

Origins of Open Source and Free Software

To best appreciate the context from which the software system called Linux arises, we must first understand the history of sharing software. Two trends were evident back in the 1970s. One trend was the implicit cooperation among manufactures and their customers. The other trend began with AT&T's release of Version 6 Unix to universities.

Computer Manufacturer-Sponsored User Groups

Over the years, computer architecture and computer system packaging has gone through roughly three stages of evolution that can be characterized as main-frame, minicomputer, and microcomputer. Within each of these broad stages, manufacturers brought to market many types of computer architectures. Software written for one architecture could not be used on another. Consequently, in order to ease the transition to new architectures, manufacturers encouraged the sharing of free source code software through manufacturer-sponsored user groups. Typically, user groups maintained libraries of open source and free software that were shared among group members. Annual or semi-annual meetings were also held to discuss software.

AT&T's Free Distribution of Version 6 Unix

In the mid and late 1970s, AT&T was prevented by the FCC from competing in the computer industry. Hence, the company decided to distribute a then-unknown operating system called Version 6 Unix for study in universities and other four-year colleges. Version 6 Unix launched many significant events. Among the most notable is that it taught a generation of computer scientists practical OS concepts that otherwise would have remained theory for years to come. Version 6 Unix also became the starting point for other Unix variants, including BSD Unix.

Yet, AT&T retained a software license for Unix, which allowed them to control and market Unix in the future—so the software was not truly free. Nevertheless, the seminal concepts within, and the apparent open-source nature of Version 6 Unix acted to further encourage software development and sharing of source code that had begun years earlier in the manufacturer-sponsored user groups.

Advantages and Disadvantages of Free Software

In spite of AT&T and other software licenses, the idea of sharing source code to Unix utilities continued, and to one degree or another, Unix (and Linux) system administrators carry on this tradition today by developing their personal archive of favorite system programs downloaded from the Internet. This personal archive grows with time and is carried by the administrator from job to job, much in the same way any skilled tradesman would bring a set of tools to the job site.

> **Disadvantage of open source and free software.** The requirement of expert knowledge to maintain and administer such systems (that is, knowledge about how to uncompress, de-archive, compile, configure, and maintain large and complex subsystems called packages).

> **Advantage of open source and free software.** The time invested yields rich productivity benefits, allowing the system administrator to get a lot more done in the same amount of time than if traditional closed software products were used.

To drive this point home, there is an old joke that compares OSs to airline companies. A recent version of the joke goes like this:

Mac Airlines—All the stewards, captains, baggage handlers, and ticket agents look and act exactly the same. Every time you ask questions about details, you are gently but firmly told that you don't need to know, don't want to know, and everything will be done for you without your ever having to know, so just sit back, relax, and enjoy the ride.

MS-DOS Airlines—Everybody pushes the airplane until it glides, then they jump on and let the plane coast until it hits the ground again. Then they push again, jump on again, and so on.

Windows Airlines—The terminal is pretty and colorful, with friendly stewards, easy baggage check and boarding, and a smooth take-off. After about 10 minutes in the air, the plane explodes with no warning whatsoever.

Windows NT Airlines—Just like Windows Airlines, but costs more, uses much bigger planes, and takes out all the other aircraft within a 40-mile radius when it explodes.

Unix Air—Everyone brings one piece of the plane along when they come to the airport. They all go out on the runway and put the plane together piece by piece, arguing nonstop about what kind of plane they are supposed to be building. Eventually, the plane gets off the ground.

Linux Air—Disgruntled employees and customers of all the other OS airlines decide to start their own airline. They build the planes, ticket counters, and pave the runways themselves. They charge a small fee to cover the cost of printing the ticket, but you can also download and print the ticket yourself. When you arrive at the airport, you are given an airplane-install program and asked to setup the airplane. You find the questions on such things as wing configuration confusing but somehow you get through the setup process. When you board the plane, you are given a seat, four bolts, a wrench, and a copy of the seat-HOWTO.html. At first you have no idea what to do with the seat, but after tinkering with it you find the fully adjustable seat is very comfortable, the plane leaves and arrives on time without a single problem, the in-flight meal is wonderful. You try to tell customers of the other airlines about the great trip, but all they can say is, "You had to do what with the airplane?"

Of course, the latter two examples are based upon the idea of sharing source code, custom configuration, and being responsible for your own system maintenance.

The GNU General Public License

The GNU General Public License (GPL) was the brainchild of Richard Stallman, who came up with the GPL as a means for ensuring that free software would remain free and not be taken over by large companies and then restricted from public use. Stallman, referred to as the father of free software for this reason, gave birth to the idea of the GPL in 1984. He wanted to permit everyone to be able to participate in the cooperation that Version 6 Unix permitted for a relative few. Stallman believed that the GPL would contribute to the continued growth of communities of software developers and thus contribute to a more productive software environment, one that encourages the free sharing of ideas.

The GNU GPL, essentially, says that you are free to use the software anyway you see fit. Moreover, you may include the software in products and services being sold, as long as you observe two fundamental restrictions:

1. Only verbatim copies of software can be redistributed—this also means that all source code must be provided with the software.

2. If new software is added to the existing software, it must be prominently documented and also included with the original software.

   Disclaimer: Please note that this is a general summary of a precise legal document. Any action based upon the GNU GPL requires that the license be studied carefully.

To date, the GPL, in combination with use of the Internet, has been very successful in encouraging the proliferation of communities of software developers who share software products and ideas. The operating system called Linux arose from this environment, thanks to Richard Stallman and the GNU GPL.

The Use of Copyright to Enforce Copyleft

The genius of the GNU GPL is that with its use, free software is accompanied with a detailed software license that employs a strict copyright. To prevent the software from being taken over and kept from free public use, the license states that even though the software cannot be integrated and sold as some other software, it can be given to others. The use of a copyright in this manner runs counter to the traditional use of a copyright; hence, in the case of the GPL, it is referred to as a *copyleft*.

Said another way, copyleft creates a "ball of independent intellectual plasma." The plasma may be brought into your home or office to use in any way you wish; in fact, many not only use, but also improve the GPL software. However, since no one can control the plasma, it and any distributed improvements can be used by anyone, even your business competitors, for whatever role they may have in mind for the software.

The Microsoft Memorandums

A Microsoft memo leaked on Halloween eve 1998, referred to as the Halloween Memo, provides another perspective on open source and free software in general, and on Linux, one of the premiere examples, in particular. Even though there was only one memo leaked on Halloween eve, there are actually two lengthy and (one was leaked subsequently) detailed memos that describe Linux and the open source community and compare them to Microsoft, and both are generally referred to as the "Halloween Memos." Following are five of the Microsoft conclusions from these memos that are of interest:

1. The GNU GPL is unique. Of nine types of software licenses examined, the GNU GPL stood out as the most robust software license.

2. The GNU GPL provides long-term software survivability. GNU GPL free software has been able to survive as a long-term product where other forms of free software have failed to survive. It is thought that the GNU GPL allows software to flourish because (a) anyone may have access to the software, and (b) the GPL prevents the software from being subdivided into competing camps of developers. Even though this was not a consideration in the creation of the GPL license, it appears to have a significant effect on keeping developers sharing the same code base as the product evolves.

3. GPL open source software possesses superior quality. The GPL software is generally superior to Microsoft software.

4. GNU software tools and libraries propel development. The GPL software superiority is, in part, a result of the open source community employing a software development engine based upon standard GNU software tools and libraries that apply to all aspects of the operating system and applications. This is quite different from Microsoft where each development team may use its own unique set of development tools.

5. The open source community model leads to superior software. GNU GPL software superiority is also, in part, a result of the open source process that collects and harnesses the collective IQ of thousands of worldwide software developers employing peer-reviewed code, parallel development, and parallel debugging cycles.

Other GNU GPL Issues

The GPL will continue to change with time. The following series of questions have arisen, but there are no quick answers to these questions. As time goes on these issues will be addressed and refined as the GNU GPL continues to grow in acceptance.

GNU GPL Lip Service

Earlier we noted that the GNU GPL has two important provisions for any free software that it covers. Essentially, these are:

1. All code, including source, must be included in any redistribution of the software.

2. Any new code added to the software must be included in the redistribution.

Despite the intention of these provisions, some software vendors have managed to comply only with the letter of the license and not its spirit. For example, there have been vendors who have provided new source code that thwarts the spirit of the GNU GPL by making the new code intentionally unclear through the use of jumbled formatting, twisted logic, multi-use variables, and dead code.

GNU GPL Software Documentation

Another gray area concerns documentation. How much documentation should the software author provide with the source code? This becomes an even more pressing concern when confronted with the possibility of developing and marketing information manuals on the software. Then the question becomes how much information should the author offer in the form of software documentation and how much should be reserved for sale?

Although the GNU GPL does not address this issue, current practice favors traditional style source code commenting combined with the provision of Unix-style manual pages, at a minimum.

GNU GPL Software Contamination

Some open source software modules (for example, parts of the X11 system) have a copyright but no other restrictions. Thus, the software may be integrated and sold as another software product by a number of companies. In this way, each vendor's version of the free software competes for business in the open market.

It is said that GNU GPL will contaminate or poison X11 software since the use of GPL code anywhere in the proprietary product would require releasing other source code that directly uses the GNU GPL code.

GNU GPL Copyright Holder

Copyright plays a key role in copyleft but the copyright holder may decide to change his or her mind and re-issue new versions of the software under a different software license. What happens if the copyright owner dies and the copyright passes to the holder's estate? What happens if the copyright for a given software system is given to a not-for-profit organization and the organization decides to change its software licenses? What happens to GNU GPLed software when the copyright expires? These and other copyright issues have yet to be addressed in a general and systematic fashion.

Commercial Use of Free Software

People who are unfamiliar with free software usually assume that it is unfit for, or incompatible with, business use, but this could not be farther from the truth. Free software, however, will require that businesses think out of the box when upgrading the company software.

The Nature of Free Software Development

In addition to a deep appreciation for the work of those that have come before us, inherent characteristics of GNU GPLed software are as follows:

1. GPL software is continually modified and redistributed.
2. There is a strong sense of trust and community among those who use the software.
3. Individuals continue to improve the software (even though they do not own it).
4. It evolves into an independent software product (package).

According to Richard Stallman, who originated the GNU GPL, these characteristics create communities of programmers who help each other by sharing examples of their craft. And this sharing benefits from the synergy of the community—the group is more productive than individuals working in isolation.

Viewed from another perspective, GNU GPL software lives by itself, growing and maturing from the tender care of many but not being controlled by any particular individual, group, or company.

The Free-Software Model in the Business World

In the past, users of free software have routinely GPLed the improvements they made to the free software by distributing the modifications. But what about the business community and the millions of new Linux users? Presumably, the business community will see the long-term economic benefit of choosing not to treat software as a proprietary product and choosing not to compete but share their Linux software with a worldwide community of developers.

The Business of Selling Free Software

How do we sell free software? By changing the focus—once the focus is moved away from the software as a product and centered on the idea of providing a service, businesses have been very successful at selling free software.

An Example of Refocusing

For example, one Linux vendor, Red Hat, has a business model that includes offering their software free over the Internet, yet they still sell hundreds of thousands of CDs filled with the same software for $50 to $80 each. Red Hat has changed its focus from selling the software as a whole to selling a particular type of configuration and service. Through its distribution, Red Hat provides the service of making installation and setup much easier than setting up the software via the Internet.

Steps to Marketing Free Software

On a smaller business scale, consider a business that has created a user mail agent that will allow mail to be manipulated in a multi-operating system environment, regardless of which operating system is booted. In other words, if the mail was received and saved under MS-Windows, the user would still be able to view and edit it under Linux.

Furthermore, while continuing along a path that will allow a business to make a profit while continuing to keep the software a free source entity, a business might take the following steps:

1. After the software has been created with source code comments and the Unix-style manual pages, it is GPLed and posted to the Internet for downloading.

2. Through various newsgroups, others are invited to try the software. Then, one waits and listens for general comments, bug reports, and bug fixes.

3. Assuming the software stabilizes and the company is satisfied with its functionality, a CD is mastered that makes the program easy to manage for the naive user.

4. As a maintainer of the software, the company would set up a Web site based upon the name of the software and offer the CDs for sale.

5. Given how other GPL authors have sold more detailed documentation, tutorials, or user manuals, the company may want to offer the more detailed documentation as part of the CD or as a separate book(s).

Can GPL Software Be Better than Proprietary Software?

One interesting aspect of this process is that since the business that issued the software does not control it, the open source software is now free to follow the needs of its users more closely than traditional closed-source software that must put the economic interests of the company first.

The users' needs can be met in a variety of ways: by the company in response to user requests, by users reprogramming the software, by independent developers, or by a combination of programmers.

Said another way, the software is no longer the responsibility of the issuing company, but rather its maintenance is taken over by the open source community in general.

Using Software without a Warranty

Taking on and using Linux in a business environment may require a Gestalt switch—a shift in the way we view and interact with software. Unlike traditional closed-source software, free software comes without any warranty and without an official vendor to complain to about problems and bug fixes. If this seems a little unnerving, there is a fast-growing industry of Linux consultants who will be happy to step in and fill the gap—for a fee, of course.

On the other hand, if the idea of not having the safety net of a warranty is not bothersome, then you may find Linux to be the operating system of choice. You simply need to remember to rephrase common "vendor-dependency" questions. For example,

INSTEAD OF...	THE QUESTION BECOMES...
Does Linux support xyz function?	How do we reconfigure Linux to get xyz function? Which Linux consultant should we call to reconfigure our system?
Does Linux support xyz peripheral?	Can you perform a quick Web search for xyz peripheral driver on the Internet?
When will the next service pack be released?	Has there been an alert? And, if so, let's do a search to see who has the patch for it.

In other words, the use of Linux represents not only the adoption of a unique software product, but it represents a fundamentally different way of viewing both software and the software development process. The company has two choices: (a) bring in high-priced consultants or (b) rely upon its staff and Internet resources for the software warranty.

Linux System Concepts

Now that we understand the concept of free software, let's move on to the overall structure of the software system called Linux. Although the Linux kernel is new, the system as a whole has been evolving for over twenty years as a series of interlocking puzzle pieces.

The Modular Structure of Linux

Modularity is the idea that software should be written so that it can run independently of other modules, yet work with other modules to achieve an effect larger than any single module. If one module needs a function contained within another module, then the function is reused as opposed to being recreated. Modules begin as small programs, or subroutines, that are grouped to form larger subsystems that, in turn, are grouped into larger systems, and so on.

There are six major independent systems, or modules, within Linux. These include: (1) the kernel, (2) the network, (3) init, (4) daemons, (5) login, shells, utilities, and (6) the X Window System. A short description of each follows.

> **Kernel.** The kernel's job is to hide the hardware details of the computer and its peripherals from users and programmers. This hiding is accomplished by creating general abstractions that refer to hardware. For example, access to the CD-ROM drive is accomplished by reading the directory /cdrom. It is the kernel's responsibility to know what type of CD-ROM drive exists and to be able to read from the drive.
>
> There are other independent subsystems within the kernel such as the file manager, data cache, memory management, and device drivers. For now, we will treat the kernel as one component even though it contains other components. The Linux kernel stands apart from other Unix-like kernels in that it has loadable device drivers, file managers, and other kernel components. These components are installed at runtime with the install module or insmod command.
>
> **Network.** The network accepts both incoming network traffic from the environment and outgoing local user requests for service, and combines the two data streams in such a way that the user has the illusion of being directly connected to other computers. Even though the network and kernel coexist in the same memory space (protected mode memory), they are independent.
>
> **Init.** To understand the init program, you must first understand that the only way a Unix-like or Linux user program can run is to have another user program start it. If this is true, then where does the first program come from? The answer: init is a user-level program that is started by the kernel at boot time and is responsible for getting the ball rolling. It is the ancestor of all the other user programs in the system.
>
> The init program plays a silent but critical role in system operation. After the kernel completes its initialization, it runs the init program. The init program checks a key systemwide file called /etc/inittab, which lists other programs to execute before other users log into the system. Init then reads from the /etc/inittab file which terminals should be used to accept users for login, and it begins the getty program for each terminal

listed. Finally, init waits for signals from any of its programs or other system events (such as power failure) and dispatches other programs to handle the event.

Daemons or system processes. One of the services that performed by the init program at boot time is to begin a series of programs, called daemons. These programs are special in that they do not communicate directly with any user; instead, they sleep in the background until needed to provide a service.

Since these programs provide helpful services, they are referred to as friendly spirits, or daemons (pronounced DAY-mons), and not as evil spirits, or demons. A typical Linux configuration employs a minimum of 15 separate daemons running in the background and may run 50 or more daemons.

Two examples of typical daemons are:

bdflush. Flush daemon moves the contents of the data cache to the hard disk(s) to limit file system corruption in the event of a system crash.

Httpd. Hypertext transfer protocol daemon—the Web server.

Login, shells, and utilities. These are system programs that run as user programs (i.e., they run in user mode, not in protected mode as the kernel does). The login utility establishes a user ID. Shells accept and oversee the execution of user commands. There are many utilities that provide user-level services.

Linux supports many types of command interpreter shells that are available for compatibility with other versions of Unix and ease-of-use. However, for purposes of simplicity, we will use just one shell, the bash shell.

The X Window System. The X Window System is made up of a series of modules that provide services for a graphical user interface (GUI). The X Window System provides the foundation for various display managers, window managers, desktop environments, graphical utilities, and applications.

Preemptive Multitasking Software

Multitasking operating systems (OSs) such as Linux exploit the fact that most programs spend the majority of their time waiting for events to take place. To prevent the system from stalling, a multitasking OS will release the CPU from these waiting intervals by suspending the waiting program and selecting from a list of other ready-to-run programs.

Examples of waiting programs that can be suspended in order to allow the CPU to continue execution on a ready program include the following: programs waiting for a user to type a character, programs waiting for the hard disk to read a sector, or programs waiting for a network packet to arrive.

A Brief Description of Linux Preemptive Multitasking

While Linux is running a program, an environmental event may occur, such as a clock tick or an interrupt from another device. This event causes the current program to be suspended and the interrupt service routine (ISR) to be entered for the device in question. The ISR transfers data between the device and the computer. Upon completion of the data transfer, the ISR may either (a) return to the program it was executing before the environmental event took place, or (b) it may preempt this program in favor of the program associated with the device event.

If (a) is the chosen action, then the ISR may change the status of the program that was waiting on the device event from a suspended state to a ready-to-run state so that the scheduler will eventually select and run the program associated with the device in the next few milliseconds. Meanwhile, the CPU returns to, and continues to run, the original program that was interrupted.

If (b) is the chosen action, then the ISR may both switch the program to a ready-to-run state and increase the priority of the program to guarantee that it will run quickly (within a few microseconds), thus preempting the first program.

Although you may not ever see an ISR or a process scheduler, being aware of these concepts allows us to understand how Unix-like OSs are able to continue to run in spite of a higher-level component crash and how they are able to allow hundreds of simultaneous users.

Single-User versus Multi-User Software

As the name suggests, single-user systems allow only one user at a time. Single-user systems may have special programs that allow two physical users to be connected to the machine at the same time, but as far as the operating system is concerned, there is only one user. Some single-user systems have login accounts giving the impression that they are multi-user operating systems, but these systems still only support one user at a time and are referred to as sequential single-user systems.

Just as with other Unix-like operating systems, Linux is designed from the bottom up as a multi-user operating system. This means that access to the machine must be done through logging in to a user account that has been previously set up. It also means the machine may be accessed by the same account through multiple ports of entry at the same time (that is, a single user may login to the same account, or a different account, multiple times).

The use of the term port is intended to convey access to the machine from one or more of the virtual consoles (TTY 1-6), from an X11 terminal window, from serial interfaces (TTYs), from the network (PTYs), or from any combination of these devices.

Users exploit the parallel login feature by switching among these access ports. A long-running job can be initiated on one port, followed by a switch made to another port where other jobs may be initiated or progress on the first job can be viewed.

Finally, any time a file is created, it must be done within the context of a user account. If users switch among access ports and switch user accounts, they may not have access to files created by the other account.

Switching Virtual Terminals and Page Scrolling

The Linux physical console supports a series of virtual console terminals that provide access to multiple login sessions. Users may switch among virtual consoles regardless of the application or application state (for example, the application may be hung up) in any of the virtual consoles.

Terminal switching works because (a) Linux is preemptive multitasking and (b) the console keyboard driver waits, at the lowest level of the Linux operating system, for special keyboard scan codes. One of six consoles can be selected by typing <Ctrl><Alt>Fx, where <Ctrl><Alt>Fx means pressing the Control key, the Alternate key, and one of the Function keys simultaneously. Thus, the user at the console may quickly save the contents of one login session and switch to another. If desired, the user may even switch from the desktop GUI to a fresh command-line session by using the Ctrl><Alt>Fx keys.

Most significantly, however, virtual consoles permit the user to switch from a locked up session to another screen in order to kill the locked process without having to reboot the operating system.

One other convenient but nonobvious feature associated with the console terminals is the ability to review earlier pages that have scrolled off the screen. To see an earlier page type <Shift><Page Up>. Type <Shift><Page Down> to go back down. Typing any other key will reset the display and insert the typed character on the command line.

CLI versus GUI System Administration

If you have worked with MS-DOS in the past, you have a notice a similar "look and feel" to Linux. This look and feel is common to all Unix-like operating systems and sparks lengthy debates among users.

The look and feel results from command line interpreter (CLI) versus a graphical user interface (GUI). As you will see later on, the command line interpreters (shells) are highly advanced tools that perform many repetitive operations with just a few keystrokes. Once these tools are mastered, many

Linux users prefer the CLI to a GUI. Because of this preference, it is common to see that many Linux users employ a GUI but also have a number of windows with a CLI running to quickly dispatch the various jobs that must be done on a day-to-day basis.

As a result of the modular and layered nature of the operating system, all programs are implemented with command line activation as well as GUI activation. Because of this modularity and cross-user-interface compatibility, there is a very thin implementation line between the command line shell and a GUI. The GUI window manager splashes up a desktop and icons, monitors mouse movements and mouse clicks, and runs selected programs by calling the shell with the appropriate program arguments. Said another way, except for interactive graphics, all of Linux functionality can be accessed from a command line shell.

Unfortunately, the Linux GUI-based system administration programs are not well-enough developed so that we can exclusively rely upon them. Furthermore, these GUI tools silently perform multiple steps that may break one or more other configurations. For example, configuring a network requires three distinct steps: loading the device driver with the `insmod` command, attaching the network interface with the `ifconfig` command, and putting the network address in the routing table with the `route` command. Consider the scenario in which an inexperienced administrator is using a GUI-based program to perform the steps of the configuration. If one of the steps were to fail, and if the GUI-based program did not report the error, then it might be impossible for the inexperienced administrator to recover from the misconfiguration.

Therefore, we must understand the basic configuration steps that are carried out from the command line before we can rely upon the GUI tools to support and ease system administration tasks.

Mainboard Configuration Issues

This section provides an overview of the personal computer (PC) system architecture. It should be noted that other system architectures are supported by Linux, such as the Alpha, MIPS, PowerPC, Acorn, and PowerMac. However, to accommodate the vast majority of Linux users, this book is focused upon the PC system architecture. References to other system architectures can be found in the Linux Hardware Compatibility HOWTO. Please refer to the section "Getting More Information."

To understand the Linux installation process, we must understand how the generic personal computer (PC) is constructed. The personal computer mainboard (or motherboard) holds the majority of integrated circuits, printed wiring, and bus connectors for the system. The mainboard also contains firmware (also referred to as the basic input output system or BIOS). Thus, to use Linux, we must understand the components contained on the mainboard and how their configuration effects Linux.

The Personal Computer Bus Architecture

Figure 1.1 shows the overall PC system architecture. The center of the figure shows the central processing units (CPUs). One CPU is what would be contained in a 386 chip; one CPU plus the floating point processing unit (FPP) is contained in a 486 chip, and the 586, or Pentium class processor, contains two CPUs, the FPP, and a high-speed cache memory.

System Buses

Although there is only one physical row of adapter sockets, there are multiple physical and logical buses contained on the mainboard. The physical buses are the peripheral component interconnect or PCI bus (usually white connector sockets), the industry standard architecture or ISA bus (usually larger black connector sockets), advanced graphic port or AGP (usually the dull-green connector socket), and the memory bus (the SIMM or DIMM sockets). Each bus has its own adapter card edge pattern, so only a PCI card can be plugged into a PCI connector slot, etc. Access to I/O buses require separate program actions, and access to main memory and shared peripheral memory, such as video memory, is through the memory bus.

The main memory bus runs at 66 or 100 MHz on recent mainboards. Access to peripheral controllers is done through an input/output or I/O bus. There are two types of I/O buses: PCI and ISA. The PCI bus protocol allows its connections (adapters) to communicate with the CPU as peers. The ISA bus, on the other hand, employs only "slave" adapters that must be configured manually at installation time. To programs, the AGP adapter appears to be on an I/O bus, but it is physically attached to the CPU's local bus for increased access speed to video memory.

Possible ISA Adapter Difficulties

The difficulty with the ISA bus is that each adapter must select values for I/O parameters from a small group of possible values and no two adapters may use the same values. Furthermore, the four parameters must be configured manually. The four parameters to be configured are:

1. *I/O address.* Although there are many possible addresses, adapter hardware allows the selection of only a few addresses that may or may not conflict with another adapter.

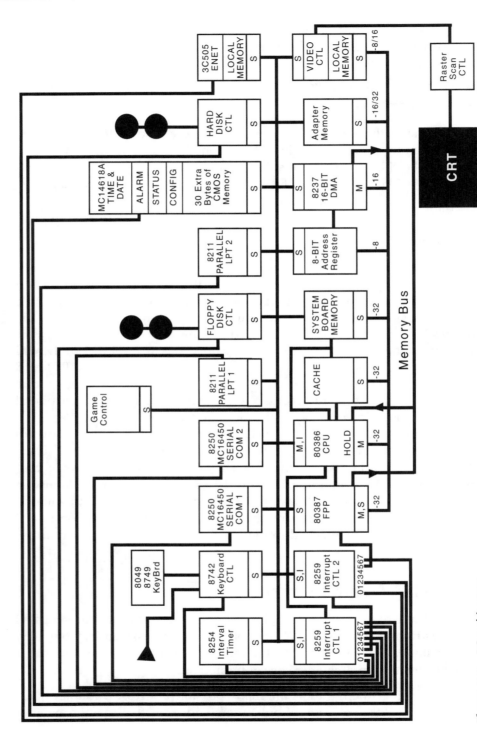

Figure 1.1   PC architecture.

2. *Interrupt Request (IRQ).* There are only about five free IRQ lines and another adapter may already have allocated the IRQ line you are trying to configure.

3. *Address area of memory shared by adapter and CPU.* Adapters generally offer only a few address options and another adapter may already be using the memory address range.

4. *Direct Memory Access (DMA) channel.* There are only seven DMA channels available and another adapter may already have allocated the DMA channel you are trying to configure. Even though there are four possible parameters, only three of them may be in conflict. The reason is that ISA adapters communicate with the CPU either via shared memory or via DMA, but not both ways.

Possible PCI Incompatibilities

Note that PCI adapters have changed firmware versions since they were first introduced, and it is not uncommon for an older PCI adapter to fail in a newer mainboard PCI slot. Also, note that if the PCI modem or Ethernet adapter employs the same ISA interrupt values (for backward compatibility), then IRQ conflicts may exist among PCI and ISA adapters, not just among the ISA adapters. Finally, be aware that each PCI slot priority is based upon its physical location. The lowest priority PCI slot is next to the ISA slot and the highest priority slot is towards the CPU. Sometimes high-speed small computer system interfaces or SCSI PCI adapters may have intermittent problems as a result of being placed in a lower priority PCI slot than other PCI adapters.

Troubleshooting Techniques

When multi-adapter reconfiguration problems appear, the best general solution is to remove all adapters except the video card, and perform a test boot. If successful, turn off the power and reinstall one more adapter and test boot. Failure to boot or failure to detect the adapter indicates a conflict with the adapter just added and an existing adapter. Reconfigure the adapter parameters until the conflict is removed.

There are generally two cautions that apply to removing and inserting adapter cards and our experience confirms these cautions! Caution one: **Turn off the system power before removing and inserting an adapter card.** This means the system must be brought down, power turned off, the adapters swapped, power turned on, and the system rebooted. All of this takes time, but it will insure that a screw is not dropped on a hot mainboard or that the power connector leads do not touch a signal lead when the card wiggled in and out of the connector. Caution two: **Physically touch the new adapter antistatic bag**

and yourself to the system box metal chassis before removing the adapter
from the bag. This will insure that you are at the same voltage level as the new
adapter and system box. In other words, touching the chassis prevents an
exchange of static electricity between you and system box through the new
adapter. Also, **if you walk away from the system box, be sure to touch the
metal chassis when you return.** Do this before touching any component such
as an adapter card, stick of memory, hard disk electronics, or the mainboard.

RAM Requirements and Configuration Issues

Random access memory (RAM) requirements vary depending on application
needs and installation requirements. Linux can run with as little as 2 MB of RAM.
The Linux kernel requires about 1 MB of main memory and the rest of RAM is up
for grabs by daemons, applications, and the data cache. Exact memory requirements depend on many factors that revolve around knowing which programs
will be running with each other and the amount in memory data that each will
be processing. Said another way, predicting RAM requirements is more of an
art as opposed to a science.

The following general numbers are based upon our experience with different applications and configurations. These numbers may not be the same for a
particular mix of programs that we have not experienced and, therefore, these
numbers should be used with a grain of salt. On the other hand, they offer a
good rule-of-thumb.

Network firewall configurations can run in 4 MB systems. Network servers
seem to run fine with 16 MB of memory. The GUI and its related graphical programs, however, require more memory.

APPLICATION	MINIMUM	TYPICAL	SWAP SPACE
Network gateway	4 MB	8 MB	None required
Network server	8 MB	16 MB	Usually none required
Network multi-user	16 MB	32 MB	64 MB
X workstation	32 MB	64 MB	100 MB
X with image processing	64 MB	128 MB	100 MB
X with Star Office Suite or vmware	128 MB	256 MB	100 MB

As for the amount of required swap space, some like to use the rule-of-
thumb "twice the size of RAM," but as RAM increases beyond 64 MB,
increased swap space has a minimal impact on system performance and it is
difficult to justify more than 100 MB of swap space for suspended programs.

When the GUI is run, RAM requirements climb. X11 components use approximately 30 MB. Netscape uses approximately 10 MB of RAM. Image processing requires that large bit-maps be held in memory using tens of MB. The Star Office Suite Version 5.0 uses a minimum of 50 MB of RAM.

Another consideration involves the use of hardware emulators such as vmware to run MS-Windows inside of one or more X11 windows. In these cases, 128 MB may be required for each virtual machine to achieve higher performance levels in both Linux and MS-Windows applications.

Difficulties with Aging Mainboards

Unfortunately, there are two common problems with older mainboards using SIMM memory configurations larger than 64 MB:

Problem 1 is a configuration problem. Linux uses a BIOS service to size memory, and many BIOS sizing routines do not go above the 64 MB boundary. Therefore, you must configure the LILO boot up script to pass a memory size argument to the kernel. The command line argument is "mem=xxxM" where xxx is the amount of memory in megabytes.

New kernels solve problem 1. The memory size problem has been fixed in the later kernels. If you use a kernel more recent than version 2.2.1, it will find all of the available RAM.

Problem 2 is a performance problem. To save on cost, many mainboards do not include all of the "tag" RAM required for large amounts of main memory. Therefore, as installed memory grows beyond the 64 MB, 128 MB, or 256 MB boundary, the mainboard may no longer be able to cache those memory addresses so that the system slows to the access speed of main memory. If there are extra "tag" sockets on the mainboard, then extra tag RAM will solve the problem; otherwise the mainboard will have to be replaced.

New mainboards solve performance problem 2. New mainboards that employ high-speed DIMM PC 100 memory do not use a cache on the mainboard. These 100 MHz memory modules have a 10 ns or less cycle time that make them faster than the 20 ns system cache on older SIMM-based mainboards, so there is no need to use mainboard-based cache in these newer systems.

Vast Amounts of RAM Transform the Hard Disk into a File Server

Availability of large amounts of inexpensive RAM allow the computer system to be viewed from another perspective. For example, consider the use of four 512 MB PC 100 DIMMs on a mainboard. System memory would total 2 GB of

RAM. There would be no need for a swap partition or a swap file on the hard disk and the complete system working set of all programs and accessed files would reside in main memory. Thus, requests to the hard disk would be greatly reduced and leave the hard disk to act more as a file server rather than as a traditional hard disk.

We have experimented with similar configurations and discovered that initially much of the large memory space goes unused since it is not required for programs or data access. However, as I/O continues over the days and weeks, memory slowly fills with hard disk information and subsequent "infrequent hard disk" accesses are very fast indeed.

Role of the BIOS and Device Detection

All of today's computers employ firmware, or Read Only Memory (ROM), programs that the CPU executes upon power-up. These firmware programs perform diagnostics on the CPU, main memory, and installed peripherals. The firmware also allows the user to configure basic system functions such as the time of day.

In the PC system architecture, the firmware is called the Basic Input Output System (BIOS). In addition to the mainboard BIOS, each adapter contains a ROM-based BIOS diagnostic routine that is used to ensure the adapter is working on system power-up.

The PC BIOS also contains routines to access the hard disk and other peripherals. On power-up and after the BIOS executes various diagnostic routines, the first sector of the hard disk (the master boot record or MBR) is read into memory and executed. The MBR contains the first stage of the Linux loader (LILO) program. LILO, in turn, uses the BIOS service to read other blocks from the hard disk so that it can boot the Linux kernel (or another OS). Unlike MS-DOS or MS-Windows, the Linux kernel does not subsequently use BIOS service routines to access hard disks or other peripherals (except for the time-of-day clock). There are a number of reasons for not using the BIOS, but the essential problem is that the BIOS design does not use interrupts and, therefore, cannot support the preemptive multitasking that Linux requires.

Plug and Play

Plug and play is a BIOS enhancement designed to eliminate the need for manual adapter reconfiguration by automatically adjusting the four I/O parameters I/O address, IRQ, DMA channel, and shared memory address range. Plug and play was never able to achieve its goal of full adapter transparency and the Linux kernel has not used the plug and play routines up through the 2.2.0 kernel. Plug and play functionality is more achievable on the PCI bus and there are Linux utilities that will show the plug and play adapter status for the PCI adapters.

Peripheral Configuration Issues

As a system administrator, you must be able to fine-tune various parameters during the install process to optimize Linux for the application at hand. If the following appears too esoteric and detailed for installation, just remember that only by understanding the various configuration issues can you fine-tune the system. Moreover, once these decisions have been made, then a reinstall is usually necessary to change these basic parameters.

Hard Disk Partitions

In the old days of the seventies and eighties, clusters of small disk drives were used in parallel to improve disk access performance and only the OS accessed these disk drives. Today, there is usually just one very large hard disk that is accessed by the mainboard firmware and subsequently the OS. The firmware, therefore, divides the hard disk into partitions for the OS.

Partitions

For at least the last 10 years, hard disk storage advancements have outpaced file system design and firmware design. Thus, when configuring an operating system, you must decide how to best slice up huge hard disks into slices that are manageable by the operating system(s) and the file manager(s).

The lowest level slice is the *partition*. Partitions are recognized by the firmware but not by the operating system. In this way, the firmware allows you to select which operating system (OS) to boot up. Once the OS is running from one of the partitions, it can see other partitions as named or mounted volumes.

The term "volume" is an OS relative concept meaning the "file system as I see it." Generally, there is a one-to-one relationship between volume and primary partition except as noted below.

Primary versus Extended Partitions

Since the BIOS contains the routines for system boot up, the BIOS defines the layout of the hard disk and the layout consists of one to four *primary* partitions. They are primary in the sense that there can be no more than four BIOS partitions. There are special purpose partitions, but primary partition usually defines an OS file system that contains secondary loaders that boot up that particular OS.

An *extended* partition occupies one of the four primary positions, meaning that if an extended partition is defined, then a maximum of three other primary partitions may be defined. Said another way, if an extended partition is defined, then the BIOS will boot from a maximum of three primary partitions. Only one extended partition may be defined. The role of the extended partition is to allow additional "logical" partitions contained within the extended partition.

Note that these logical partitions also become OS volumes creating multiple volumes within one extended partition. Assuming the BIOS begins the boot up process from a primary partition, the secondary boot loader may load one or more OSs from any logical partition.

If these partition details seem unnecessary, consider the layout of a 50 GB hard disk. Dividing 50 GB by four partitions means that the average size of a partition would be 12.5 GB, which is too big for some file managers. Extended partitions permit dividing the hard disk into even smaller chunks that can be managed both within and across operating systems. Furthermore, there are other hard disk partition considerations such as creating swap space, running multiple operating systems, reducing boot up time, and reducing the size in which files may grow. The swap space guidelines have been discussed earlier.

Multiple Operating System Booting

Why would we want to be able to boot more than one OS from the hard disk? Because this would allow the user to switch among applications that are unique to each OS. Also, many users are not sure they will like Linux and by dual booting they feel that they can return easily to the more familiar OS.

If multiple operating system coexistence is desired, then it is possible to share the disk using multiple partitions. Since the other OS is most often a form of MS-Windows, it is instructive to consider the steps that would be required to establish separate partitions for Linux and for MS-Windows. Note that MS-Windows' default action is to format the entire hard disk as one partition, and that this scenario assumes that this was done when Windows was installed.

Steps to share a hard disk between MS-Windows and Linux are as follows:

1. Back up the existing OS in the event that one of the following steps fail.

2. Boot MS-DOS and run SCANDISK to find and replace any bad disk blocks.

3. Run DEFRAG to move all files from scattered locations on the hard disk to one end of the hard disk.

4. Run FIPS or another partition manager to search the hard disk for empty space and to offer to place the empty space in a new partition. FIPS also

allows the changing of the partition type to "Linux native" or "Linux swap" so that MS-DOS will ignore the new partitions when it reboots.

Emulation Instead of Coexistence

For those who may want access to MS-DOS or MS-Windows applications, but who do not necessarily relish the idea of having to reboot every time they want to switch, Linux offers an intriguing option. Linux supports both MS-DOS and MS-Windows emulation.

In one form, there are the DOSEMU utilities that access native MS-DOS partitions and directly execute MS-DOS files. There are also emulators for Windows 3.x programs and another emulator for 32-bit Windows9x applications.

A second form of available emulation is the proprietary product vmware that emulates the PC hardware inside of the X11 environment. In other words, it is possible to install an OS such as MS-Windows98 and to run its applications inside an X11 window or full screen. In fact, you could install Linux inside of Linux or have different OSs running in each X11 window.

It must be noted, however, that these emulators require access to a native MS-DOS partition and a native MS-DOS file system. These file systems can be allocated as a partition (for DOSEMU) or as a large Linux file (for vmware).

Hard Disk Partitioning Strategies

One hotly debated topic in many Linux circles is whether Linux provides too many installation options. One of the debated installation options to be considered here is hard disk configuration.

The first two configuration issues that confront the system administrator when installing Linux to the hard disk are whether to participate in decisions affecting the partition of the hard disk, so that you can customize and fine-tune the workings of disk operations within the OS, or whether to select a Linux release that will not require any administrator input (and which will, essentially, automate the partitioning process), but which will not have the benefits of a customized disk setup.

   Noncustomized, automated partitioning. If, as system administrator, you do not want to be bothered with decisions about the hard disk, then either the Red Hat 6.0 or Caldera's OpenLinux 2.2 release of Linux may fit the bill. For Example, Red Hat 6.0 offers "server" or "workstation" installation options that erase the entire hard disk and repartitions it for Linux.

   Customized, participatory partitioning. Other Linux releases require that the person installing Linux make a decision on how to divide (partition) the hard disk by: (a) partitioning for multiple volume configurations, and (b) partitioning in order to customize and improve swap space.

a) **Multiple volume configurations.** Similar to other Unix-like operating systems, Linux generates event logs and accepts mail without user intervention. If, for one reason or another, logging or mail gets out of hand, then the hard disk could fill up and cause other programs to fail. To eliminate this possibility, many companies create separate partitions for the log and mail files. Thus, as the separate partitions (volumes) fill up, only the programs that write to that volume will be affected. Programs writing to other volumes will continue to execute.

b) **Swap partition configuration.** The other reason for having hard disk partitioning options during the installation process is due to the desire for swap space.

The purpose of swap space is to provide the system with the ability to run more programs than can fit in physical memory. This is accomplished by saving suspended programs on the hard disk and creating the illusion to application programs that they all fit in physical memory (RAM). In order for swap space to be used, two conditions must be met. First, an application or program must request memory space by beginning to execute. Second, RAM must be full. Next, the least recently accessed pages of a process are copied to the swap partition and room is made for the new program.

As a general rule, swap space should be twice as big as the amount of RAM on the system. This rule holds true for up to 64 MB of RAM. As RAM increases past 64 MB, the increase in swap space has a minimal impact on the system. It is difficult to justify swap space over 100 MB given the number of programs that would have to move between memory and the hard disk. When the system spends more time moving programs between swap space and memory than it does executing programs, the system is said to be "**thrashing.**"

Many operating systems swap (save) the programs in a special file. Just as with other Unix-like operating systems, Linux saves programs on a separate disk (or disk partition). The rationale behind the Linux choice is to avoid engaging the file manager, since the disk I/O speed is slow enough as it is, without taking on the added delay that would be incurred by asking the file manager to process each swapped page.

It is also possible for Linux to swap programs to a file with the swapon command; however, the command generally is used only as a temporary measure. If you do need more swap for some special reason, you can create a swap file in addition to the swap partition. A swap file is almost like any other file in your file system. The file should be sequentially allocated so that it occupies the amount of allocated swap space. For example, to create a contiguous 1 MB swap file, begin with the command:

```
dd if=/dev/zero of=/my_swap_file bs=1024 count=1024
```

In this example, the device dump command is used to read zeros from a system abstraction called /dev/zero and to create an output file named my_swap_file. The output file is created in chunks of 1024 bytes, and there are 1024 chunks created. The file size should be a multiple of 4096 bytes since the kernel swaps pages or units of 4096 bytes.

The file, /my_swap_file, is now a candidate for a swap file. The second step is to format the contents of the swap file so that it contains a list of swap pages available for use. The mkswap command creates this list, but be careful with this command since it does not perform any checks on the specified file and the command will overwrite everything in any specified file. The format of the command is:

```
mkswap /my_swap_file 1024
```

where /my_swap_file is the file to be formatted and 1024 is the file size in KB. The swap file is now made. The third step is to inform the kernel so it can use the new virtual memory area. Use the command:

```
swapon /my_swap_file
```

to tell the kernel that it is all right to use the swap file. The swapon may be automated at boot time by adding the line:

```
/my_swap_file    none    swap    sw    0    0
```

to the /etc/fstab file.

The fstab file will be covered in more detail in the system administration book. Swap space may be removed with the swapoff command, which is not usually necessary.

One last comment on swapping: Swapping is not a requirement. Rather, it is an option that allows the system to run with high memory allocation demands. There are probably just as many or more situations where swapping may not be configured; for example, in embedded applications using read only memory or CD-ROM drives.

CD-ROM Controllers

Given the size of a typical Linux software release, installing from a CD-ROM drive is almost always required. An exception to this generality occurs when other computers are located on the same high-speed network; only then are network-based installations practical. Yet, even though CD-ROM–based installations are frequently mandated, there can be a potential difficulty with installing Linux from a CD-ROM.

The CD-ROM is a special type of mass storage since it is an adaptation of the audio Compact Disc or CD-ROM. CD-ROM drives were introduced into the computer market with custom interfaces on each CD-ROM drive model and the CD-ROM drives were attached through sound cards. In these early designs, the manufacturer provided custom MS-DOS device drivers to access the sound card and, in turn, the CD-ROM drive.

Linux has a minimum of 12 types of sound card CD-ROM drivers. Each sound card brand requires its own device driver, such as the Sound Blaster and compatibles (sbcd.o) or the Sony CD (sonycd535.o). Generally, the administrator "guesses" which type of sound card is present in the machine and then loads and tests the various Linux drivers to see if one works. If so, the CD-ROM drive may be mounted via the device driver entry point (for example, /dev/sbcd for the sbcd driver). Although Linux drivers work on a fair number of these sound-card based CD-ROM drives, there is still a chance that none of the drivers will recognize a particular CD-ROM drive.

CD-ROM drives have also been attached to general-purpose SCSI interfaces. Linux device drivers have done quite well with the SCSI-based CD-ROMs. Access to a SCSI CD-ROM drive is not as described previously. Instead, the CD-ROM drive is read by a SCSI driver and accessed through the regular SCSI device such as /dev/sdc, or SCSI disk c.

More recently, another interface was developed for CD-ROM drives so that they could be attached to the common integrated device electronics or IDE controllers. The new standard is referred to as the attachment packet interface or ATAPI, and is combined with the IDE interface creating the ATAPI IDE CD-ROM drive interface. Access to the ATAPI is through the regular IDE device drivers. For example, access to an ATAPI IDE CD-ROM drive is through /dev/hdb, or hard disk b.

The other details on CD-ROM drivers may be found at <ftp://metalab .unc.edu/pub/Linux/docs/HARDWARE> or <ftp://metalab.unc.edu/pub/ Linux/kernel/patches/cdrom/>. You may also wish to check out the Linux CD-ROM HOWTO.

Early ATAPI Incompatibilities

Generally, Linux does well with all SCSI and ATAPI IDE CR-ROM drives; however, when installing Linux on an older machine that employs an ATAPI CD-ROM drive there will probably still be incompatibilities. Also, not all CD-ROM drives will support booting from the CD-ROM drive. In these cases, the floppy disk boot image must be read and written to a floppy disk drive with the MS-DOS rawrite command or the "dd" command.

The Video Adapter

Video adapters generate the video signal that ultimately appears as an image on the monitor screen. These adapters are sometimes referred to as video cards, graphic cards, or VGA cards. All video adapters accomplish their function via three major components, which are outlined briefly below.

The Video Controller
(Video Processor)

The video controller chip determines the type of I/O commands required to save, manipulate, and display information on the monitor screen. These chips are complex—many times exceeding the complexity of the CPU chip—therefore, video adapters are classified more by the type of video controller chip used on the adapter and less by the video adapter manufacturer. Controller chips are classified according to chip manufacturer and chip family. Trident, Tseng, and S3 are examples of well-known chip manufacturers. The Tseng ET6000 series and the S3 ViRGE series are families of video controller chips produced by the manufacturer. The S3 ViRGE/DX and S3 ViRGE/GX are two members of the ViRGE family.

Video Memory (RAM)

Video memory is shared between the CPU and the video controller chip. The CPU places display data in video memory and commands the controller chip to process and display the data. Also, the amount of video memory determines the maximum amount of information that may be displayed. If the video information is "shallow," such as a black and white drawing, then a large amount of information can be displayed. On the other hand, if the video information is "deep," such as a true-color photograph, then a much smaller amount of information may be displayed using the same amount of video memory. The trade-off between shallow and deep is resolved with the use of graphic modes.

Graphic Modes

A graphic mode specifies the number of picture elements and the amount of information each element may hold. For example, 4 MB of video memory will be able to hold one 2250×1750 pixel image with 256 colors per pixel, but the same amount of video memory will hold only one 1280×1024 pixel image with 16 million colors per pixel (or two-thirds fewer pixels).

Many times video controllers are switched to graphic modes that do not use all the available video memory. However, the X Window System exploits this situation by providing multiple virtual desktops that you may switch among, thus allowing the use of all video memory.

Based upon the current graphic mode, the video controller establishes a fixed number of "scan lines" and a fixed line length. The video controller sends this information with the contents of video memory as a series of bytes to the DAC.

Example Graphic Modes

Table 1.1 contains a list of commonly used graphic modes. The column labeled "Resolution" shows the number of pixels on the X (horizontal) axis, the Y (vertical) axis, and the number of colors. The "Memory" column shows the minimum amount of memory required for a given graphic mode. The column labeled "Horizontal" lists typical row-to-row raster scan sweep rates, and the column labeled "Vertical" provides typical refresh rates for the whole display.
Table 1.1 demonstrates three key graphic mode characteristics:

- The higher the resolution, the greater the amounts of video memory required to hold the information.
- The higher the resolution, the faster the monitor must sweep the display horizontally.
- The vertical sweep rate tends to increase with resolution, but most any vertical sweep rate may be used with most resolutions.

The Monitor

A monitor's display is painted by an electron gun driven by a raster-scan circuit. The gun sweeps from top to bottom, row by row. The total display area is cov-

Table 1.1   Example Graphic Modes

RESOLUTION	MEMORY	HORIZONTAL	VERTICAL
$640 \times 480 \times 16$	154 KB	31.47 KHz	60 Hz
$640 \times 480 \times 256$	308 KB		
$800 \times 600 \times 256$	480 KB	37.88 KHz	60.31 Hz
$1024 \times 768 \times 256$	787 KB	78.9 KHz	74 Hz
$640 \times 480 \times 32K$	615 KB		
$640 \times 480 \times 16M$	922 KB	37.86 KHz	72 Hz
$800 \times 600 \times 32K$	960 KB	57.9 KHz	72 Hz
$800 \times 600 \times 16M$	1.44 MB	56.5 KHz	70 Hz
$1024 \times 768 \times 32K$	1.58 MB	81.2 KHz	76 Hz
$1024 \times 768 \times 16M$	2.36 MB		
$1152 \times 864 \times 16M$	2.99 MB		
$1280 \times 1024 \times 16M$	3.94 MB		
$1600 \times 1200 \times 16M$	5.76 MB		

ered a minimum of 60 times per second or, said another way, the total display area is refreshed 60 times per second. If the graphic mode has a low enough resolution, the monitor will have time to refresh the display more often. A refresh rate of 70 or more times per second make the monitor easier to read and leads to less eye strain, so for best viewing, the goal is to set the refresh rate as high as possible.

However, if the graphic mode is a high resolution, it may drive the refresh speed too high, thereby causing the raster-scan circuitry to fail. Even when the monitor is able to process a given high resolution graphic mode at a given refresh rate, if the refresh rate is increased beyond the monitor capabilities (to improve viewing comfort) then the raster-scan circuitry may fail.

Monitor Characteristic Examples

Table 1.2 provides example data taken from various monitor user manuals. The "Units" column represents the number of phosphor dots per millimeter in the monitor's CRT. "Display Area" is the total display-surface area of the CRT. "Addressability" is the maximum resolution graphic mode that the monitor can accept. Also, the "Horizontal" and "Vertical" columns show the minimum

Table 1.2   Display Parameters Taken from Monitor User Manuals

MONITOR	UNITS	DISPLAY AREA	ADDRESS-ABILITY	HORIZONTAL	VERTICAL
Samsung 14"	.39mm	(not reported)	640 × 480	31.5 KHz	60–70 Hz
Samsung 14"	.28mm	(not reported)	1024 × 768	31–35 KHz	60–70 Hz
Seiko 14"	.25mm	240 × 180 mm	1024 × 768	31–50 KHz	50–90 Hz
old Magi 17"	.28mm	300 × 225 mm	1024 × 768	24–64 KHz	55–90 Hz
new Magi 17"	.28mm	322.8 × 242 mm	1280 × 1024	30–69 KHz	50–120 Hz
ViewSonic 17"	.27mm	300 × 225 mm	1280 × 1024	30–70 KHz	50–120 Hz
OptiQuest 19"	.26mm	365 × 275 mm	1600 × 1200	30–95 KHz	50–150 Hz
Seiko 20"	.31mm	360 × 270 mm	1280 × 1024	30–77 KHz	50–90 Hz
Sony 20"	.30mm	350 × 280 mm	1280 × 1024	28–85 KHz	50–160 Hz

and maximum frequencies that the monitor can accept for each graphic mode. Note that exceeding these frequencies will damage the monitor.

Examination of Table 1.2 reveals three striking features with regard to monitor characteristics:

- Advertised monitor size in inches has little to do with the actual display area.

- Monitors accept graphic modes (addressability) approximately 10% greater than what can be supported by the number of phosphor units. (In other words, the problem is not with a person's eyes—those high resolution images really are fuzzy!)

- Graphic mode and refresh frequency are independent. Total display refresh rates can be much higher than generally used; these higher refresh rates offer improved viewing comfort.

Graphic Mode Notes

Older monitors (from the early 1990s), like the first two entries in Table 1.2, would support only one or two graphic modes. Newer monitors were designed with the ability to "sync up" with additional modes. Thus, the term "multi-sync monitor" came into use; however, since all new monitors are multi-sync, the term is now falling out of use.

Changing Graphic Modes or Refresh Frequency

As the video adapter card switches graphic mode frequencies, many monitors will "chirp" or make clicking sounds. The chirp comes from the change in frequency at which a large capacitor is being charged and discharged. The capacitor is used to adjust the sweep rate of the electron beam as it paints the screen.

The first time a monitor "syncs up" with a graphic mode refresh frequency, the CRT will have to be adjusted, or fine-tuned, for each frequency. Once tuned, the monitor stores these values for later reference. As an aside, most every Linux distribution uses a different default refresh frequency for the same graphic mode. Also, if you switch between MS-Windows and X11 using the same graphic mode, the display image may still change size or shift position. The reason is that MS-Windows is using one refresh frequency while X11 is using another refresh frequency and your monitor can only save one refresh frequency for each graphic mode. To fix this, re-adjust the X11 refresh frequencies until they match the MS-Windows refresh frequencies.

Is It Possible to Break Your Monitor?

The short answer to the question is yes. We have had the unique experience of observing a student randomly select refresh frequencies and subsequently break the raster-scan circuit of a monitor, so it is possible to kill your monitor.

Nevertheless, monitor capabilities have significantly improved over the years and there should not be a problem with a newer monitor accepting the default refresh rates stated in the Linux configuration files. In fact, these refresh rates should be increased to improve viewing comfort.

Diagnostic and Setup Floppy Disks

There are many solutions to configuring the ISA bus parameters for a new peripheral, but one of the most convenient solutions is to keep an MS-DOS bootable floppy and copies of the various maintenance programs that vendors offer for their adapters. (The most convenient, of course, is when the adapter's BIOS announces that you can enter its configuration program by typing a special character at boot time.)

For example, consider the task of configuring a network firewall with two Ethernet adapters (let's say they are SMC adapters). Plug in the first adapter, power up the machine, and boot the MS-DOS floppy. Then insert the vendor's floppy and run the configuration program (in this example, it's "ezstart"). Select the I/O address, IRQ number, and shared memory address range (these adapters do not use the DMA channels) that do not conflict with other existing adapters. Also, be sure to note the values selected. Next, turn off the power and install the second adapter. Repeat the preceding steps but configure the second adapter with unique values for the three parameters.

Note that if you do not have these vendor configuration programs, they can usually be found on the vendor's Internet site and downloaded.

Network Configuration

We will devote a complete text to network configuration and services, but for now all we have to do is to tell the machine how to communicate with the local network. To accomplish network connectivity, we have to provide parameters for the four network concepts describe below.

IP Address, Mask, Gateway, Name Server

An essential part of a Linux installation concerns network access. There are four key parameters that hold the answer to providing network access: the IP address, the network mask, the gateway, and the name server. Each is considered briefly here.

> **IP Address.** The IP address is a unique, logical Internet address that identifies the geographical location of the computer. This number cannot be guessed at—it must be assigned by the network administrator. The format of an IP

address is w.x.y.z, where each letter represents a decimal number from 1 to 254 and the "dots" act as separators among the four decimal numbers.

Network Mask. The mask has the same format as the IP address, except that the least significant bits are zero and represent the size of the subnet to which the host is connected. For example, w.x.0.0 is a subnet with 65,534 possible computers. The pattern w.x.y.0 represents a subnet with 254 possible computers. Finally, the pattern w.x.y.240 represents a subnet with 15 possible computers. Note that host addresses 0 and 255 are not permitted since they mean "subnet size" and "broadcast address" respectively.

Gateway. A gateway (or router, bridge, firewall) is the IP address of a host that accepts messages destined for the Internet.

Domain Name Service. The Domain Name Service refers to the IP address of a host that accepts a domain name (an ASCII string) and returns its IP address, or it will accept the IP address and return the domain name (if there is one).

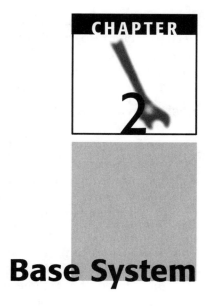

CHAPTER

2

Base System

Installation Media

There is a vast array of open source and free software available. Companies and non-profit entities have gathered "chunks" of this software around the Linux kernel. Our role here is to describe these chunks and let you decide which one best fits your needs. To understand and use Linux as a system administrator, you must have experience installing several, if not most, of these chunks. And even though there are detailed installation walk-through sections in Appendix A, it should be noted that we do not test on specific install steps of a given distribution. We will now examine the installation process.

Media Choices

Linux comes as a "distribution," meaning that an organization has packaged the software and bundled a special install program with the packaged software. Install programs are, in fact, stripped down versions of Linux that use RAM disks and shell scripts to perform the install operations. Distributions tend to use their own set of install programs, which run off of various media. However, several distributions use the Red Hat install mechanism.

There are a number of media that can be used to install a Linux distribution. Each has their respective advantages and disadvantages, considered later. The six media types fall into two basic categories: local device installation and network access installation.

Local Device Installation

CD-ROM. As indicated in the previous chapter, CD-ROM is the preferred installation media. Depending on which software release is installed, the 500 MB of archived CD-ROM data uncompresses and expands to anywhere from 800 MB to 1 GB on the hard disk. This dearchiving process usually takes one or more hours with older computers. With today's faster CPUs and CD-ROM drives, it may take less than eight minutes.

MS-DOS partition. In this scenario, Linux installation archives have been copied to the MS-DOS partition. Although this may seem like a strange thing to do, it overcomes the "older CD-ROM" problem described in the previous chapter. Once the MS-DOS disk archive image is set up, the installation program can be directed to the hard disk.

Floppy. In this case, a minimal system archive is placed on a set of 10–50 floppy disks. Each disk contains a fraction of the installation archive. The remainder of the distribution is downloaded from a network server.

Network Access Installation

FTP. Using this method, you connect to a server that already has the archives stored. One problem that continues to occur when downloading a Red Hat distribution is that its download process is not interactive. After specifying the FTP password and directory, Red Hat attempts the connection without feedback. Consequently, an error as simple as forgetting to specify the FTP root directory /pub/can prevent a successful installation.

NFS. This method is very similar to the FTP scenario just described. Following this method, the archive has been stored on another Unix or Linux box, and the user simply specifies the NFS server host name or address and the shared directory path. Once set up, NFS works very well, but as with FTP, there are a number of small configuration problems that usually prevent you from setting up a Linux install host and an NFS server at the same time.

SAMBA. As with FTP and NFS, SAMBA uses the network to "share" a hard disk with an MS-Windows SMB server. Again, little details—such as using the wrong case for the password—can prevent establishing a connection.

Reserve Time for Internet-Based Installations

It took me three days of on-and-off tinkering to set up the correct directory structure, transfer Red Hat 4.2 installation files over the Internet, and confirm that all files were properly located in each subdirectory. Thus, any non-CD-ROM solution requires a serious time commitment from the installer. A compromise solution is to mount the CD-ROM on a network server and read the CD-ROM archive via FTP, NFS, or SAMBA. Recently, complete CD-ROM images have been made available on the Internet. These 650 MB files are called "isos" since they are ISO9660 formatted and the file name ends with ".iso". If you can afford the download time, note that these images are usually burned onto a CD-R disc.

Component Compatibility Issues

One indication of the acceptance of Linux is the inclusion of Linux device drivers with new hardware, such as Ethernet or video adapters. Unfortunately, many adapter cards do not come with Linux drivers, which means that system administrators and system builders will have to pay close attention to hardware compatibility issues.

Configuration Responsibilities

When purchasing hardware for a new Linux box, it is always tempting to purchase the least expensive clone PC that can be found. Although this strategy works sometimes, it seems just as often the administrator is stuck with incompatible hardware. Incompatibilities arise when the appropriate device drivers are not available for the new components. Thus, it is the system administrator's responsibility to review the new PC components to ensure that there are Linux drivers for all the desired peripherals.

Generally, incompatibilities can be avoided by purchasing a more up-scale PC and components. These machines generally do not use short cuts that strip out hardware components and replace the hardware with MS-Windows drivers.

To be completely sure about hardware compatibility, the administrator must compare the listed PC components against a compatibility list such as:

```
www.linuxdoc.org/HOWTO/Hardware-HOWTO.html
```

Unsupported Devices

Since Linux does not use the BIOS firmware, it is responsible for knowing the hardware details of all peripherals. This is generally not a problem with well-established hardware interfaces. However, Linux gets into difficulty when new hardware products appear with their design details deliberately hidden by the manufacturer behind proprietary device drivers that are provided only for a particular OS. Example devices are printers, video cards, and modems. Here are a few examples:

Printers. On some types of ink or bubble printers, a custom communication protocol is required between the printer and the device driver. Many other printers can handle the PostScript language, but some printers require a custom graphic mode protocol. Unless a driver for a specific printer is available, it will not be "Linux-friendly."

Video Adapters. Video adapters are another problem area. Although the XFree86 project supports many types of video adapters, new ones are released every few months. System resellers tend to configure systems with the most recent and inexpensive video adapters. The result is that the Linux system administrator must check in advance to see whether Linux supports the video adapter hardware before purchasing the new system.

Modems. One innovation in modem design has been the development of controllerless, or "Winmodems." These devices have fewer components than traditional modems and require more operations by the device driver. These additional operations also require a special protocol between the CPU and the modem adapter.

Since these new designs generally attempt to tap into "unused" CPU cycles to do the task that the peripheral normally does, it is not clear whether there should be Linux drivers developed for this type of minimal hardware since the new drives will, by definition, have to slow the system down to attend to the less functional adapter.

Nine Linux Distributions

Here we provide an overview of a "few" of the available Linux distributions. With the limited space it impossible to do justice to all Linux distributions. Please note that these distributions are specific to the PC system architecture.

All Linux software has version numbers. The Linux kernel and each Linux distribution have independent version numbers. The kernel employs three numbers separated by decimal points. For example, the kernel version number 2.4.10 would mean that it is the second major version and it is at the fourth minor version with the tenth patch in place. The middle number or minor number has two modes. If the minor number is even, then it is considered to be a stable version of the kernel. If the minor number is odd, then the kernel is said to contain untested or not-fully tested experimental code that appears to work and, therefore, it is an unstable version.

Linux distribution numbers have two digits separated with a decimal point. From left to right, these are the major and minor version numbers. Distribution version numbers do not refer to the Linux kernel version, but instead they refer to the type and default configuration of all software in the distribution. A distribution tends to change once or twice per year as major kernel revisions are provided by the open source community. A large distribution version number has a psychological suggestion that one distribution is newer than another even though version numbers have little to do with differences among distributions. Nevertheless, expect the more popular distributions attempt to leapfrog each other with larger and larger version numbers.

An overview of nine Linux distributions is provided next. The distributions considered are: Debian 2.1, LinuxGT 1.0S, Mandrake 5.3, OpenLinux 2.2, Red Hat 6.0, Slackware 4.0, Stampede 0.1, SuSE 6.1, and TurboLinux 3.0.

In general, installation programs vary among distributions, but kernel differences tend to be relatively minor. The X11 environments and default configured applications also vary among distributions. In this section, we will paint differences among distributions in broad strokes and let each distribution publicist speak for themselves. Each of these distribution descriptions will toss around terminology about advanced topics. If all of the terminology does not make sense, do not worry, all the topics will be revisited in due course.

Debian 2.1—www.debian.org

The Debian distribution is one of the oldest and probably the least known distribution. Debian can be found on CD-ROM, but it was designed to be distributed over the Internet as well. The primary goals of the Debian distribution are to provide an easy upgrade technique and high-level security components. Because of these goals, it is preferred by Linux "power users." With Debian, you install a basic Linux kernel, and then use the Debian select (`dselect`) utility to download the various components or upgrades over the Internet. As you install a Debian distribution and select from among the 2250-plus software packages available over the Internet, you begin truly to sense the magnitude of the worldwide open source effort.

Debian stands out as the most unique of the distributions. Both the Debian configuration files and the Debian default installed system components, such as the secure shell and smail, tend to differ more from what is typically provided by the other distributions. Debian also has its own software packaging system, deb, that historically has been more robust than the more common Red Hat package management (`rpm`) system. In Debian's own words. . .

> Debian GNU/Linux is a free distribution of the Linux operating system. It is maintained and updated through the work of many users who volunteer their time and effort.

Debian is a free, or Open Source, operating system (OS) for your computer. Debian uses the Linux kernel, a free piece of software started by Linus Torvalds and supported by (probably over 1000) programmers worldwide. A large part of the basic tools that fill out the operating system come from GNU, which are also free. Of course, the thing that people want is software; tools to help them get what they want to do done, from editing documents to running a business to playing games to writing more software. Debian comes with over 2250 packages (precompiled software bundled up in a nice format for easy installation on your machine) all of it free. Debian 2.1, which is also known as "slink," is now available.

LinuxGT 1.0S—www.greysite.com

The "GT" in LinuxGT stands for Grey Technology. It is designed to be a quick install for a particular preconfigured application. The first distribution is for network servers. Here is the company's description of LinuxGT...

LinuxGT Server Edition Version 1.0S. This is a streamlined Server Solution for everything from file and print server to Internet Gateway to E-Mail and Web Server. We've included a prime set of applications and tools to make any administrator happy, and bring extreme power and flexibility to your current network.

Here's what is included: the LinuxGT Server Edition CD, QuickStart Installation Guide, Administrators Handbook (covers a variety of topics!), and telephone customer support for 60 Days.

On the CD -Sendmail The most popular E-Mail server available, Apache SLL (in the U.S.) or Apache Web Server (Outside the U.S.), mySQL ANSI SQL Database Server, Webmin for Web-Based Administration, GUI Admin Tools, KDE and GNOME Desktops, IPLimit for limiting the possibility of attacks, Big Brother Remote Security Monitoring, Big Brother Web Statistics and Trend Monitoring, and the standards (telnet, ftp, and ssh servers + clients, PERL5, C/C++, tons more!).

Mandrake 5.3—www.mandrake.org

Several distributions build on top of GPLed Red Hat! Mandrake is one such distribution, and we will let Mandrake 5.3 speak for itself...

Linux-Mandrake is 99% compatible with Red Hat' Linux 6.0. This means that you can install any RPM package made for Red Hat 6.0 in Linux-Mandrake. Linux-Mandrake is inspired by Red Hat Linux, with many improvements and preconfigured applications which make it easier to use for the beginners. Linux-Mandrake uses the Red Hat GPL distribution and extends it with the X11 KDE environment.

Improvements and add-ons—Installation procedure in many languages (several boot images, 21 languages). Creation of a non-privileged user when installing. X test while installation, permitting to boot directly into X when it's finished.

CD-ROM and Floppy-disks can be mounted by non privileged users, just by typing "mount /mnt/cdrom" or clicking on the CD-ROM icon. Multiple graphical interfaces choice: KDE, Gnome, AfterStep, WindowMaker, IceWM with session choice in KDM/GDM. Scalable fonts support in all X applications and for printing (with ready-to-use True Type' fonts provided) KDE and Gnome languages follows installation language Many KDE themes available. Mandrake KDE customization, with preconfigured desktop. Easy printing under KDE by dragging and dropping documents onto the printer icon. Power-saving management control under KDE. Laptop control under KDE. Better accents (and special characters management under X and console. Better locale man-pages management and displaying, following the $LANG environment variable Easy automatic distribution update system from the graphical desktop saving diskspace (bzip2'ed man pages, ext2compr support in kernel-source). SVGALib support for all VESA 2.0 compliant VGA cards.

Applications—Many supplementary KDE apps and Gnome apps like ktop, kvirc, knetmon, kpackage, klyx, gaddr, gtkzip... Office extensions (Killustrator, Gnumeric, Maxwell, Check Book Balancer, sane-1.0.1...) BeroFTPD (with easy configuration from kBeroFTPD), BeroList, Netscape 4.6 with optimized keyboards-shortcuts and flash plugin, Gimp 1.0.4, Apache 1.3.6 with PHP integrated, Wine 990518, XEmacs 20.4, and Postfix [sendmail installed by default].

OpenLinux 2.2— www.calderasystems.com

This distribution, from Caldera consulting, sets itself apart from other distributions with the first fully graphical installation procedure. The unique install is a result of their Linux Wizard, or Lizard, tool as well as an advanced graphical system administration tool called Caldera open administration system, or COAS. OpenLinux has been predicated upon the Red Hat distribution and provides all of the programs that come with Red Hat. In Caldera's own words. . .

What's new in the Linux 2.2 Kernel? Improved performance of machines with at least 16 megs of RAM. Power management for laptops. Linux will now read NTFS (Windows NT) drives and Windows 98 FAT32 drives (also used by some later versions of Windows 95). Recognizes the Joliet system for long filenames on CD-ROMs. Completely rewritten CD-ROM driver system for more standardized support. Support for more than 4 serial ports. Supports higher data transfer rates with newer modems. Many new sound devices are supported. Support for a growing number of TV and radio tuner cards and digital cameras. Enhanced support for Ethernet and ISDN devices. Additional rewritable CD-ROMs are supported under Linux 2.2. SMP: up to 16 processors are supported, with amazing performance. Linux 2.2 includes enhanced support for spanning a file system across several disks transparently. Presently, this support can be used in RAID 0, 1, 4, and 5 modes as well as a simple linear mode. OpenLinux 2.2 comes complete with Linux kernel 2.2.x; multi-user; multi-tasking; glibc 2.1 (and libc5 for backwards compatibility); as well as PalmPilot-capability.

Installation—Lizard, (LInux wiZARD).

Administration—COAS Administration System 1.0, Disk Quotas, IP firewall and accounting

Office, WordPerfect 8, personal edition, Daily schedule/organizer

Internet/Network, Protocols: TCP/IP, Ethernet, PPP, SLIP, PLIP, UUCP, SMTP, POP, IMAP, NFS, SMB, IPX Client/Services: DHCP 1.0, NFS 2.2, NIS 2.0, Samba 2.0.3, DNS (bind 8.1.1), Telnet, WU-FTP 2.4.2 Internet: Communicator 4.51, Apache 1.3.4, Sendmail 8.9.1, News (inn 2.1), Majordomo 1.94.3, Dial-in (mgetty 1.1.8 & ppp 2.3.5), Dial-out (kppp 1.1)

Development—Symbolic debugger (gdb & ddd), Python 1.5, Perl 5.005 Tcl/Tk 8.0.4, Java Development Kit 1.0.2, Java Virtual Machine (Kaffe 1.0)

Desktop—K Desktop Environment, (KDE) 1.1 XFree86 3.3.3.1

Red Hat 6.0—www.redhat.com

Red Hat is the clear volume leader in Linux distributions. The Red Hat distribution is mass-marketed and, therefore, the most commonly available. Like the other distributions, the Red Hat goal is to provide an easy-to-install, preconfigured system that comes complete with many applications, including a Web server and X11 environment. It also has an X Window configuration tool manager. Beginning with distribution 5.2, Red Hat now allows workstation and server options that can automatically partition the hard disk. Red Hat is distributed primarily via CD-ROM and is sold over the Internet and in bookstores ($78.95–$99.95). Although you can download Red Hat from the Internet, it usually requires about three days—a lot more time than using the CD-ROM version. Here is the Red Hat self-description…

NEW FEATURES in Red Hat Linux 6.0 that benefit the technical workstation

The 2.2 kernel is included as the base for the operating system. It has significant speed and performance from your workstation because of the 2.2 kernel. This kernel also supports more peripheral hardware, such as television and radio cards.

The GNOME Graphical User Interface provides a Drag and Drop protocol to the desktop.

GNOME gives users the ease of a Drag and Drop protocol with the practicality of included applications. Just a few of the new applications include File Manager,

GnoRPM, gftp, calculator, URL handlers, any many desktop settings tools. Use this new interface as an alternative to command line tasks such as file management and launching applications. Customizing the desktop is a cinch with the GNOME Control Center. Extras such as a CD player and calendar are bonuses that enhance the convenience of this GUI.

Red Hat Linux 6.0 as a SERVER.

Red Hat Linux is widely known as a server for many reasons. In general the simple fact that Linux is a stable operating system makes it a winner when you can't afford to have any server downtime.

Red Hat Linux can be used as a: file server, web server (Apache included), mail server, DNS server, Usenet news server, and Print server.

NEW FEATURES in Red Hat Linux 6.0 that benefit the server.

Improved stability and scalability with the power to scale up to 4 processors allowing you to serve even more users with one machine.

Improvements in NFS allow a 40% improvement with a single client. GNOME Graphical interface for administrators to interact with their servers.

Kernel Optimization Enjoy the power of the hardware you spent your money on so you can exploit your processor's power to the fullest.

Serial console or "headless servers" Communicate with all of your servers through a serial cable and cut down time and expenses of towing a monitor to each machine.

RPM 3.0 The latest version of RPM ensures your system's integrity through package verification. You can check to see what packages have changed which allows you to know what is going on with your servers.

Software RAID (0,1,4,5 support) Threaded rebuild process occurs in the background so that you can continue to use the system during the rethreading process. Save data and don't lose time while you repair a bad hard drive.

Slackware 4.0—www.slackware.com

The Slackware distribution is probably the second-best known Linux distribution, and it has a loyal following. In Slackware's own words. . .

Slackware 4.0 Runs the 2.2.6 version of the Linux kernel from ftp.kernel.org. Generic IDE (bare.i) and SCSI (scsi.s) boot images work with nearly all Intel-based (and compatible) computer systems. Additional precompiled kernels (62 varieties in all) and boot images. Provide specialized support for hardware such as new Adaptec aic7xxx 7890 SCSI controllers, parallel-port IDE devices, IBM PS/2 machines with the Microchannel bus, SGI Visual Workstations, Symmetrical Multiprocessing machines, and much, much more.

Includes additional boot disks, precompiled kernels, and source for the 2.2.7 kernel, for those who need its features. System binaries linked with the stable libc5 C libraries, version 5.4.46. Includes glibc-2.0.7pre6 shared libraries for glibc binary runtime support. XFree86 3.3.3 patch 1, plus X servers for Neomagic and Intel i740 chipsets. GhostScript and APS-filter included to support many common PC printers. Among these are: HP670, HP690, HP850, HP855, HP870, HP890, HP1100 and HP1600 Installs both egcs-1.1.2 and gcc-2.7.2.3 compilers to provide a more flexible development environment. By default, C code compiles with gcc, C++ code compiles with egcs (or specify your own PCMCIA, CardBus, and APM support for laptops (pcmcia-cs-3.0.9). New development tools (autoconf and automake) as well as the LinuxThreads libraries are now available. GIMP 1.0.4 image manipulation program. (with gtk+-1.2.2 libraries compiled with multithreaded support enabled) Includes Netscape Communicator version 4.51. The K Desktop Environment version 1.1.1 is fully integrated into the Slackware distribution. Updated versions of the Slackware package management tools, making it easy to add, remove, upgrade, and make your own Slackware packages. Large repository of contributed software compiled and ready to run. This includes GNOME 1.0, various window managers, bash 2.02, support for 3Dfx gaming cards, JDK, and more (see /contrib). Many more improved and upgraded packages, including: apmd_3.0beta3-2, bzip2-0.9.0b, cdrecord-1.6.1, cvs-1.10, e2fsprogs-1.14, emacs-20.3, fetchmail-4.6.3, gpm-1.14, gv-3.5.8, ibcs-2.1-981105, ipchains-1.3.8, jdk_1.1.7-v1a, libgr-2.0.13, loadlin-1.6a, pciutils-1.10, man-pages-1.23, minicom-1.82-3, modutils-2.1.121, net-tools-1.52, netkit-routed-0.12, nfs-server-2.2beta40, perl-5.005_03, pidentd-2.8.3, pine 4.10, procmail-3.13.1, procps-2.0.2, procinfo-16, python-1.5.1, Qt-1.44, rpm2targz, samba-2.0.3, sendmail-8.9.3, shadow-990307, svgalib-1.3.1, and kde-1.1.1.

ZipSlack

ZipSlack installation provides a full-featured text-based Linux system as a 37 megabyte ZIP archive. Simply unzip on any FAT or FAT32 partition, edit your boot partition in the LINUX.BAT batch file, and you can be running Linux in less than five minutes. Even boots on machines with only 4MB of RAM. The ZipSlack installation includes everything you need to network with Linux (including Ethernet, token ring, SLIP and PPP), develop Linux applications with C, C++, and Perl, and extend the system with additional software packages such as X. A ZipSlack system will even fit on a Zip disk, so you can carry a personal Linux system with you to run on any PC with a Zip drive.

Stampede 0.1www.stampede.org

With a kernel that tends to be more up-to-date than others, Stampede is optimized for the Pentium and has newer libraries, but it is untested and has no installation manual. In Stampede's own words. . .

> Stampede Linux is an innovative, new approach to Linux distributions. We wanted a distribution that was fast, easy for the new user, and awesome for the power user. So, we decided to create Stampede. These are the features that Stampede offers:
>
> Based on GNULibC2, the newest in innovative libc technology. NFS installation. FTP coming soon! A package based distribution, with all packages being compatible with non-Stampede Linux machines. Compiled with Pentium GCC 1.1, to make the system 10-30% faster. Debugging flags removed on stable software (installing software with debugging turned on is optional), increasing system speed, and decreasing binary sizes. Comes with the latest stable versions of ALL software. BSD-like init scripts. These are the easiest way to manage a system, and arguably the most configurable. Automated installs (optional). Don't feel like digging through every package? Choose a Stampede Linux predefined install script. Development is steam rolling ahead. Perhaps one of the fastest distributions from scratch ever.
>
> Please note that this is a beta release. Although it is stable, it is not very easy to install (Yet).

SuSE 6.1—www.suse.com

SuSE (pronounced "SUE-suh") works closely with the XFree86 Project, and its distribution has the most recent modifications to, and device drivers for, the X11R6 X Window System. Also, the SuSE CD-ROM distribution has the most bundled applications; consequently, a full installation requires over 4 GB of disk space. In SuSE's own words. . .

> SuSE Linux 6.1 includes version 2.2 of the Linux kernel! Kernel 2.2, was in development for 2-1/2 years, offers significant enhancements, including: Even faster kernel performance, much improved performance and support for Symmetric Multi-Processing (SMP) devices, driver support for many more kinds of devices, especially multimedia (video, digitizers, and sound), and there is support for more non-Intel processors and different workstations (e.g., Sparc).
>
> SuSE Linux offers KDE 1.1 and now GNOME 1.0. KDE (K Desktop Environment) is extended by several interesting features. The disk navigator now allows direct, menu-driven access to the complete file system. The Window Manager functions

can be executed using keyboard shortcuts. Mouse key mapping is freely configurable and you can display the menu bars of the windows at the top edge of the screen, just as with MacOS.

A popular alternative to KDE, GNOME 1.0 is on SuSE Linux. It can also now be combined with any window manager, including WindowMaker, icewm or Enlightenment—which are part of SuSE Linux 6.1.

SuSE Linux 6.1 includes both StarOffice 5 Personal Edition, a complete office package which can be used free-of-charge for private purposes, and the Personal Edition of Corel WordPerfect 8 as well. Both allow you to import MS Office files and other popular formats. As for cross-platform compatibility, Corel WordPerfect 8 for Linux uses the same file format as Corel WordPerfect for Windows 95, Windows NT, Windows 3.1x and UNIX.

Kernel 2.2.5, XFree86TM 3.3.3.1, Support for all 3Dfx cards, KDE 1.1 with koffice, GNOME 1.0, Ghostscript 5.10, ijb (non-cacheing HTTP proxy server that filters contents as described in the configuration files), freeamp (MP3-Player), netbeans (Cross-platform Java IDE, Demo).

English installation, free package selection "susewm": tool to keep the window manager menus up-to-date with the actually installed software. Extensive online help system in HTML, graphical desktop XFreeTM 3.3.3.1 (X11R6.3), easy to configure with SaX or XF86Setup, boot from CDROM—no boot floppy needed, tools for internet access (mail, news, WWW), complete source code. Emulations for: DOS, Atari ST, Amiga, C64, C128, VIC20, PET, ZX Spectrum, Gameboy, Nintendo Entertainment System, Atari VCS2600, Coleco Vision, ZX81 ... and much more!

We provide installation support to help our registered customers with problems they may have when installing and running a "normal" SuSE Linux system. You may receive support up to 60 days from date of purchase. You can contact us via email (support@suse.com), call 1-510-835-7879, or fax 1-510-835-7875. Of course you can always check out our support database, which is full of solutions to common (and not-so-common) problems.

TurboLinux 3.0—www.turbolinux.com

Like Mandrake and Caldera, TurboLinux is based upon Red Hat. TurboLinux tends to be used more outside the USA than inside. At the time of this writing, version 3.6 was announced with the newer 2.2.x kernel. TurboLinux is also specializing in configuring high availability Linux clusters. In its own words. . .

Updated Kernel—TurboLinux 3.0 uses the 2.0.35 kernel, which provides support for such new features as parallel-port IDE devices and Fat32/Windows98 partitions. We've added in the 5.1.2 revision of the Adaptec aic7xxx driver, to allow support for dual-channel cards and the aic7890 chipset. This patch also fixes some serious lockup problems on systems with aic7xxx-based SCSI cards. We've also increased the size of the file table for better performance on network servers. In addition to the standard kernel which is installed by TurboLinux, there is also an optional APM-capable kernel which can be installed after the main installation is finished. Updated PCMCIA Support XFree86 3.3.2.3 (with X-TT)—Our new XFree86 package is based on the standard XFree86 3.3.2 distribution, but includes support for 3D Labs chipsets through the SuSE 3DLabs X Server. We also have included the XBF-Neomagic server for neomagic-based PCs. This version of TurboLinux also includes TrueType font support built-in to the X server through the X-TT extension. **Note—the '3.3.2.3' refers to the fact that we are using XFree86 3.3.2 with all three of the official XFree86 patches. The X servers report themselves as version 3.3.2.3 as well.

Updated Installation Program—Many new features have been added, and many bugs have been fixed. As always, the installation program is capable of automatically detecting most hardware, both ISA and PCI, and these routines have been improved for TurboLinux 3.0. This version will also allow you to install from a parallel-port IDE CD-ROM drive, and will allow you to configure your default X desktop before the initial boot of your new TurboLinux system. New Compiler—TurboLinux 3.0 comes with the egcs 1.1b compiler system, a faster, more robust replacement for the standard gcc compiler. gcc 2.7.2.3 is also included for doing kernel compiles (this will be unnecessary once the 2.2.0 kernel is released, however, and is currently unnecessary if you plan to build a 2.1.x kernel—2.1.x and 2.2.x kernels can be correctly built with egcs).

Updated Package Manager (TurboPkg)—TurboPkg was written from scratch at Pacific HiTech to provide a simple front-end for system package management that does not require X. It is used by the TurboLinux installer, and can also run as a standalone program. It can even obtain and install upgrades via FTP. This is basically the same as the version that shipped with TL 2.0, but this version has numerous bug fixes, some new hot keys, and some other handy new features. TurboNetCfg, TurboUserCfg, TurboFSCfg—These three tools are new for TurboLinux 3.0, and they configure what their names imply (networking, users/groups, and filesystems). TurboFSCfg can also configure LILO options. All three have X-based counterparts, making system administration even easier than before. Timeserver Support—The 'turbotimecfg' package in TurboLinux 3.0 will now let you configure your system to synchronize itself to a time server using the rdate or ntp protocols.

Improved Desktop (TurboDesk 2.4)—Many tweaks have been done to the desktop interface to make it easier to use and more visually appealing. We've also fixed some bugs in the desktop configuration tools. We've updated the mail and modem icons so that they're better looking and more functional (the new modem icon, for example, has working send/receive lights). XTurboAppMgr—This is an all-new, window manager-independent application launcher bar. It was written in-house at Pacific HiTech, specifically for TurboLinux. It is written in GTK+ and is both easy to use and highly customizable. It's available from the pulldown menus in TurboDesk as well as the TurboDesk Control Panel.

Updates to Mission-Critical Packages—TurboLinux 3.0 includes the latest versions of all the important server and application packages that you've come to expect. We monitor BUGTRAQ daily and provide fixes via FTP when bugs are uncovered. More Programs—TurboLinux 3.0 comes with even more new packages that were not part of 2.0. Some of these include the XessLite spreadsheet (shareware/commercial demo—the 'full' version is also available for Linux), the Code Crusader development environment, the Simple DirectMedia Layer (SDL) library for creating multimedia applications, MagicPoint (a presentation-graphics package), numerous system administration utilities, and others.

Common Distribution Installation Steps

All distribution installation programs must go through the following steps. The essential difference is whether the installation program displays these steps explicitly and possibly requests user input, or whether it performs the steps silently.

1. *Miscellaneous*—Select language, keyboard format, etc.
2. *Hard disk allocation planning:*
    1. Choose either a single OS Linux installation or a dual boot installation.
    2. If the dual boot option is selected, decide whether to share the same hard disk or whether separate hard disks will be used. If the same hard disk is to be shared between both OSs, then repartition the hard disk with FIPS or another partition manager. If separate hard disks will be used and if DOS or Windows emulation is desired, then allocate DOS and Linux partitions on the separate hard disks.
    3. Regardless of the number of OSs and hard disks, decide on the number and size of Linux partitions. A minimum of two is usually required, one for swap space and one for a root file system. Generally, the swap partition should be twice the size of physical memory, up to a maximum of 100 MB.
3. *First, boot from installation media*—Boot the install kernel and install program from the CD-ROM or from boot floppies. If the BIOS cannot boot directly from the CD-ROM, then boot floppies must be constructed by employing the DOS-based program `rawrite` to copy a minimal Linux kernel image and install the program onto the floppy disk. Alternatively, a boot disk could be created from another Unix or Linux box by typing the command:

```
dd if=/kernelimage of=/dev/fd0 bs=1024
```

Here the device dump command takes an input file name, an output file name, and a block size argument. The command works without the block size argument, but it takes a while to individually write the small 512 byte default blocks. Most any large block size argument also works and everyone seems to have a personal favorite for the bs argument.

4. *Creating Linux partitions*—Note that the hard disk is being shared with another OS; the following assumes you have prepartitioned the hard disk with FIPS. Use the `fdisk`, `cfdisk`, or `disk druid` program to write native file systems and swap partitions.

   Sometimes, the question of which partition should be placed first on the hard disk is brought up. Overall, ordering has little effect on performance; however, usually the size of the swap partition has been determined, but not the size of the root partition. Thus, it is easier to specify the swap partition first, as well as any other predefined partitions, and then let the root partition fill the remainder of the hard disk.

5. *Format file system and swap partitions*—The installation program will use `mke2fs` and `mkswap` to lay down the second-level disk format so that it will be able to access these partitions.

6. *Copy files*—Dearchive the software and create the default configuration files from the CD-ROM, network, or floppies onto the newly partitioned hard disk and reboot.

   Sometimes, the new hard disk is updated with configuration files from a running Linux system. Often, this is done when the administrator wishes to install an updated version of the OS onto the currently running system with a minimum of down time. Generally, the configuration files of the running system are copied to the new system via an FTP connection. After copying the configuration files of the running system and moving them to the new system, this new system should behave just like the running system. After testing the new system to make sure that it performs as expected, the administrator can power down the running system, remove the current hard disk, and replace it with the new hard disk. In this way, a running system can be updated with the newest version of Linux while experiencing a down time of only a few minutes.

7. *Configure a boot up sequence mechanism*—There are many possible configurations and many booting possibilities as well. Three general possibilities are:

   1. Have the LILO write itself to the primary master hard disk drive MBR. Use the LILO to boot Linux or the (optional) other OS. The LILO can boot either OS as the default.

2. Use a DOS program called System Commander to boot Linux or Windows.

3. Leave the old boot program intact so that it boots the other OS, and use a floppy disk to boot Linux.

8. *Setup network*—If the network was not used as the installation media, then configure the network driver, network address, and routing table.

9. *Setup the X Window System*—Select the correct X server for the video adapter and configure the mouse type, monitor resolution, applicable video RAM, and pixel depth.

General Distribution Installation Comparisons

Among the preceding distributions, OpenLinux 2.2 is the most silent with just 13 user prompts, and Debian 2.1 is the most interactive with 140 user prompts. Selecting the full distribution options, some distributions installed as little as 623 MB (Slackware) to as much a 4,200 MB (SuSE) of programs and data. The other distributions installed approximately 1000 MB each. Installation time ranged from approximately 12 minutes for OpenLinux 2.2 to 39 minutes for Debian 2.2.

Assuming that you have yet to install several Linux distributions, now is the time to begin practicing installing different distributions. Appendix A contains several walk-through sections that show step-by-step how to install Debian, OpenLinux, Red Hat, Slackware, and SuSE distributions.

Start Up and Shut Down Sequence

After developing the skills to install Linux, the next step is to learn how to properly boot up and shut down the system. Also, we will review system initialization mechanisms.

The Linux Loader

The Linux loader (LILO) was written by Werner Almesberger. It is the program that resides in the first sector or master boot record (MBR) of the hard disk. LILO reads a list of internal parameters from the MBR to decide when and which OS image to load and execute. For example, assume the following setup from the file /etc/lilo.conf:

```
# Tell the kernel we have two Ethernet cards and 128 MB RAM
append="ether=11,0x280,eth0 ether=5,0x300,eth1 mem=128M"
```

```
boot = /dev/hda      # Which device to boot from
root = /dev/hda2     # Which partition contains other boot data
prompt               # Prompt for interaction if key pressed
timeout = 50         # Wait up to 5 seconds for interaction
image=/boot/vmlinuz # 1st boot image on hda2
    label=SUSE6.0  # Name of OS for prompt
    root=/dev/hda2 # Its file system is also on hda2.
    read-only
image=/boot/vmlinuz-2.0.36-3.mandrake  #2nd boot image on hda2
    label=Mandrake # Name of OS for prompt
    root=/dev/hda3 # But its file system is on hda3.
    read-only
```

These parameters, also known as boot stanzas, become fixed in the executable boot image and are placed in the MBR. This is accomplished with the LILO command. In other words, the LILO program is a front-end program that copies its boot code and the preceding parameters (from the file /etc/lilo.conf) into the MBR.

In the preceding example, the LILO append parameter has been used to pass three parameters into the kernel. The first two parameters tell the kernel where to look for Ethernet adapters and the logical names of the Ethernet adapters. The third parameter tells the kernel that the system has 128 MB of main memory. The timeout parameter tells LILO to wait five seconds (i.e., 50 tenths of a second = five seconds) for the user to press the <Tab> or <Shift> keys. Pressing the <Tab> key causes LILO to display OS labels SUSE6.0, Mandrake, and the prompt Boot. The user then enters the OS name (label) and presses <Enter> to begin the boot process.

Note that both boot images are on the hda2 partition, but the second OS entry (Mandrake) has its file system on hda3.

System Boot Up Sequence

System boot up goes through several phases that include LILO, kernel initialization, running shell scripts that activate system services, and initializing the login process.

Steps Common to All Distributions

All distributions begin the boot up sequence in the same way. First, the BIOS runs LILO from the MBR. Second, LILO executes and locates the boot file system. Third, LILO runs its secondary loader /boot/boot.b which, in turn, loads the Linux kernel and runs it. As the kernel initializes itself, many messages are displayed on the console screen including messages about the CPU, its speed, the type of instructions it can execute, the various peripherals it discovered (autoprobed), and the low-level network protocols being activated.

These messages can be reviewed with the dmesg command after the system comes up and the user logs into the system.

After initialization, the kernel runs the first application (user space) program, called init. The init program is the ancestor of all other programs and its task is to read the various resource control (rc) files, run the background system programs, and launch the login programs. Note that messages continue to be displayed on the console screen during the boot up sequence described later, and that the final step in this sequence is the appearance of the Login: prompt.

Steps Unique to Distributions

Linux distributions differ in how the init program reads the resource control files and executes the boot up programs (shell scripts). This may seem to be a fundamental difference among distributions, but in reality the strategies are not only similar, but easy to understand and easy to modify. Note that these are the same resource control files discussed in the next section.

As noted, the kernel simply runs ancestor init with a run level as a command line argument. For the various distributions, the subsequent system boot up sequence is as follows:

1. Red Hat and OpenLinux

   Both employ a directory called /etc/rc.d/ that contains shell programs and names of shell programs. The programs are contained in a master directory called /etc/rc.d/init.d/. There are other directories named after the run levels, such as /etc/rc.d/rc0.d/ for run level zero. Each of these /etc/rc.d/rc?.d/ directories (where ? represents a run level) contains a list of program names that are in the master directory /etc/init.d/. A master program called /etc/rc.d/rc accepts a run level argument (0,1,2, etc.) and runs the programs in the specified directory. Finally, the /etc/rc.d/rc program runs another program called /etc/rc.d/rc.local, where programs unique to this site installation can be run.

2. SuSE

   The SuSE run-level directory is located in sbin/init.d; however, SuSE links to it through the traditional etc/rc.d/name. SuSE functions in the same way that Red Hat and OpenLinux do, except the master directory /etc/rc.d/init.d/ links back to the current directory /etc/rc.d/ where all the scripts are held.

3. Debian

   Debian functions the same as Red Hat, except that it employs a master directory called /etc/init.d that contains all the shell programs. There are other directories named after the run levels, such as /etc/rc0.d for run level zero. Each of these /etc/rc?.d directories (again, where ? represents a run level) contains a list of program names that are in the master directory /etc/init.d/. A master program called /etc/init.d/rc accepts a run level argument (0, 1, 2, etc.) and runs the programs in the specified directory. Finally, the last program name in the /etc/rc?.d/ directory is the program called /etc/init.d/rc.local where programs unique to this computer can be run.

4. Slackware

Like Red Hat and OpenLinux, Slackware employs the /etc/rc.d/ directory that contains shell programs run directly by ancestor init. Unlike Red Hat and OpenLinux, Slackware does not use the symbolic file-linking indirection method of the other distributions. Instead, the files contain directly executed shell scripts.

Init and Run Levels

As noted in the previous section, after the kernel completes its initialization, it runs the first user space program, called init. The init program is key to the whole system since it is responsible for starting all the other user space system programs. A series of resource control files determine which system programs should be run or stopped, and an argument or signal to the init program tells it which resource control file to run.

Thus, the concept of a run level is nothing more than an argument or signal number sent to the init program to tell it the where to find the list of programs (shell scripts) that must be run to switch from one run level to another run level. Here is a list of typical Linux run levels:

0	Shut down—Terminate the programs begun at system start up.
1 (or S)	Single-user—Skip the multi-user login step and just run a command line shell on the console terminal. Note that the S is allowable since the run level argument is a string passed from the kernel to the init program. In the event that signals are sent to the init program, then the run level argument is numeric.
2 (or 1)	Multi-user—The normal operating mode (sometimes without network).
3	Varies among distributions (maybe multi-user with networking).
4	Varies among distributions.
5	Varies among distributions.
6	Reboot—Go to run level 0 then to multi-user (run level 2 or 3 depending on the distribution).

As indicated, the middle levels (3–5) vary in function, but more often than not, one or two of them are unused and the third run level starts the GUI window manager or starts the login sequence (the xdm display manager).

For example:

- Red Hat 6.0 and OpenLinux 2.2—In both Red Hat and OpenLinux, level 3 is multi-user with networking, level 4 is unused, and level 5 runs an X11 window manager.

- Debian 2.2—Debian equates run levels 2, 3, and 4 to run the same multi-user plus networking configuration, and level 5 runs a login display manager.

- SuSE 6.1—SuSE does not have levels 4 or 5, and level 3 runs the xdm display manager.

- Slackware 4.0—Slackware level 3 is multi-user plus networking, 4 runs the xdm display, and 5 runs the default X11 window manager.

Finally, it should be noted that the default start-up run level is controlled by the following line in the /etc/inittab file:

```
# default run level
id:2:initdefault:
```

Here, the number 2 (meaning multi-user) can be replaced with another run level. For example, if you wanted to run a graphical login sequence automatically and you were using the Slackware distribution, then replace the number 2 with the number 5 (meaning the xdm display manager).

Logging In and Out

At the virtual consoles and whenever there's a remote login via the network, Linux presents the Login: message. In response, the user enters an account name followed by (or ending with) the <Enter> key. This causes the login program to run and to present the Password: message. Next, the user enters a password followed by the <Enter> key. For example:

```
Login: jjones<Enter>
Password:<Enter>
```

Successful Login Activates a User Shell

If an existing account name and valid password is entered, the login program will initiate a command line shell program for the user. The name shell comes from the idea of encapsulating layers. Back in 1975, it was considered a revolutionary idea to move what was then called the monitor out from the kernel and into user space. In this sense, the shell encapsulates kernel services much like the shell of an egg encapsulates the embryo and nutrients. Today, of course, the shell itself is encapsulated by the GUI.

Logging Out

Logging out of the system depends on how the shell has been configured. By default, the shell will accept the end-of-file (EOF) character <Ctrl>D as the termination command and return the user to the Login: prompt. Alternatively, some shells may be configured to prompt the user to use the built-in shell commands logout or exit.

Data Cache and System Shut Down

The goal of a data cache is to reduce long disk I/O delays by saving previously accessed disk blocks in main memory so that they are quickly accessible when needed (the blocks are flushed to the hard disk when they are no longer needed).

As an aside, the Linux kernel has a unique data cache mechanism when compared to other Unix-like OSs. In Linux, the data cache grows and shrinks in size depending on the amount of memory not used by other programs. Approximately 1.5 MB of memory is left unallocated for new programs, and the remainder is given over to the data cache. As a result, it is not uncommon to see the data cache occupy one- to two-thirds of physical memory. This is one reason why Linux is one of the fastest OSs being used today.

The problem, of course, is what happens in the event of a power failure, or if someone turns off the computer? The simple answer is that the disk blocks in main memory are lost, and the file system is corrupted and must be reconstructed. Linux will minimize this problem by periodically saving any outstanding modified disk blocks. Therefore, to turn off Linux, you must first terminate the system programs that reset open files and flush the data cache before termination.

Shutting Down Linux

Linux can be turned off with signals or commands given to the ancestor, or parent, of all Linux programs—the init program. Anyone can generate the bottom-up I/O signals sent to init, such as "power failure" or "reboot," but only the superuser may issue commands to the init program. The central program is named "shutdown," and it is called from other programs in various ways:

shutdown now	A direct call to the utility with the English argument "now."
halt	Effectively the same as issuing "shutdown -h now."
reboot	Effectively the same as issuing "shutdown -r now;" that is, the shutdown program is called with the reboot option indicated via the -r switch.

Typing `<Ctrl><Alt><Del>`	If there are MS-Windows NT users around, this option may be removed from the `/etc/inittab` file to prevent them from shutting down the Linux box inadvertently when using the NT login technique.
Imminent power failure	Some machines provide a signal from an UPS, indicating power failure in X minutes. This signal initiates the count down for system halt in X minutes. If power is restored, the UPS will provide another signal that will terminate the countdown and restore Linux to its normal state.

File System Structure

The key to using Linux is knowing the ins and outs of its file system structure. This means knowing how to use hierarchical file name conventions: conventional placement of files, traversing physical volumes, accessing removable media, and understanding file system abstractions.

Global File System Hierarchy

Linux follows the Unix tradition of employing hierarchical file names where the target file is specified with a path. The path contains a starting point, optional directories, and the file name. There are two types of paths: absolute and relative. Absolute paths take the form:

```
/var/spool//lpd/lp/lock
```

where the first forward slash (/) means the beginning or *root* directory. Subsequent forward slashes separate directory names and the file name. The double slash (//) was included to show that Linux, like its predecessors, skips extra slashes when looking up file names. Relative paths take the form:

```
mail/fred/letter5
```

where the absence of the first slash means the current directory path should be prepended to the relative path in order to create an absolute path. This situation takes advantage of the fact that the system remembers the position of the current, or working, directory. The command `pwd` prints the working directory.

File System Hierarchy Standard

In general, Linux distributions have the root file structure shown in the following display. It is recommended that as few as possible additional directories be added to the root directory. The file system hierarchical standard is shown later.

The root directory is recognized at system boot-up time. Other volumes must be mounted onto directories that begin with the root directory. In the following list, the word essential refers to programs that must always be available even though other volumes are not mounted.

/ --	The root directory
--bin	Essential commands that are always mounted
--boot	Boot loader and kernel images
--dev	Device driver access points
--etc	Host-specific system configuration
--home	User account home directories, a large branch
--lib	Libraries, runtime load libraries, and kernel modules
--mnt	Mount point of removable media
--opt	Local add-on application software packages
--proc	Kernel status routines
--root	Home directory for the root user—always mounted
--sbin	Essential system administration command binaries
--tmp	Temporary files—use /usr/tmp for applications
--usr	Secondary hierarchy—large branch
--var	Variable data—dynamic logging, spooling, and status information

Volume Referencing

Since the firmware controls access to hard disk partitions as well as subpartitions (BIOS extended partitions), then each partition appears to the operating system (OS) as a separate and independent volume. Assuming that there are multiple hard disks or hard disk partitions, the OS file manager must have a way to move among these independent volumes. Many OSs have followed a convention where each volume is given a logical name like C:, D:, etc. But in Unix-like OSs, each physical volume has been hidden within one large, logical directory hierarchy. Consequently, this means that **movement** among the logical directories results in physical movement among the hard disk volumes.

To view the physical volumes that make up the logical directory hierarchy, the mount command can be used. Furthermore, the mount command will reveal where in the hierarchy the switch is made between (physical) volumes. For example:

```
hostname:~$ mount
/dev/sda1 on  /     type  ext2 (rw,errors=remount-ro)
proc      on /proc type  proc (rw)
/dev/sda3 on  /usr  type ext2  (rw)
```

Here, we see that there are three partitions on SCSI disk a (although the second partition is for the proc file system, which is a pseudo file system). The first partition (sda1) is the root volume. We will discuss the /proc file system in a later section. The third partition (sda3) provides read-write access to any of the files on its physical volume through the /usr directory. That is, as you negotiate the logical directory /usr, you are also negotiating the physical volume of /dev/sda3.

Mounting Removable Media

There are two basic classes of mountable devices—read only and read/write. To place a read only disk volume into the directory hierarchy, you must mount the volume with the mount command. For example, to mount an ATAPI type CD-ROM drive, enter a command such as:

```
mount /dev/hdb /var/src
```

The first parameter on this command line is the device name, and the second is the name of the mount point within the logical file system. Now, enter the mount command again but without arguments. This will show the mount table:

```
hostname:~$ mount
/dev/hda2 on /       type ext2 (rw)
proc         on /proc   type proc (rw)
/dev/hdb  on /var/src type iso9660 (ro,noexec,nosuid,nodev)
```

By examining this mount table data, you can see that entering the directory /var/src switches over to the CD-ROM drive. Also, it should be noted that the eject button is disabled while the CD-ROM is mounted. Use the unmount command (called umount) to unmount the CD-ROM and reenable the eject button on the CD-ROM drive. Finally, the CD-ROM is mounted "read only," meaning that when a program attempts to write to the CD-ROM, it is refused permission as opposed to receiving a write error from the device.

Another class of mountable devices are the read/write devices such as a floppy disk, the LS120 superdisk, and Zip drives. If desired, these other types of disks may be mounted in a similar fashion to the CD-ROM drive. The `mount` program probes the disk to see if it contains an MS-DOS format or Linux format and mounts the drive according to its type of file system. Auto-probing allows work to be moved more easily between systems, should the need arise. For example, an MS-DOS formatted floppy can be mounted, Word-Perfect files could be saved onto the floppy, and the floppy unmounted. The floppy disk could then be taken to a Windows machine and the MS-Windows version of WordPerfect could read the files.

Conventional Mount Points
for Removable Media

Disk volumes may be mounted on any directory. Sometimes it is advantageous to mount a volume in a user's home directory; however, most removable media mounts are done in the `/mnt` directory. Sometimes there are subdirectories `/mnt/floppy` and `/mnt/cdrom` in the `/mnt` directory, and other times there are `/floppy` and `/cdrom` mount points set up in the root directory. Remember, the mount point is used to switch over to the drive that would contain Linux or MS-DOS files.

A Fast Way to Read/Write MS-DOS Disks

Continuing the WordPerfect example, using Mtools provides an alternative to the mount command. You can use the `mtools` program suite to check, read, or write a Linux-based WordPerfect file to or from a floppy with MS–DOS-based WordPerfect files on it. In other words, instead of saving the files on a floppy disk through Linux-based WordPerfect, you would enter the command:

```
mcopy document.wpd a:
```

where the file name `document.wpd` would be copied to the floppy disk. The file transfer could be confirmed with the command:

```
mdir a:
```

to show the directory of files on the MS-DOS formatted floppy.

File System Abstractions

The Linux kernel is unique among other Unix-like OSs in its use of the file manager. Even though the user views a single file manager front-end, there are a minimum of 12 back-ends. A given kernel may not have all of the various back-end file managers precompiled internally, but additional back-ends can be loaded as kernel modules.

Part of the original Unix design is the idea that file names could be avenues to information other than just hard disk data. These special files can lead directly to physical devices or to logical constructs often called system abstractions. The Linux kernel has been able to exploit abstractions with its ability to dynamically load file manager back-ends. One of the best examples is a pseudo file system to report the status of programs, device drivers, and kernel internal events. Access to this pseudo file system, or "system abstraction," is accomplished by going to the directory /proc.

In other words, displaying the contents of a file within the /proc directory does not switch hard disk volumes, but instead, switches to a kernel routine that shows system status as a series of directories, files, and file contents. Here is a list of conventional abstractions:

/proc	Provides direct kernel status routines.
/dev/xxx	Provides direct access to device xxx.
/dev/null	Returns EOF when read and ignores all input when written into.
/dev/zero	Returns any number of characters requested, but they are always the null (zero) character.

Basic System Navigation

So far we have reviewed kernel installation, system initialization, shutdown and boot up, logging in, and the file system structure. Next, we need to know basic command navigation, basic system administration, and GUI initialization and start-up methods.

Case Sensitivity

When logging onto a Linux system or another Unix-Like OS, you'll notice how most output is displayed in lowercase characters. For example, to view files within a directory, use the ls command.

```
[hostname]$ ls
alpha.txt    edolog    input    mbox
clog         edulog    lc.tz    olog
edclog       flog      llog     wish
[hostname]$
```

The command ls is in lowercase, as are the file names. If the command LS is typed, the result will be:

```
[hostname]$ LS
bash: LS: command not found
[hostname]$
```

The reason is that the name of the directory program is ls and typing LS is a request to the bash shell to look for a program named LS. Unlike other operating systems that automatically map uppercase characters to lowercase for file names, Unix-like operating systems use upper- and lowercase characters in all file names.

In fact, you can use most any ASCII character for a file name including the <space> character. The security implications of file names made up of spaces will be discussed in the security study guide, but for now, be aware that all files are case sensitive and that they may include most any character or sequence of characters.

The cd and ls Commands

The two key commands in any operating system is movement among directories and the display of file names. Directory movement is accomplished with the cd command, and file name display is accomplished with the ls command. For example, let's assume the shell prompt has been configured to show the account name and host name followed by the name of the current directory. In this case, the shell prompt would be:

```
[name@host home]$
```

where name is the user account, host is the network name of the computer, and home is the current directory. Assuming the directory named mail was below the directory named home, then issuing the command cd mail would result in the current directory switching from home to mail like so:

```
[name@host home]$ cd mail
[name@host mail]$
```

The ls command displays file names as described in Chapter 3 and it also displays the owner and access permissions for other user accounts. For example, the command ls -l * gives the long form display for all files in the current directory, except those that begin with a dot character.

```
[name@host mail]$ ls -l *
-rw--------  1 jordan     users          49 Jul 17  1998 clog
-rw-rw-r----  1 jordan     users          46 Jul 29  1998 edclog
-rwxr-xr-x  1 jordan     users          49 Sep 13  1998 edolog
```

These files are owned by the account named jordan and they belong to the group users. Jordan may or may not be a member of the group users, but the account name is usually also a member of the group associated with the file.

The owner, group, and all others have separate read (r), write (w), and execute or search (x) permissions for each file in the directory as well as for the directory itself. Thus, in the preceding example the file `clog` has read and write permission for the owner, but no other permissions are provided for group members or others. The middle file `edclog` is readable and writable for the owner and group members, but only readable for others. The last file `edolog` is readable and executable by all, but only the owner may write (change the contents of) the file.

One more point about permissions. The execute (x) permission is interpreted as a search permission when the file is a directory. For example, the command `ls -ld` displays the access permissions for the current directory:

```
[name@host mail]$ ls -ld
drwxr-xr----  3 jordan   users   1024 Jun 25 18:09   .
```

Note that the leftmost character has switched from a dash (-) or regular file in the previous example to a "d" meaning directory-type file. Now, the meaning of x has changed to mean that the owner and group members have directory search permission, but not others. Since the x was replaced with a - for others, now the `ls` command will not display file names in this directory for others. However, since the x permission only refers to searching, the files in the directory may still be accessed *via* their file relative permissions if the file names are already known. In other words, even though others could not see the files `clog`, `edclog`, and `edolog`, others can still read the files `edclog` and `edolog`.

Finally, the number to the left of the file creation date is the size of the file in bytes. Directories are allocated in logical OS blocks so, in Linux, their size will always be a multiple of 1024 bytes.

The Process Status (ps) Command

As users log into the system, additional programs are created. The first set of programs are created by the system, and they can be viewed using the `ps` command. By typing `ps` at the shell prompt immediately after login, the following output would be produced on Red Hat Linux:

```
PID    TTY  STAT TIME  COMMAND
13977  p0   S    0:00  /bin/login -h hostname domain.com -p
13978  p0   S    0:00  -bash
13992  p0   R    0:00  ps
```

Aside from the process identifiers (PIDs), we can also see from the display that the user logged in from the network (TTY type p0), that the two system programs (login and the bash shell are sleeping (STAT type S), and that the process status (ps) program is running (STAT type R).

In Red Hat versions, the login program waits in the background. On other versions of Linux, you would see:

```
PID     TTY   STAT TIME COMMAND
397     3     S    0:00 -bash
13978   p0    S    0:00 -bash
13992   p0    R    0:00  ps
```

In these versions, the login program terminates before the shell is run. In this display, there is also a second shell program run from TTY 3 by the same user.

As an aside, note that the terms process and program are used interchangeably here. To be more precise, program refers to just the code that makes up the application or utility. However, programs need the assistance of I/O libraries and the kernel. A process, therefore, is said to be the action of a program as it invokes actions from library routines as well as kernel services.

Revisiting the idea of a concurrent, multi-user system, the output of the ps command shows only the current user even though there may be other users logged into the system. There are other forms of the ps command that show more information, such as ps eax, which shows all system processes.

The kill, nice, and renice Commands

As we saw earlier, the ps command allowed us to see how many other programs have been created and owned by the current user account. Two other basic commands allow you to exercise control over these programs. The kill command sends signals (software interrupts) and can be used to terminate a specified process, and the nice command lowers the scheduling priority so that other programs may be selected to run.

The kill command is typically used in combination with other status commands such as the ps command. If the ps command has produced the following display:

```
  PID TTY STAT TIME COMMAND
  397   3   S  0:00 -bash
13978  p0   S  0:00 -bash
13992  p0   R  0:00  ps
```

Then the kill command could be used to terminate one of the bash shells. For example the command:

```
[name@host home]$ kill -KILL 397
```

would send the terminate signal to PID 397 and cause its termination. On the other hand, the nice (as in be nice to others) command could be used to start other programs at a low priority. The `renice` command will lower the priority of a running process. For example, the command: `renice 15 397` would lower the program's scheduling priority from the default of 0 to 15. The lowest priority provided by the GNU utilities is 19 and the highest priority is –20. (Note that Linux keeps the old convention of larger numbers meaning lower priority.) In case you are wondering, only the superuser may use the `nice` command with a negative value to raise a processes' priority.

The who and w Commands

To see if other users are logged in or if there are other virtual terminals with login sessions, use the commands `who` or `w`. For example:

```
hostname:~$ who
lindsay     tty1       Apr  2 08:58
lindsay     ttyp0      Apr  2 11:01  (host1.yourcompany.com)
lindsay     ttyp1      Apr  3 07:59  (host1.yourcompany.com)
lindsay     ttyp2      Apr  1 13:53  (sales.offsite.com)
```

The user `lindsay` is logged in four times; once on a virtual system console (`tty1`), twice over the network from a computer called `host1`, and once more from a computer called `sales`. For example:

```
hostname:~$ w
11:54am  up 2 days, 14:16,4 users,load average: 0.00,0.00,0.00
USER     TTY   FROM            LOGIN@ IDLE   JCPU  PCPU  WHAT
lindsay tty1                   Fri 8am 2:26  0.91s 0.91s -bash
lindsay ttyp0 host1.yourcompa Fri11am 1.00s  2.91s 0.30s w
lindsay ttyp1 host2.yourcompa 7:59am  1:38m  2.89s 1.81s bash
lindsay ttyp2 sales.offsite.c Thu 1pm 44:21m 0.88s 0.88s -bash
```

The `w` command reports the same information as the `who` command, but with additional details on system usage. The additional information at the top of the display is the up time of the kernel, the number of user accounts logged in, and the number of processes waiting to run now, 5 minutes ago, and 15 minutes ago. The value 0.0 means that there is idle time in the system. The CPU is able to run and complete all tasks before another task requests service. On the other hand, a value of 2 or more means that two or more processes are waiting for service. In these cases, the system will become sluggish.

The Superuser

Generally, the shell is configured to provide two types of command line prompts. The $ symbol represents nonprivileged (or positive value) UIDs whereas the # symbol represents superuser status (a zero value) UID, which tells the file manager to ignore the file system protection scheme. The superuser is also the only account that may request certain system services such as changing date/time, adding a new user account, and increasing a process' priority as described earlier.

Routine Tasks as Superuser

The problem with running as superuser to accomplish routine tasks is that even the simplest of mistakes can lead to a catastrophe. Consider, for example, what would happen as a result of typing the following commands when running as superuser:

```
rm * .bak

rm -rf / home/fred/tmp
```

In both examples, the inadvertent extra space results in deleting all files in the current directory or in the whole file system, respectfully.

Moreover, the problem of accidental file deletion is further complicated by the design of the Linux file system. As with other Unix-like systems, Linux employs a fully indexed file system with direct access to the free-block list. When a file is deleted, its contents form the first-come-first-served free blocks of the next created file. Thus, once a file has been deleted and a new file has been created, the old file blocks have been reused.

Another largely unforeseen consequence of working as superuser has to do with the files that are created while operating under superuser status. These files will have very restricted access permissions associated with them as a result of being created by the superuser. This means that there will be a higher probability of having to run as superuser in the future to access the files created earlier.

Use Superuser Status to Switch Among Users

Administrators can quickly switch from user to superuser status with variants on the `su` command, which changes the current user account effective UID to 0 to allow access to files or services. Another form of the `su` command is the command `su - useraccount` where the dash means switch from the superuser account to that user account environment. Said another way, it is just like logging in as that user.

To return to the superuser account, simply log out of the user's shell and to return to the original account, then log out of the superuser shell.

Starting a Display or Window Manager

The final step in system setup and installation is to launch the graphical user interface (GUI). The X Window GUI has three basic components: a display manager called xdm (that provides a GUI login), an X server (the device driver for the monitor), and desktop (window) managers. Both the X server and the window manager are launched with the startx command.

The console is configured for six virtual terminals, F1 through F6. Starting the display manager with the xdm command or launching the window manager GUI with the startx command may be done from any of the virtual terminals, but the GUI is subsequently displayed on virtual terminal F7.

Once the display manager is launched with the xdm command, it never terminates. Instead, the xdm program presents a graphical login screen, waits for someone to login, and starts up a desktop (window manager) for the user. Upon session termination, the xdm program automatically restarts the login request screen and waits again for someone to login. Since the display manager is intended for a multi-user environment, only the superuser may execute the xdm command. To begin the display manager automatically at system start-up time, change the default run-level, or add the xdm command to one of the distribution-specific system boot-up files described earlier in the system start-up section.

One of the window manager GUIs is launched either from the xdm program or directly from the user's virtual terminal with the startx command. Again, the window manager desktop GUI is displayed on virtual terminal F7 and the other six virtual terminals remain available for use with a command line shell.

X Windows System Initialization Files

The xdm login manager, X server, window manager desktop, and applications each have one or more configuration files with initialization parameters. Furthermore, there are both systemwide initialization files and user-specific initialization files. Also,

- The user-specific files have precedence over the systemwide files.
- If the xdm display manager is running, its initialization files have precedence over the startx initialization files.

Systemwide initialization files are found in /etc/X11, where:

- /etc/X11/xinitrc is read by startx.
- /etc/X11/Xsession is read by xdm.

Many times the xinitrc file name is linked to the Xsession file. In this way, any changes to the xinitrc file go directly into the higher priority Xsession configuration file.

More recently, OpenLinux 2.2, Red Hat 6.0, and SuSE 6.1 distributions have moved the systemwide configuration files. The new location is `/etc/X11` `/xinit/xinitrc` for `startx` and in some cases the Xsession start-up file has been renamed to `/etc/X11/xinit/Xclients`.

The user-specific initialization files are in the home directory for each user. These files are:

- `.xinitrc`, read by startx
- `Xsession`, read by xdm

Finally, as various GUI applications run, they create and maintain history files in the user's home directory. For example, Netscape creates the .netscape directory that holds, among other things, the last size and position of the Netscape window. In this way, Netscape can position its browser window in the same place that it was the last time the program was run.

The Virtual Display and Other GUI Tips

The power of the X Window system is that any visual and interactive element can be configured, and as a result, most things are configured in unique ways. Additionally, unlike other OSs, it is difficult to make generalizations about Linux GUIs since a large number of GUIs have been written for the Linux OS (and there is considerable variety among them).

Each GUI's look and feel is controlled by its particular window manager. Furthermore, Linux GUIs generally have only the most basic features in common. Some of the common features of Linux GUIs are considered briefly here. The K Desktop Environment (KDE) is a general exception. KDE's basic GUI controls were inspired by the MS-Windows GUI and, therefore, make an excellent transition to Linux for users more comfortable with Microsoft products than Unix-like products.

Pop-Up Menus

A right-click, middle-click, or left-click on the desktop will reveal one or more pop-up menus that provide access to programs, exit the desktop, configure the desktop, or switch to another area of the virtual display. It should be noted that this is not true for the KDE window manager.

The Virtual Display

Unlike other OS GUIs, the X11 window managers can exploit unused video memory by creating a virtual display that is four, six, or more times larger than the screen. The details of navigating the virtual display depend upon which window manager is used. Generally, there is a "pager" that always remains in the same position on the desktop on top of other visual elements. Clicking on one of the quadrants within the pager switches to that area of the virtual display. Also, many window managers provide virtual display navigation via the desktop pop-up menus. One default configuration for window managers, such as Afterstep and Enlightenment, permits movement among virtual display quadrants as the mouse cursor travels to the edge of the display. The KDE window manager provides a pop-up menu (from the title bar) that allows the window (as opposed to the user) to be sent to another virtual display area. Finally, the most common window managers are Afterstep, Blackbox, Enlightenment, KDE, FVWM, and Window Maker.

X Window Scrolling

Each window manager employs a widget set that provides common controls within a window, such as scrolling. Most X11 scroll bars work as expected. However, the default X Window scroll-bar widget is found in older X11 applications, and it is unusual compared to other GUIs. Moving the mouse cursor along the scroll bar creates a double arrow cursor. Regardless of where the cursor is located in the scroll bar (top or bottom) clicking on the left mouse button scrolls the window down and clicking on the right mouse button scrolls the window up. Moving the cursor from the top towards the bottom of the scroll bar results in larger "chunks" of scrolling either up or down with each mouse click.

X Window Resizing

Generally, windows have a title bar with buttons; the left-hand button(s) on the title bar, if any, allow the focus to be switched from window to window. The right-most title bar button usually contains an X, and clicking it will terminate the window. The two title-bar buttons next to the right-most button control window size. One will usually contain a dash symbol and clicking it will pull the window up much like a window shade (that is, it will be minimized). The other button contains a window symbol; clicking it will maximize the window, but sometimes not enough to fill the screen.

The full screen effect can be achieved by right-clicking the same button. Sometimes the full screen operation places the window resize button under a floating control panel (such as a pager or "wharf") where the resize button cannot be reached. The full-sized window now hides windows below it and the pager or wharf hides the resize button as well. Thus, it appears that you are stuck, and the only way out is to kill the X Window environment with the <Ctrl, Alt, Backspace> key. But there is another way out; simply double-click the title bar and the window will come to the top and occupy the entire screen. Windows may also be resized by clicking on and dragging the corner edge.

Although this solution may appear to be handy, be aware that it has its problems as well. For example, you may have made Netscape full screen, but a requestor or dialog box pops up and is waiting for your input. If the window title bar has been double-clicked and is on top, the requestor/dialog box will be hidden under the Netscape window. Thus, the system will appear to be locked up, but the real problem is simply that a hidden requestor box generated by the program is waiting for the OK button to be clicked. Double-clicking the title bar again will allow the other windows to appear.

Copy and Paste

Unlike other OSs, the X Window System does not have a fully evolved clipboard with edit commands such as undo, cut, clear, and select all. There is, however, a minimal copy and paste mechanism.

To copy, drag the cursor over the desired text. Move the focus to the destination window and position the program cursor (not the mouse cursor) to the desired position for insertion, and click the middle mouse button to paste the highlighted text.

Note that this only works between the highlight operation and the next paste mouse click. If the left mouse button is used to highlight other text, even in another window, then the previously highlighted text is forgotten.

If the mouse has only two buttons and three-button emulation has been enabled, then click both mouse buttons before releasing either one to emulate the third mouse button. The copy and paste operations generally work among X Window applications; however, large applications such as Star Office may not support the importing or exporting of the X Window copy and paste operations.

X Terminal Font Sizes

Many times a high-resolution display in combination with small default fonts make text difficult to read. To enlarge the font size, position the cursor in the X terminal window and press the <Ctrl> key and the right mouse button simultaneously. A menu of font sizes will appear. Move the cursor to the desired font size, then release the <Ctrl> key and mouse button. Again, some window managers, like KDE, provide their own Kterm windows, which offer this feature with a right-button mouse click in the KDE terminal window.

GUI Utilities: Linuxconf, Lisa/COAS, and YaST

Probably the most significant advancement in system setup is the all-in-one system configuration utilities. These programs are interactive, meaning that the operator does not have to remember the myriad Linux and GNU configuration commands, much less their various arguments. Instead, these configuration utilities take the operator through a given configuration process in a step-by-step fashion. The GUI mega-utilities can be invoked from the command line and from the X GUI. Some can even be invoked from the Web. At the time of this writing, `Linuxconf` is GPLed but is generally found only on Red Hat. `Lisa` is also GPLed and found only on OpenLinux 3.6. `YaST` is copyrighted to the SuSE Corporation and comes with SuSE 6.0. Debian and Slackware do not have default all-in-one configuration utilities.

Use Configuration Utilities with Care

Ease-of-use is a characteristic that makes these tools appealing; yet, since they irreversibly modify the system, they should be used with care. The term irreversibly is dramatic, but it is used to make the point that if the operator does not understand what is being asked by the configuration utility, or the reason why, then the program will silently perform multistep operations that could render the system inoperable. Furthermore, if the operator does not know how to reverse the operations performed, the system will have to be reinstalled.

Another reason these programs can be dangerous is that they cannot know the context behind, or the reason for, the attempted change. In other words, they are very conservative in their approach and check for all possible system interactions. As a result, programs like `Linuxconf` can introduce a few, or a long list of, additional configuration issues. Again, these new issues usually require parameter modifications about which the operator may have no prior knowledge.

In terms of system configuration, the ability to use these all-in-one configuration tools versus manual configuration is similar to the difference between driving and walking, but you must know the rules of the road, driver responsibilities, and have the skills to drive before being able to use a car. Therefore, as the various configuration utilities are discussed, we will revisit these tools to see how the configuration process may be automated.

Maintenance of User Accounts

Since Linux is predicated upon being a multi-user OS, user account creation and deletion form the foundation of system administration. In this section, we will review the basic steps in account creation and then review a series of system administration tools that make the task easier.

Creating a User Account

The first task to be completed after installing Linux is to create user account(s). Although various programs that can be used to facilitate this process will be reviewed in a subsequent section, it is important to understand the basic operations required to maintain user accounts, since this is the only way you can tweak and troubleshoot automated account creation.

One of the key files in Linux is the user-account `passwd` file. Each line of the `passwd` file has seven categories (fields) that are written flush against each other and delimited with colons, as follows:

```
AccountName:EncryptedPassword:UserID:GroupID:UserName:HomeDirectroy:FirstProgram
```

Steps to Set up New User Accounts

New account creation consists of modifying the `passwd` file according to the following eleven steps:

1. Check to see if the shell prompt begins with a # and, if not, issue the `su` command to become the superuser.

2. Edit the file `/etc/passwd` and duplicate the last line, which will look something like this:

   ```
   jordan:0yqyTCla8iFGw:501:100:Jordan K.Jones:/usr/home/jordan:/bin/bash
   ```

3. Assuming the new account name was `meredith`, modify the duplicated line to look like this:

   ```
   meredith:0yqyTCla8iFGw:502:100:Meredith M. Smith:/usr/home/meredith:/bin/bash
   ```

   Note that the account name field was changed to `meredith`, the encrypted password was left unchanged, the user ID was incremented to a new value (502) that is unused by other accounts, the group remained unchanged, the user's name was replaced, the new home directory was inserted, and the first program to run was left unchanged as the bash, or Borne again shell (a play on words used to identify the revised version of the `sh` program that was written by Mr. Borne).

4. Change directory (`cd`) to `/usr/home` and create the user's home directory with the commands:

   ```
   cd /usr/home
   mkdir meredith
   ```

5. Change the owner of the directory from root to the account name:

   ```
   chown meredith meredith
   ```

6. Change the group of the directory from root to the account group:

   ```
   chgrp 100 meredith
   ```

   Note that numbers or names from the file /etc/group work with the chgrp command. There is no requirement that group numbers be consistent from computer to computer. The number 100 was used because it was copied from the previous user in the password file, and the system administrator did not want to look up the group name in the group file. The group number 100 is usually associated with the group "users."

7. Give the new user a password with the command:

   ```
   passwd meredith
   ```

   The passwd program will prompt for a password for the account. The program will also complain about passwords that have too few characters or that appear to be too obvious, but entering the same password again in response to a second prompt will force the program to accept the password. (But only the superuser can insist on a poor quality password.)

8. Change the system administrator's identity to the new user (this will automatically switch to the new user's home directory) with the command:

   ```
   su - meredith
   ```

9. Copy the per-user initialization files from the system standard file /etc/skel into the new user's home directory with the command:

   ```
   cp /etc/skel/.* .
   ```

   Per-user account initialization files begin with the "." (dot) character, which tells the system utility programs to routinely ignore these files. Thus, to copy the files we must explicitly specify the dot. To make matters more confusing, the dot character is also the name of the current directory. In this example, the copy command is specifying that ".*" or all files beginning with the dot character are to be copied to "." or the current directory.

10. Type <Ctrl>D twice—once to log out from the user's shell and return to the superuser environment and a second time to log out from the superuser (root) account.

11. At the Login: prompt, log in as the first user. From now on, do not log in as root. Instead, log in as a user and use the su command to switch to superuser status.

Restricted Accounts

The login procedure normally runs a command line shell, but other programs may be run instead of the shell. For example, it is possible to run just an editor that provides access to a text editor or just a Telnet session. To do this, you simply need to place the full pathname of the program (text editor or Telnet) in the seventh field of the password file for the particular user. In this way, a restricted account could be set up.

ADDUSER

There are a number of programs that assist with the creation and removal of user accounts. Each of these programs assume that the /etc/skel/ directory has the proper default initialization files for the new account. Again, remember that only the superuser can add or update user accounts.

The older GNU utility (written by Guy Maor, Ted Hajek, and Ian Murdock) for performing automated account creation is adduser. It takes a number of arguments, which may be specified in a control file called /etc/adduser.conf. However, if the control file seems like too much bother, another alternative is to create a small shell script (such as the one that follow) that will prompt for each account name and then call adduser to have the account automatically set up. The shell script can be operated interactively, with the administrator manually entering each account name, or it may have input redirected to come from a file to allow for batch operation.

```
echo -n "Enter Account Name: "
read name
while [ $name != "done" ]
do
  adduser -g users -s /bin/bash -d /home/$name -p $name $name
  echo -n "Enter Account name: "
  read name
done
```

In this script:

1. The echo command displays a prompt with new line suppressed.

2. The read command accepts an alphanumeric string into the internal shell variable name.

3. The while command evaluates the string and sets up a loop to continue processing the commands in the "do-done" block until the contents of the internal variable $name equal the literal string done (the sentinel value to be entered either at the command line or as the last line of a batch file). The program may also be terminated by simply typing a <Ctrl>C.

4. The `adduser` command installs a user account by always putting the account in the group users, giving the account a bash shell, and labeling the account with the user's name. As you can see, the `adduser` program does not create a password. The role of the -p $name argument is to insert the plain text account name into the encrypted password file, thereby disabling use of the account until a password is assigned with the `passwd` program.

5. The `echo` and the `read` commands are used again, but now they are processing a list of names.

If the name of this shell script was `newaccount`, then a batch of new accounts could be processed with the command `./newaccount < users`, where the last user account name is done.

The `adduser` program is found in Red Hat 6.0, Debian 2.1, and Open-Linux 2.2. Slackware 4.0 employs the older shell script called `adduser` that interactively collects the arguments and calls the `useradd` program (see the next section).

useradd, userdel, newusers

useradd. As described in the previous section, `adduser` is an older program that automates account setup. There are also some newer account maintenance utilities. The one that we will consider here, `useradd`, was written by Julianne F. Haugh. The `useradd` program takes arguments similar to the `adduser` program and assumes that the `/etc/skel/` directory has the proper default initialization files for the new account. Of course, only the superuser can add or update user accounts. The default arguments used with `useradd` may be specified in a control file called `/etc/default/useradd`. Like `adduser`, `useradd` does not update passwords.

userdel. The `userdel` program can disable an account in the same way that the shell script in the previous section did, or it can remove the user's files and home directory.

Newusers. Unlike `adduser` and `useradd`, the `newusers` program takes a list (batch) of names and plain text passwords to create or update user accounts. Unfortunately, the program encourages the system administrator to keep such a list, which is usually considered an unreasonable security risk.

The `useradd` series can be found in Red Hat 6.0, Debian 2.1, and Slackware 4.0.

Adding Accounts with Linuxconf, Lisa/COAS, and YaST

The configuration utilities `linuxconf`, `lisa/COAS`, and `YaST`, all employ a hierarchical menu of configuration options as the user interface. Each is considered here.

Linuxconf

To create or update a user account, the following options would be selected in `linuxconf`:

```
Config -> User accounts -> Normal -> User accounts
```

(The arrow "->" means select from the next level in the menu hierarchy.) The `linuxconf` program presents a series of requestor boxes asking for the same user account information as described earlier. Eventually, `linuxconf` will run the `adduser` program and then the `passwd` program (see Figure 2.1).

> **NOTE** Selecting a category from the hierarchy and pressing the `<Enter>` key will expand the hierarchy by revealing the subordinate categories. But be careful, since pressing the `<Enter>` key again will hide subordinate category names. Moreover, be aware that category names tend to repeat at different levels, so it is easy to become disoriented.

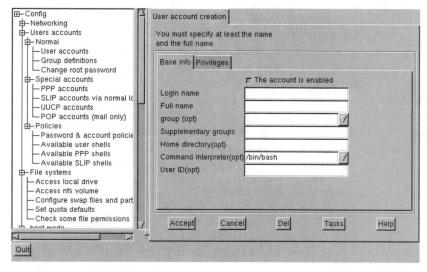

Figure 2.1 A screenshot of linuxconf.

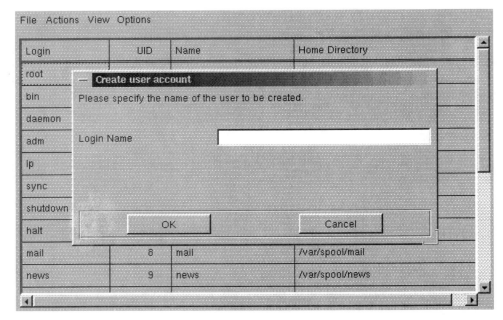

Figure 2.2 A screenshot of Lisa/COAS.

Lisa/COAS

Caldera's OpenLinux 1.3 distribution employs the `Lisa` system configuration tool, and OpenLinux 2.2 distribution employs the `COAS` system configuration tool. `Lisa` or `COAS` are the only system administration utilities offered in OpenLinux to add new user accounts. Focusing on the newer distribution, the following `COAS` menu items must be selected to add new accounts:

```
System -> Account -> Action -> Create User
```

As with `Linuxconf`, the arrow (->) means select from the next level in the menu hierarchy. The `COAS` program also presents a series of requestor boxes asking for the same account information as described earlier. The screen shot in Figure 2.2 shows the requestor box that starts the user account create sequence.

```
Config -> User accounts -> Normal -> User accounts,
```

YaST

In SuSE 6.1, run YaST (it will ask for the superuser password if you are logged in as a regular user). Then select:

```
System administration ->  User administration
```

```
┌─────────────────────USER ADMINISTRATION─────────────────────┐
│ In this mask you can get information about the existing users, create new │
│ users and modify and delete existing ones.                                │
│                                                                            │
│ User name                          :█████████████:                         │
│                                                                            │
│ Numerical user ID                  :             :                         │
│                                                                            │
│ Group (numeric or by name)         :             :                         │
│                                                                            │
│ Home directory                     :                         :             │
│                                                                            │
│ Login shell                        :                         :             │
│                                                                            │
│ Password                           :             :                         │
│                                                                            │
│ Re-enter password                  :             :                         │
│                                                                            │
│  Detailed description of the user                                          │
│ :                                                                        : │
│                                                                            │
│ ▐F1=Help▌  ▐F3=Selection li▌ ▐F4=Create user▌ ▐F5=Delete user▌ ▐F10=Leave mask▌ │
└────────────────────────────────────────────────────────────────────────────┘
```

Figure 2.3   A screenshot of YaST.

A mask will appear (see Figure 2.3). Enter the user account information into each field of the mask.

CHAPTER

3

Shells and Commands

The Shell

There are many different shells included with Linux distributions. Some of these shells are ash, bash, csh, ksh, tcsh, and zsh. Everyone has a favorite shell, but the bash shell tends to be deployed in Linux as the default shell, and it appears to be the most commonly used shell. To keep complexity to a minimum, we will only describe the bash shell in this section.

Command-Line Interpretation

The bash shell is a command-line interpreter that provides the following services:

- Program invocation
- Simple command-line editing
- Program execution and flow control in the execution of other programs (batch jobs)

Probably the most commonly sited reason for using bash is its default use of command history and command completion. We will use the bash shell for our examples unless otherwise noted. Bash is an acronym for Bourne Again Shell and is named after the creator of the first programmable shell for Unix, Stephen Bourne.

Two important shell characteristics are interactivity and script execution. Both are considered briefly here.

Interactivity

Recent versions of the `bash`, `tcsh`, and `zsh` shells all offer command history review and command name completion. Command history is the ability to use the `<up arrow>` and `<down arrow>` keys to display and redisplay previous commands from the most recently typed command to the least recently typed command. The bash shell maintains a history of the most recent commands. By entering the command `history`, you can see a list of all of the commands that have been typed, up to the recall limit. By modifying the `$HISTSIZE` shell variable, you can change the number of commands that can be recalled. Consider the example:

```
bash$ HISTORY=1000
```

This would give the Bash shell the ability to recall the most recent 1000 commands.

Command completion is the ability of the shell to complete the directory name, file name, or command name when the `<Tab>` key is pressed. If there are several name possibilities, then the shell only completes the name as far as it is unique, beeps, and waits for the user to type more characters to make the name unique. Pressing the `<Tab>` key twice tells the shell to display all possible names so that the user may select the desired name.

For example, if the directory contained the file names `julie`, `angus`, `meredith`, `allison`, and `lenny`, typing a command such as bash$ m followed by the `<Tab>` key will display: bash$ `meredith`.

Script Execution

In addition to running programs, shell commands allow the use of variables, variable testing, and branching based upon the value of shell variables. Format of shell variable assignment and testing depend upon which shell is used. In other words, `sh`, `bash`, `ksh`, and `zsh` employ flow control constructs (for example, while and for loops) that are different from the Berkeley-derived `csh` and `tcsh`.

Environment/Shell Variables

A shell variable provides a means of (a) getting the command-line information into a shell program when it is called with parameters, and (b) temporarily storing information within the shell program. Furthermore, shell variables can have values assigned to them as follows:

```
bash$ varName=abcdef
```

When a shell variable is used in any other way than value assignments, the name of the shell variable must be preceded by a dollar sign. However, when assignments are made, as in the preceding example, a $ should not be used. In the next example, the shell variable is not being used in an assignment of value; thus, a $ is required to precede the variable name.

```
bash$ echo $varName
```

An environment variable is similar to a shell variable except that it is a string constant. An environment variable is passed to a child process for the purpose of program initialization.

Another difference between shell variables and environment variables concerns their "visibility" both within and outside of the shell program. Environment variables are global variables. Since every shell program has access to them, we can say that environmental variables are visible to every shell program. Shell variables on the other hand, are local variables; that is, their visibility is restricted to the particular shell in which they are located. A shell variable that is established and used inside one shell will not be accessible by another shell, unless it has been exported via the export command. Consider for example the following:

```
bash$ export varName
```

The variable, varName, that is being exported here will now behave like an environment variable in the sense that it, too, will have global visibility.

Naming Conventions

Yet another difference between shell and environment variables concerns naming conventions. A common practice is to use all uppercase letters for environment variables and mixed case for shell variables. In addition, shell variables can consist of letters, digits, and underscores, but they cannot begin with a digit.

The PATH Variable and the Dot Debate

The PATH variable is a special shell variable. To look at the setting of your path variable, type echo $PATH.

```
bash$ echo $PATH
/usr/local/bin:/usr/bin:/bin:/usr/home/meredith/bin
bash$
```

You will see a list of directory paths, where each directory path is separated from another by the colon (:) character. Note that this is the same directory list that the shell will search for an executable file when the shell is instructed to run a program.

How the PATH Variable Facilitates Program Execution

While in the home directory, if you wanted to run a program in /usr/bin, there are two ways this can be accomplished:

- Explicitly call the program with the full pathname: /usr/bin/myProgram.
- Have /usr/bin in your path as shown, and then you can just type myProgram at the command line to have the shell search all the directories contained in the $PATH variable for the executable.

Even if the program resides in the current directory, the full pathname must be used or it must be in the $PATH variable. However, there is one shortcut that can be used if the executable is in the current directory. Simply type ./myProgram to tell the shell to look in the current directory for the program.

The rationale behind the "dot slash" requirement originates from a past security problem, and as a result, many distributions do not include the current directory, "." in the $PATH variable. The security problem revolves around the routine access of commands and utilities located in the system directories /bin/ and /usr/bin/, such as the directory list (ls) command. If the dot is listed in the $PATH string before the system directories, then a program by the same name in the current directory would be executed instead of the command or utility in the system directory. In this way, a "Trojan horse" could be planted in the current directory that has the same name as a common program, such as the ls command. When the user types ls expecting a directory listing, the Trojan horse would execute and display a message similar to the one here in an attempt to gain the user's password:

```
Session error - terminating program
Login:
Password:
```

In response to this message, the naive user would enter the account name and password. This would allow the Trojan horse program to acquire the user's password and subsequently erase itself so that the next time the ls command is entered, everything would work as expected, leaving the user unaware that his/her password has been stolen. Thus, for security reasons, the dot character is not usually included in the $PATH variable. Some distributions do include the dot character in the $PATH string but *after* the system directories.

Passing Special Characters to the Shell

There are some characters that have special meaning to the shell. A common example of such a character is the * (asterisk). The * is used by the shell as a wild-card character. If a situation should arise in which there was a need to use the * as a literal argument to a command, you would have to tell the shell not to interpret the asterisk as a wild-card character. This can be done by character quoting, also know as "escaping the character." There are a couple of ways that the special meaning of a character can be turned off just for that instance in the Linux shell. These are considered next.

Escaping an Individual Character

To escape a single character, place a backslash immediately before the character. For example, if you wanted to list all of the files that had an * in the file name, the following command would be used:

```
ls -a *\**
```

This would cause the shell to interpret only the first and the third * but not the middle *.

Escaping Multiple Characters

To escape an entire string of characters, use either a pair of double quotes (") or a pair of single quotes ('). The single and double quote delimiters have somewhat different meanings. When using the single quotes, everything that falls between the single quotes will not be shown to the shell for processing. If you use the double quotes, the shell will continue to process any shell variables starting with the $ sign. You can also use the single quotes to turn off the meaning of the double quotes and vice versa.

For example, to search all files in the current directory for a string containing special command characters use:

```
bash$ grep  "I'll find your $name "   *
```

Here the single quote in the word "I'll" will be ignored by the shell (as will the spaces between words), but the shell variable, $name, will be evaluated to determine its value. This value will be placed into the string, replacing this instance of the shell variable.

Back-Quoting Strings of Characters

Single back-quote characters (`) can be used in pairs to delimit strings of characters in the shell. Placing an item in back-quotes means that anything between them will be executed as a separate command and not as part of the arguments to the original command. Here is an example of back-quoting:

```
echo The exact date is `date
```

The output would look like:

```
The exact date is Wed Apr 14 15:07:33 CDT 1999.
```

As you can see, the date command was executed, and the output from it was inserted into the string that was subsequently echoed with the echo shell command.

Shell Aliases

Even the experienced Linux-user admits that seemingly easy commands can become harder to remember when switches are added to them. This is where the convenience of command aliases becomes important. Command aliases provide the ability to make up an easy-to-remember name for a more complicated command.

For example, let's assume that you want to see a full (long) directory listing every time you type the ls command. Using an alias, this can be accomplished easily, as follows:

```
alias ls='ls -l'
```

After this alias is created, each time the ls command is typed, you will see the output just as if you had entered the ls -l command.

To remove this alias, simply type:

```
unalias ls
```

Here are some examples of commonly used aliases:

```
alias ..='cd ..'
alias ...='cd ../..'
alias dir='ls -l'
alias l='ls -alF'
alias la='ls -la'
alias ll='ls -l'
alias ls='ls $LS_OPTIONS'
alias ls-l='ls -l'
alias md='mkdir -p'
alias o='less'
alias rd='rmdir'
```

Unfortunately, aliases are user account specific and, as a system administrator, you'll find yourself continually switching among user accounts and multiple systems. Therefore, the convenience of aliased commands is overridden by the inconvenience of not having the aliases available as you move among systems. Also, it should be noted that by default Red Hat 6.0 aliases the commands cp, mv, and rm with the –i or interactive switch. Some users find the question "Are you sure?" annoying every time they want to copy, move, or delete a file.

By the way, if a command behaves in an unexpected fashion, use the backslash to escape any aliasing. Thus, the command \ls would escape the preceding 'ls $LS_OPTIONS' command and just perform the simpler ls command.

I/O Redirection

In Unix-like systems such as Linux, input and output are handled via three I/O channels known as standard input (stdin), standard output (stdout), and standard error (stderr). Just as the names imply, input comes from the stdin I/O channel, output goes to the stdout I/O channel, and any error output that gets generated is directed toward the stderr I/O channel.

Normally, the stdin I/O channel is associated with the keyboard and stdout is associated with the computer's display. However, there are some special characters that can be used to redirect the input for stdin or to redirect the output for stdout. These characters are ">" and "<". Stderr can be redirected as well, should the need arise.

As an example of output redirection, consider the following:

```
bash$ ls > directoryListing.txt
```

If ls alone were typed, the output would be sent to stdout, which is usually associated with the terminal screen. However, in this example, a redirection operator has been used to send the output of ls to the file named directoryListing.txt. This means that the current value (output) of ls has been saved in a file so that it can be viewed again or manipulated.

Standard input, or stdin, works very much the same way that standard output does. It allows you to redirect a program's input so that it may come from a source other than the keyboard. If, for example, there was a program called printNames, and the input was to come from a text file called names, then the printNames program would be executed as follows:

```
bash$ printNames < names
```

Table 3.1 contains a list of the redirection operators and their functions.

Table 3.1 Redirection Operators

REDIRECTION CHARACTER	WHAT IT CAN DO
>	Redirects output of the left-side command to the right-side device or file, overwriting any file if it already exists.
>>	Has the same effect as the > command, but appends to the end of the file if it already exists, rather than overwriting the file.
2>	Redirects the error output of the left-side command to the right-side device or file, overwriting any file if it already exists.
<	Redirects the input of the left-side command to the right-side device or file.

Program to Program I/O Channels or Pipes

When a pipe character (|) is used between commands, the pipe connects the output of the command on the left-hand side of the pipe to the input of the right-hand command. For example, the following command:

```
bash$ ls -l | more
```

causes the output of the directory listing to become the input of the more command. The only limit to the number of commands that can be piped together is the amount of system resources.

Many commands in Unix-like systems such as Linux read from the standard input and write to the standard output. Pipes take advantage of this fact by providing a shorthand way to connect the output of one program, or command, to the input of another program, or command.

Background Program Creation versus Virtual Terminals

One of Linux's most powerful features is its ability to do more than one thing at a time. This is commonly referred to as multitasking. There are different ways you can exploit multitasking in Linux, and some of these are considered here.

Command Line

When working at the command line, you don't have to wait for a program to finish before beginning another command. Programs can be made to execute in the background by simply following the command with the & character. For example, the following command runs in the background, searching the entire directory structure for the file named `filename`.

```
bash$ find / -name filename &
```

After starting a command, if you subsequently realize that it may take longer to complete than originally thought, you can suspend that command by pressing `<Ctrl>Z`, and push it to the background by issuing the `bg` command. For example:

```
bash$ find / -name filename -print
<Ctrl>Z
bash$ bg
bash$
```

Virtual Terminals

Another way that more than one task can be accomplished at once is by using the Linux virtual terminal feature. By pressing `<Ctrl><Alt>F1` through F6, different virtual terminals may be accessed. For example, you can login on `F1` and begin a task, then switch to `F2` to do other work while the job on `F1` is finishing.

X Window Environment

In the X window environment, you can, of course, have more than a single program (window) open at a time, and you may also have multiple desktops. The multiple-desktop feature is dependent on the window manager being used. Most window managers have a default of four desktops that are laid out in a two-dimensional array. The Enlightenment window manager, however, takes this concept to the extreme: Some default Enlightenment configurations provide the ability to have 32 desktops on the horizontal and vertical axis, plus an additional 32 desktops on the Z axis!

Basic Commands

The remainder of this chapter will present a subset of commands based upon the frequency of use. After each command is presented, examples are provided that show how the command is used in context.

Command Name	`ls` —List directory entries
Synopsis	`ls [ -a -s -F -i -l -r -R -t -u ] pathname`
Description	Each file has not only a name, but certain attributes that are associated with it: name, size, and various dates of modification, owner, group, and permissions. The ls command displays this information in a variety of formats depending on the switches used with the command.
Options	`-a` Includes all files and directories in the listing, including those with a name starting with the character dot.
	`-s` Prints the size of the files in blocks.
	`-F` Appends a character to each file name to indicate its type. It appends an "*" for executable regular files, a "/" for directories, an "@" for symbolic links, a "|" for FIFOs, and a "\" for Unix domain sockets.
	`-i` Includes the index node number (internal file number) in the display. This option is useful if you want to see whether file names are synonyms. If the index node numbers are the same and the files are in the same disk volume, then they are just different names for the same file.
	`-l` Displays a long listing of the file information, including permissions, size, owner, and modifications.
	`-r` Reverses the order of the sort (default is alphabetic).
	`-R` Recursively accesses files in all subdirectories.
	`-t` Sorts the listing by last modification date.
	`-u` Sorts the listing by last access time.

For example, the ls command in the current directory could provide the following results:

```
luke@xwing:~/test > ls -lF
total 560
-rw-rw-r-     1 luke          users        56780  Aug 21 10:39    file1
-rwxr-xr-x    1 luke          users       568832  Aug 21 10:40    prog2*
drwxr-xr-     2 luke          users         1024  Aug 21 10:40    file3/

Permissions   links Owner     Group    File size Creation time   Name Type
```

The output of the `ls  -lF` command has eight basic parts: permissions, links, owner, group, file size, creation date, file name, and symbolic file type. *Permissions* will be discussed in more detail later. *Links* refer to the number of directory entries that contain references to the file. Links are described in more detail under the `ln` command. *Owner* and *group* are the user account (`luke`) that owns the file and the group account (`users`) that owns the file. It is possible to allow a group with no members to own a file. *File size* is the size in bytes. Files may be zero bytes in length (empty). Directory files are created with the mkdir command, and are a multiple of the logical OS block size or 1024 bytes. At the right-most side of the display the symbolic file type is displayed after the file name and without a space. In the preceding example, we see that the "*" means that prog2 is executable and that the "/" means that file3 is a subdirectory.

Permissions

The output of the long form of the ls command reveals a coded permissions field on the left-hand side. The left-most column describes the type of file. The dash "-" character for the first and second rows means they are regular data files containing a stream of bytes. The third row has the "d" character as its left most entry; this means that the file is a subdirectory that contains pairs of file names associated with index nodes.

 The next three permission columns from the left contain a combination of dashes and the characters rwx, where r means read permission, w means write permission, and x means execute permission. The dash character means negation of read, write, or execute permission.

 As you can see from the display, there are three sets of the three columns making a total of nine columns; but remember, *only one of the three sets is applicable at any given point in time*. The first set of permissions refers to the owner of the file, in this case luke, and are active only if the user account luke is attempting to access the files. The second set of permissions refer to the group owner or the group users, and this set is active only if a member of the users group is attempting to access the file. The third and final set of permissions refers to others, or any user account that is not the owner or a member of the group that is trying to access the file.

 Data files cannot be executed, yet the execute permission may be set for these files with no effect on the system. If a data file is set executable and an attempt is made to execute the file, then it is evaluated by the bash shell and an error message is returned indicating that it "cannot execute binary file." If an ASCII data file has been set executable and the user is trying to run the executable file, then bash shell will attempt to interpret the file contents as a series of shell commands. If a particular interpreter is desired, then the ASCII file may begin with the characters "#!" and the path to the interpreter. For example, the following line will have the perl interpreter read the file contents:

```
#!/usr/perl
```

 Directories are much like any other data files in that they cannot be executable, yet they have the x permission. Thus, the x permission for directories means that the file name may or may not be viewed by the owner, group, or others. This only refers to viewing. If the read permission is valid for the user account, then the file may be read even though its name cannot be viewed with the ls command. Also, if the read or write permission is not set for a given directory and owner, then none of the files in the directory may be read or written, respectively.

There are other permission attributes, such as set user ID, set group ID, and set the sticky bit. These are discussed with the chmod command.

Another handy form of the ls command is with the arguments ls -ltr:

```
-rw-r-r-    1 dmw      users      118272 Aug 21 00:02 file
-rw-r-r-    1 jmm      users       53248 Aug 21 00:05 freda
-rw-r-r-    1 dfm      users       20480 Aug 21 02:47 Temp
-rw-r-r-    1 dfm      users       24576 Aug 21 02:47 Temp2
-rw-r-r-    1 jmm      users       45568 Aug 21 07:43 comma
-rw-r-r-    1 cpt      users       28672 Aug 21 12:36 v
-rwxrwxrwx  1 dfm      users          24 Aug 22 01:08 t
-rw-r-r-    1 dfm      users       50688 Aug 22 02:51 commands
```

In this example, we see that files have been listed based upon creation time (because of the –t switch) and that they have been sorted in reverse order (because of the –r switch). In this way, you can quickly review and remind yourself of which files have been most recently created.

The cd command is not a standalone program like most other commands. Instead, it is part of the shell and called a built-in command. Most people use the cd command in its simplest form. By typing cd <dir>, you can move to that directory. In the following examples the bash shell prompt has been set up to show additional information. The prompt shows the account name, john, followed by the host name, sith, followed by the current directory name. For example:

```
john@sith:~ > cd /etc
john@sith:/etc >
```

Here the ~ sign indicates John's home directory /home/john/. The cd command means change working directory. The use of . (dot) and .. (dot dot) allows reference to the present working directory and its parent directory. An example of the use of the dot is:

Command Name	cd
Synopsis	cd [-P -L] <dir>
Description	Changes from the present working directory to the <dir> specified.
Options	-P Changes to the physical directory and does not follow symbolic links.
	-L Forces symbolic links to be followed.

```
john@sith:/etc > cd ./opt/gnome
john@sith:/etc/opt/gnome >
```

The .. (dot dot) move to the parent directory, such as:

```
john@sith:/etc/opt/gnome > cd ..
john@sith:/etc/opt >
```

There is a special class of files called symbolic links. These files usually contain a path to the real file, but they may also contain a path to another directory. If the cd command is used to switch into a symbolically linked directory, the symbolic link is automatically followed. By default, the cd command uses the –L option and shows the symbolically linked name. If the –P switch is used, then the real (hard-linked) directory name is displayed.

Typically, you will change directory temporarily and then return to the home directory. Since the bash shell remembers the previous directory, it is possible to move back and forth between two different directories by using cd -. For example, if the previous directory was the home directory, /home/john, and the current directory is /bin, then the cd - command would have the following effect:

```
john@sith:/bin > cd -
/home/john
john@sith:~ > cd -
/bin
johnos@sith:/bin > cd -
/home/john
```

Associated with the cd command are the shell commands dirs, pushd, and popd. There is a list of currently remembered directories maintained by the bash shell. The dirs command will display this list. The dirs syntax is:

```
dirs [-clpv] [+N] [-N]
```

This list of directories works like a stack. The pushd command pushes a directory onto the list, and the popd command removes a directory from the list. This may sound a bit tricky, but it can be very useful when working between several directories. To see how this works, here is an example of the pushd and dirs commands. This example starts from the home directory (~) and moves throughout several directories within the system.

```
john@sith:~ > dirs
~
john@sith:~ > pushd /etc
/etc ~
john@sith:/etc > pushd /bin
/bin /etc ~
```

```
john@sith:/bin > pushd /etc/opt
/etc/opt /bin /etc ~
john@sith:/etc/opt >
john@sith:/etc/opt > dirs
/etc/opt /bin /etc ~
```

As you can see, there are now four remembered directories. The -l option for the `dirs` tells `dirs` to not use shorthand versions such as ~ for the home directory.

```
john@sith:/etc/opt > dirs -l
/etc/opt /bin /etc /home/john
```

The -v option will cause `dirs` to print each directory on its own line with the associated number entry.

```
john@sith:/etc/opt > dirs -v
0   /etc/opt
1   /bin
2   /etc
3   ~
```

The -p option is the same as -v without the associated number entries.

```
john@sith:/etc/opt > dirs -p
/etc/opt
/bin
/etc
~
```

The +N and -N options displays the Nth entry starting with zero. The +N will count from left to right and the -N will count from right to left, such as:

```
john@sith:/etc/opt > dirs +1
/bin
john@sith:/etc/opt > dirs -1
/etc
john@sith:/etc/opt >
```

Finally the -c option will clear all elements in the directory stack. Pushd and popd allow you to manipulate the directory stack. The `pushd` command places a named directory to the top of the directory stack. Pushd without any arguments causes the top two directories to be exchanged. Pushd without any arguments acts just like `cd -` command. The options available to `pushd` are:

```
pushd [dir | +N | -N]
```

The `dir` option will add the directory listed to the top of the directory stack and make it the present working directory.

```
john@sith:~ > pushd  ~/download/games/
~/download/games ~
```

The +*N* and -*N* options will manipulate the stack such that *N*th directory is at the top of the stack and the present working directory. The +*N* starts counting from the left of the list and the -*N* starts counting from the right of the list. For example:

```
john@sith:/home > dirs
/home /bin /etc ~/download/games ~
john@sith:/home > pushd +3
~/download/games ~ /home /bin /etc
john@sith:~/download/games >
```

Popd removes the directories from the directory stack. If no arguments are given it removes the directory from the top of the stack and changes your working directory to the new top directory.

```
popd [+N | -N]
```

The +*N* and -*N* option is similar to pushd's +*N* and -*N* options except that it removes the *N*th entry from the stack. For example:

```
john@sith:~/download/games > dirs
~/download/games /home /bin /etc
john@sith:~/download/games > popd +3
~/download/games /home /bin
john@sith:~/download/games > dirs
~/download/games /home /bin
john@sith:~/download/games >
```

There are two commands used to view and navigate within ASCII documents: more and less. More is the older command with fewer features, so we will describe the less command. With the less command you can use the up and down arrow keys to move one line at a time or else you can also use the page up and page down buttons to move one page at a time.

With the less command you can specify a search pattern with the -p option and less will browse the file and highlight all the hit keywords. If you want to search for a particular pattern you can start the less command at the prompt with your search pattern as follows:

```
nilesh@yoda:~ > less -p linux filename
```

This command will search for the word linux in the file called filename and highlight all the hits.

You can also search for word occurrences within the less program environment by pressing:

Command Name	less
Synopsis	less [-p pattern] [-N] [-f] [-C] <file name>
Description	Similar to more, but it allows backward movement in the file as well as forward movement. Also, less does not have to read the entire input file before starting, so with large input files it starts up faster than text editors like vi.
Options	**Command line arguments:**

Command line arguments:

-N	Causes a line number to be displayed at the beginning of each line in the file.
-f	Forces nonregular files to be opened.
-C	Clears the screen before proceeding with output.

Commands used once less has been run:

space	Scrolls a full screen.
z	Scrolls forward a full window if N is not specified.
? command	Indicates that the command should be applied to the end of the file first (if relevant or meaningful to do so).
-I	Followed by one of the command line (i) options letters (see later) this changes the setting of that option and prints a message describing the new setting. If the option letter has a numeric value (such as –b or –h), or a string value (such as –P or –t), a new value may be entered after the option letter. If no new value is entered, a message describing the current setting is printed and nothing is changed.

```
<Esc> -/searchkeyword
```

and less will search for that new word. The less command can also take several files at the command prompt and permit navigation through them. For example, type:

```
nilesh@yoda:~ > less filename1 filename2 filename3 filename4
```

to load multiple files at the same time. While viewing one file, you can move to another file, using these two commands:

```
:n  to go to the next file

:p  to go to the previous file
```

While in the less command, an editor may be invoked to edit the file currently being viewed. To do so, just type v and it will invoke the editor specified in the environment variable VISUAL or EDITOR. But, if it is not defined, the default is set to the `vi` editor. After you edit the file and exit, it comes back to the `less` command.

You can also display line numbers before all lines with the less command. You just have to start the `less` command with the -*N* option and each line in your file will have a line number before it. This is helpful when doing a quick search for a line number containing an error. For example:

```
nileshd@yoda:~ > less -N filename
```

The `cp` command makes a copy of files or directories. This command will preserve the properties of a file, but will not preserve the ownership of file. This behavior can be overcome with the "-P" option, which will preserve all the properties of a file. Notice in the following example that the passwd file, which was originally owned by root and by the group root, is now owned by the user ajneel and by the group users. Also, make note that there are now two copies of the passwd file on the system.

```
ajneel@maul:~ > ls -l /etc/passwd
-rw-r-r-   1 root       root            1869 Aug 22 18:07 /etc/passwd
ajneel@maul:~ > cp /etc/passwd .
ajneel@maul:~ > ls -l ./passwd
-rw-r-r-   1 ajneel     users           1869 Aug 23 16:57 ./passwd
ajneel@maul:~ >
```

The `cp` command does not copy directories by default. The "-R" switch can be specified in order to copy a directory. This switch instructs the `cp` command to recursively copy directory contents as well as regular files. For example, if the command `cp /etc/* /etc_backup` was issued then only the files in the top level of this directory would be copied. However, if the same command were

Command Name	cp
Synopsis	cp [-f -i -p -R -u -v] source_file dest_file_or_directory
Description	Copies file or files to new directories or files.
Options	-f Forces overwriting existing destination files.
	-i Interactively prompts whether to overwrite an existing file.
	-p Preserves the original file characteristics including owner, permissions, and modify time.
	-R Recursively copies directories as well as regular files.
	-u Overwrites a file only if the file being copied is newer than the destination file.
	-v Verbose mode. Prints out the name of each file as it is copied.

issued with the -R option, then all files and directories would be copied. In the following example, the files and directories of /usr are copied to the /tmp.

```
ajneel@maul:/tmp > ls
ajneel@maul:/tmp > cp -R /usr/* .
ajneel@maul:/tmp > ls
IBMdb2          doc             i486-linux-libc6  local
X11             empress         i486-linuxaout    man
X11R6           etc             i486-sysv4        openwin
X386            games           include           sbin
bin             i486-linux      info              share
dict            i486-linux-libc5 lib              spool
ajneel@maul:/tmp >
```

In some cases, a file being copied may already exist at the target. Therefore, cp has a couple of options that are useful in these cases. The first is the "-f" option, which forces the copying of files without the complaint. The second is the "-i" option, which causes the cp command to pause and ask for user intervention when a file being copied already exists. Finally, the "-u" option overwrites a file only if the file being copied is a newer file. Note that Red Hat 6.0 aliases the cp command to cp -i.

The ln command is used to create a link between two files or directories. A link is simply a pointer to another file name or directory name. By default, ln will create a hard link to join two or more file names or directory names. Files with only one name have a directory entry made up of the file name and an associated index node (inode) number that points to an inode. The inode describes the contents of the file. Hard links are implemented by creating another directory entry with a new name but the same inode number. To track the number of hard links, the inode also contains a link count number. Thus, a hard link is a path to another file or directory such that if the contents of the link are changed then the original file is changed. For example,

```
ajneel@maul:~/temp > cat original
This is the original file!
ajneel@maul:~/temp > ln original new
```

Command Name	ln
Synopsis	ln [-s -v -i] source_file dest_file_or_directory
Description	Creates a link to directories or files.
Options	-s Creates a symbolic link instead of a hard link (which is the default).
	-v Verbose mode.
	-i Interactive mode.

```
ajneel@maul:~/temp > echo This is text added to the file new  >> new
ajneel@maul:~/temp > cat original
This is the original file!
This is text added to the file new
ajneel@maul:~/temp > ls -l
total 2
-rw-r-r-    2 ajneel    users         62 Aug 24 12:57 new
-rw-r-r-    2 ajneel    users         62 Aug 24 12:57 original
ajneel@maul:~/temp >
```

In this example, we can see that the appended text to the file called new has also changed the file called original. Notice that the hard link new and the file original are both 62 characters in length. Also notice that the number between the file permissions and the user account (the number 2) is the hard link count number from the inode of the file having the names original and new. The disadvantage of using a hard link is that the hard link must be within the current mounted disk volume boundary since inode numbers are only volume relative and not whole file system relative.

However, the ln command can also create symbolic links using the -s option. A symbolic link is a file that contains the full path to another file and it can reference a file anywhere in the file system. Symbolic links behave similarly to hard links except that they are slower to access than hard links. The reason is that once the file manager discovers a symbolic link, it must restart the path lookup process. A second way the symbolic links differ from hard links is that the symbolic file size is equal to the length of the file name and not the length of the file. Notice that in the following example, the file new has a length of eight bytes and the file original has a length of 62.

```
ajneel@maul:~/temp > ln -s original new
ajneel@maul:~/temp > ls -l
total 1
lrwxrwxrwx  1 ajneel    users          8 Aug 24 13:20 new -> original
-rw-r-r-    1 ajneel    users         62 Aug 24 12:57 original
ajneel@maul:~/temp >
```

Command Name	mv
Synopsis	mv [-f -i -v] source_file dest_file_or_directory
Description	Moves a file or effectively changes the name of a file.
Options	-f Forces overwriting of destination files.
	-i Interactive move. mv prompts before each move is attempted and waits for a response.
	-v Verbose. Prints the name of each file before moving it.

The mv command is used to move a file, group of files, or a whole subdirectory between two higher level directories. The man pages calls it rename files, but most people refer to it as move. This command has two syntax usages:

```
mv [Option] <source> <destination>
mv [Option] <source> <directory>
```

The reason for the term rename comes from the first syntax usage, rename the source to the destination. The best way to explain is by example. The first syntactical usage is to rename a file, such as:

```
john@sith:~/test > ls
test
john@sith:~/test > mv test this_is_not_a_test
john@sith:~/test > ls
this_is_not_a_test
```

The file test has been renamed this_is_not_a_test. Note that Red Hat 6.0 aliases the mv command to mv -i.

In the second form of the mv command, the file may be moved to a directory like this:

```
john@sith:~/test > ls
this_is_not_a_test
john@sith:~/test > mv this_is_not_a_test ~/not_a_test/
    john@sith:~/test > ls
    john@sith:~/test >
john@sith:~/test > cd ~/not_a_test/
john@sith:~/not_a_test > ls
this_is_not_a_test
```

The file this_is_not_a_test under the test directory is now moved to the not_a_test directory.

The Linux file manager does not treat all files equally. Instead, it uses the file type field in the index node or inode to determine what to do with the file. If the inode type is special then it means that the file contents are really just access pointers to kernel device drivers. If the file type is directory then the file manager knows that the contents of the file are to be used to locate other files. Given this distinction, the mkdir command is used to create an instance of the file type directory.

The commands rm and rmdir remove files and directories, respectively. Interestingly, the kernel service that deletes a file is called unlink, which is more along the lines of how the process is implemented. The rm and rmdir commands disable the directory entries (a directory never shrinks, but it does grow to accommodate more files), and they decrement the link count in the index node (inode). If the link count drops to zero, then the file blocks are

Command Name	`mkdir`
Synopsis	`mkdir [ -p -mmode -parents -mode=mode -help -version ] directory`
Description	Creates a directory with each given name. By default, the mode of created directories is 0777 minus the bits set in the umask.

Options	`-m, -mode=mode`	Sets the mode of created directories to mode, which is symbolic, as in chmod, and uses the default mode as the point of departure.
	`-p, -parents`	Ensures that each given directory exists. Creates any missing parent directories for each argument. Parent directories default to the umask modified by the u+wx. Does not consider an argument directory that already exists to be an error.
	`-help`	Prints a usage message on standard output and exits successfully.
	`-version`	Prints version information on standard output then exits successfully.

Command Name	`rmdir`
Synopsis	`rmdir [ -p ] target_directory`
Description	Removes directories.

Options	`-p, -parents`	Removes directories and any subdirectories that become empty as a result of the original operation. This is a useful switch for removing entire empty directory trees.

Command Name	`rm`
Synopsis	`rm [ -r -d -i f ] target_file_or_directory`
Description	Removes files or directories.

Options	`-r`	Recursively removes files and directories starting from the bottom of the tree.
	`-d`	Specifies that the target is a directory.
	`-i`	Activates interactive mode.
	`-f`	Ignores all errors and never prompts the user.

returned to the free list of blocks. (Note that Red Hat 6.0 aliases the rm command to rm –i.)

There is a special case of the rm command that will also remove directories. The command:

```
fred@xwing:~ >   rm -r junk
```

removes all the files contained within the directory junk as well as the directory itself. If there are subdirectories within the junk directory, they and their subdirectories are also deleted.

The commands head and tail are helpful for quick viewing of log files or other types of status files. The head command displays the first 10 lines of a file and the tail command displays the last 10 lines of a file. To view more lines, use the numeric argument. For example, to view the last 50 lines of a log file try this:

```
fred@xwing: ~> tail -50 /var/log/messages | less
```

In this example, the last 50 lines of the messages file is sent to the pager called less, which displays the file contents one page at a time. As an aside, only the superuser can access the /var/log files.

Command Name	head
Synopsis	head [#b #k #m –n#] file
Description	Previews the beginning of a file.
Options	#b Displays the first # of bytes.
	#k Displays the first # of kilobytes.
	#m Displays the first # of megabytes.
	–n# Displays the specified number of lines as indicated by the integer value #.

Command Name	tail
Synopsis	tail [#b #k #m –n#] file
Description	Previews the end of a file.
Options	#b Displays the last # of bytes.
	#k Displays the last # of kilobytes.
	#m Displays the last # of megabytes.
	–n# Displays the specified number of lines as indicated by the integer value #.

Command Name	file	
Synopsis	file [-f namefile] [-L] file	
Description	Determines the file type of a file.	
Options	-f namefile	Uses the namefile to examine multiple files. (Note: Each line is considered a file name.)
	-L	Instructs the program to follow all links.

Most non-Unix operating systems employ strongly typed files. Thus, an executable file is named with the .EXE file name extension, or a visual basic program is named with the .VB extension, and so on. Once the files are data typed, other OS utilities can use the data type to carry out their tasks. For example, the printer subsystem may look for the .DAT file name extension to assume that the file contains printer commands as well as data.

Since Linux and other Unix-like OS designers take pride in not strongly typing files, we never really know what type of files are contained in a directory the first time we visit the directory. The find command is very helpful in finding out what is in the various files. For example, the following display confirms if a file's contents match the suggested data type of the file.

```
fred@xwing:~ > file *
90752535211:    ASCII text
Assets.PDF:     PDF document, version 1.2
BROCHURE.rtf:   Rich Text Format data, version 1, ANSI
Basic-CED.Doc:  data
Comments.txt:   English text
Desktop:        directory
Exam_costs.doc: WordPerfect document
Mgr_s-Guide.zip: Zip archive data, at least v1.0 to extract
SysAdm:         English text
allie34:        troff or preprocessor input text
att:            mail text
big_penguin.jpg: JPEG image data, JFIF standard
bookmark.htm:   exported SGML document text
ch01.doc.2.doc: Microsoft Word document data
dd.wcm:         WordPerfect document
dns.fig:        FIG image text, version 3.2
fhs-2.0.tar.gz: gzip compressed data, deflated, last modified:
                Sun Oct 26 02:36:59 1997, os: Unix
less:           English text
lind.ps:        PostScript document text conforming at level 3.0
logo.epsi:      PostScript document text conforming at level 2.0
                - type EPS
questions.dsk:  HP Printer Job Language data
t.ps:           empty
xw:             MS Windows PE 32-bit Intel 80386
                GUI executable not relocatable
```

Command Name	Grep	
Synopsis	`grep [-f -c -s] pattern file`	
Description	Searches for string matches.	
Options	`-f name_file`	Uses the name_file to examine multiple files. (Note: Each line is considered a file name.)
	`-c`	Suppress normal output; instead print a count of matching lines for each input file. With the `-v`, -revert-match option (see later), count nonmatching lines.
	`-s`	Suppress error messages about nonexistent or unreadable files.

Grep is a program used to search for patterns or strings within a file, multiple files, or standard input. Grep will display the line in which the matching pattern appears. New users usually are surprised to see the `grep` command on a short list of frequently used commands; however, once someone begins to use `grep` they always seem to come back for more. Let's say that you have been editing several files (letters, invoices, notes, or whatever), and there was a thought that you wanted to return to but you could not remember which file contained the information. Using `grep`, you search for anything having to do with the thought, say "Friday," by entering the following command:

```
fred@xwing:~ > grep Friday *
grep: Desktop: Is a directory
MIScontract.doc:\par Re-installation services performed outside of
standard operating hours (8:00 a.m. to 5:00 p.m. Monday through Friday)
$500 per location.
clet1:revisions will be completed Friday of this week.
clet2:revisions will be completed Friday of this week.
clet3:revisions will be completed Friday of this week.
jnk:06:00 PM Central Time, Monday through Friday.
jnk2:06:00 PM Central Time, Monday through Friday.
grep: wp: Is a directory
```

Where `grep` was unable to process a file it reports `grep:` and a message; otherwise `grep` reports the file name, ":", and the line in which the string match was found.

The `grep` command also accepts metacharacters as well as literal strings. For example, you can search for all words beginning with a and ending with b with the arguments " a[^]*b ":

```
fred@xwing:~ > grep " a[^ ]*b " *
note1:  attrib a.out +x
note2:  attrib a.out +x
```

In the preceding command, the <space> a and b <space> sequence are literal strings, and the [^]* sequence means any character that is not a space that occurs zero or more times. These constructions are referred to as regular expressions and will be discussed in more detail in later study guides.

The commands du and df are frequently used to check for disk space used within a directory or directories, or to check space used relative to each disk volume, respectively. Unfortunately, by default the du command reports in logical OS block size or 1024 byte chunks, and the df command reports in bytes. On the other hand, the GNU versions of these programs allow the human-readable form when the h switch is used. Output from the commands look like this:

```
fred@xwing:~ > du -h Desktop/
1.8K    Desktop/Trash
3.8K    Desktop/Templates
1.9K    Desktop/Autostart
2.4K    Desktop/Apps
14K     Desktop

fred@xwing:~ > df -h
Filesystem          Size  Used  Avail  Capacity  Mounted on
/dev/hda2           5.5G  4.8G  503M    91%    /
```

Command Name	du - directory usage
Synopsis	[-c] [-b] [-k] [-m] [-h]
Description	Displays statistics on current directory usage.
Options	-c Produces a grand total.
	-b Displays the disk usage in bytes for each disk volume.
	-k Displays the disk usage in kilobytes for each disk volume.
	-m Displays the disk usage in megabytes for each disk volume.
	-h Displays the disk usage in human-readable form.

Command Name	df
Synopsis	df [-i] [-b] [-k] [-m] [-h]
Description	Displays statistics on the current disk usage.
Options	-i Displays the inode usage for each disk volume.
	-b Displays the disk usage in bytes for each disk volume.
	-k Displays the disk usage in kilobytes for each disk volume.
	-m Displays the disk usage in megabytes for each disk volume.
	-h Displays the disk usage in human-readable form.

Command Name	tar	
Synopsis	tar c|t|x [-vkmx] [f archive] files…	
Description	The main backup utility used in Linux. Tar pushes a large amount of files that you specify into one large file. It preserves the directory structure of the original file system. Optionally tar can also call gzip to compress the file. When using tar, the pathnames of files are limited to 100 characters.	
Options	-f archive	Name of the file or device that is the archive.
	-k	Does not overwrite newer files.
	-m	Preserves file modification time.
	-v	Verbose. Lists file names and more detailed information.
	-z	Compress or decompress files.
	files	A list of the file names to archive. If a directory is specified, tar descends through that directory tree, archiving the files within those directories.

The `tar` command is the main archive program for Linux. The tar program combines many files into one file, compressing the many files if requested. The archiver must also preserve critical system information such as who owns the files, the permission settings, the directory path, as well as hard and symbolic links.

To create an archive of files in the current directory, enter the following command:

```
tar czf myarchive *
```

To view the archive table of contents, enter the following command:

```
tar tvf myarchive
```

To archive a large amount of disk space and move the files from one part of the file system to another part, use the following pair of `tar` commands:

```
tar cf - . | (cd /newplace; tar xvf -)
```

Here is a great example of multitasking at work from the command line. The first instance of the `tar` command begins reading the current directory (dot), archiving the files, and generating the archive (because of the c or create switch) to standard out (the combination f - characters). Standard out is then directed to another program through the pipe operator (|). The second program is actually two commands done in sequence, the `cd` command and the second `tar` command. The `cd` command switches from the current directory to the `newplace` where the files are to be deposited, while the second `tar` command extracts (the x switch) the archive being read from standard in (the combination of f - characters) and dumping the individual files into the current directory called `newplace`. We will revisit the tar command in the system administration study guide.

The `find` and `locate` commands help by searching the file system for programs and configuration files. A typical `find` command takes the form:

```
find / -name fruitsalad
```

where "/" is the starting point of the search and `fruitsalad` is the name of the file to be located. Find will search all directories, but it is slow. Locate is much faster since it searches a database of files, but the database may not include recent additions to the file system. Use the `updatedb` command to refresh the locate database. (Most Linux installations are configured to run the updatedb program in the evening.) A typical `locate` command takes the form:

```
locate fruitsalad
```

The `wc` command is used to discover summary information about a text file; for example, the following command string:

```
ls -l | grep ^d | wc
```

In this example, the `ls` command generates a long listing and the output is sent to the `grep` program, which shows only the lines that begin with the letter "d" or directories. The output is then sent to the `wc` program, which counts lines and reports the number of directories.

Command Name	find
Synopsis	find [path...] [expression]
Description	Searches the directory tree rooted at each given file name by evaluating the given expression until the outcome is known.
Options	-name pattern Base of file name (the path with the leading directories removed) matches shell pattern. The metacharacters ('*', '?', and '[]') do not match a '.' at the start of the base name.

Command Name	locate
Synopsis	locate [-d path] [—version] [—help] pattern...
Description	Locates list files in databases that match a pattern.
Options	-d path Gives the path to an alternative database.

Command Name	wc	
Synopsis	wc [-clw] [—bytes] [—chars] [—lines] [—words] [—help][—version] [file...]	
Description	Counts the number of bytes, white–space-separated words, and new lines in each given file, or the standard input if none are given, or when a file named '–' is given. It prints one line of counts for each file, and if the file was given as an argument, it prints the file name following the counts. If more than one file name is given, wc prints a final line containing the cumulative counts, with the file name 'total'. The counts are printed in the order: lines, words, bytes.	
Options	-c, -bytes, -chars	Prints only the byte counts.
	-w, —words	Prints only the word counts.
	-l, -lines	Prints only the newline counts.
	-help	Prints a usage message and exits with a status code indicating success.
	-version	Prints version information on standard output then exits.

Command Name	stty	Change and print terminal line settings.
Synopsis	stty [-a] [—all] [-q] [—help] [—save] [—version]	
Description	stty accepts arguments that change aspects of the terminal line operation. An optional '–' before a capability means that it is turned off.	
Options	-a, -all	Show all configuration parameters.
	-g, -save	Save the parameters so that they may be reused as input to the stty command.
	-help	Prints a usage message and exits.
	-version	Prints version information on standard output then exits.

Many of the commands that are used at the terminal are single-character commands. For example, the backspace is a single-character command, and the interrupt signal, <Ctrl>C, is a single-character command. These commands can be set or redefined using the stty command. To display all of your current terminal settings, type:

```
bash$ stty -a
```

To change an `stty` mode that is either true or false, type `stty` followed by the name to turn the mode on, and `stty` with the hyphen before the name to turn the mode off. For example,

```
bash$ stty -echo
```

disables echoing of characters to the terminal, and

```
bash$ stty echo
```

reenables echoing of typed characters to the terminal. To change the value of a terminal setting, type `stty name value`. For example, to change the `erase` command to `Ctrl+V` you would type:

```
bash$ stty erase <Ctrl>V
```

System Utilities

The preceding chapter described commands; this chapter describes utilities. However, it is difficult to be exact when describing the difference between a command and a utility. Both types of programs serve similar goals of assisting with the general maintenance of the machine, yet system administrators routinely make the distinction between command and utility programs. Some distinctions are obvious: the `ls` program, for example, is a command; the `tar` program is a utility; but what about the `vi` program?

The distinction between command and utility addresses how the program is used as well as its functions. For our purposes, commands tend to be invoked more often than utilities, and utilities tend to have more complexity (runtime options) than commands. This is not a precise definition and, as a result, we acknowledge that it is possible for one person's command to be another person's utility.

Device Driver Utilities

One obvious set of utilities are the ancillary programs that assist with runtime device-driver and logical-driver insertion into the kernel. In addition to the programs described next, there is also a kernel daemon, kerneld, which assists with bringing user-space file system images into kernel space and assists with the removal of unused kernel modules.

The use of runtime modules is a fundamental design breakthrough for Linux; however, there is a tradeoff. The obvious advantages are configurability and flexibility. Runtime modules permit the install kernels to self-configure themselves for a vast array of unique hardware configurations. Runtime modules also allow quick reconfiguration in the face of unexpected events. On the other hand, access to the installed modules must be done via a look-up table, and a "sanity" check must be done before the kernel can pass control through the jump table and onto the module. Of course, all of this checking and indirection takes time, and these modules slow down the system when compared to other modules compiled into the kernel.

Kernel Modules: lsmod, insmod, rmmod

A key role of any operating system is the masking of odd physical differences among types of devices and the presentation of a uniform logical view of all devices to the user. This is accomplished with program modules called *device drivers*, which know the details of how to communicate with a physical device and, by encapsulating these details in the driver, they present a uniform logical view to the rest of the OS. Generally, there is one device driver per type of physical device. Traditionally, these drivers are built into the kernel when it is constructed and cannot be changed unless the kernel is recompiled.

Linux, however, is unique among Unix-like operating systems because not only does it have the traditional "compiled-in drivers," but also the kernel can load other device drivers at runtime. To see the list of currently installed device drivers, type the command /sbin/lsmod:

```
hostname$ /sbin/lsmod

Module          Pages           Used by
serial          8               1
wd              2               1
8390            2     [wd]      0
nfs             12              4
3c509           2               1
rarp            1               0
```

Here, you can see that there are six device drivers loaded, which consume 27 pages of memory at 4096 bytes each. (Note that some versions of lsmod will list bytes and not pages.) You can also see that the 8390 driver is used by another driver, the wd Ethernet driver. Furthermore, by looking at the "Used by" column, you can see that three of the six device drivers have one program using them, and one driver, nfs, has four programs using it.

Adding and Removing Drivers

New drivers may be added with the `/sbin/insmod` command, and other drivers may be removed with the `/sbin/rmmod` command. The kernel will automatically load these drivers at boot time if they are listed in the file

```
/etc/conf.modules
```

Available drivers for a given kernel can be found in the `/lib/modules/` `X.X.X` directory, where `X.X.X` is the version number of the kernel. These modules will only work with that particular version of the kernel.

Linux distributions use generic kernels and the `insmod` feature to adapt to different environments at boot time; however, once an installation stabilizes, the kernel should be configured for the machine it is running on. Part of this tuning process includes compiling the drivers into the kernel for better performance.

In addition to device drivers, `insmod` will also load network protocol engines as well as file manager back-ends.

Printer Configuration

Generally, there is only one file that must be modified in Linux to set up a printer, so in many ways Linux printer configuration is as easy as falling off a log. On the other hand, there is usually some oddball aspect to the printer that requires trial and error tinkering before the printer will start up (which means falling off a log into an abyss).

Printer Modes

Printers have two basic printing modes—text and graphic. The differences between these two modes are outlined here.

Text-mode. In text mode, the printer accepts ASCII characters and prints these characters using an internal font. The internal printer font is usually a fixed-width, Courier typeface that looks old-fashioned.

Graphic-mode. When the printer is in graphic mode, it accepts separate commands and data that direct how each picture element (pixel) will be drawn. Today's word processors generally put the printer in graphic mode so that many typefaces can be printed anywhere on the page, and in many sizes. This strategy also allows graphic images to be included with the text.

Graphic-mode Commands. Printer graphic-mode commands are generally unique to each printer manufacturer and sometimes unique across models from the same manufacturer. For example, one common set of graphic mode commands is Hewlett-Packard's printer command language (PCL) format that is used with its LaserJet family of printers.

PostScript Printing Language. In an attempt to reduce compatibility problems among hundreds of different printers, each with their own graphic mode commands, Adobe Systems developed a midlevel language that interprets general commands and translates the commands into PCL or some other graphic-mode format.

Types of Printer Drivers. Historically, Linux has evolved from the midrange computer and workstation market. These system administrators have typically picked PostScript to avoid integrating various types of printers, printer filters, and printer drivers. Most Linux applications generate test format or PostScript format files, and therefore, Linux machines tend to be connected to PostScript printers.

Having said that, there is also a growing number of applications that will print graphic mode formats. The X Window application `Ghostscript` accepts various file formats including PostScript and prints a graphic mode file to popular printers (such as HP's PCL printers). Corel's Word-Perfect and other office suite programs also print graphic formats to a large array of printers.

Printer Filters. Printer filters are generic programs that convert from one file format to another. Printer filters may be executed from a command line, from an application program, or from the printer capability file called printcap. Printcap filters will be discussed in a later section.

The Server lpd and the Client lpr

Printing in Linux is based upon the BSD client/server model, where the client and server are implemented with network sockets even when the printing is done locally. The client is known as the lineprinter request program, or `lpr`, and the server is referred to as the lineprinter daemon or `lpd`. The general printing process goes like this:

1. The client `lpr` program reads the requested file(s) that are to be printed from the user's area and writes them into a spooling directory named after the destination printer, regardless of whether the printer is local to the user's machine or is located on a remote machine.

2. A control file describing which files are to be printed is also written into the spooling directory by `lpr`. Then the client `lpr` program sends a notification message (through a Unix domain socket) to the `lpd` server and terminates.

3. The `lpd` server has been scheduled to run as a result of receiving the notification message.

4. The lpd server begins by reading its configuration file and searching for valid printer directories that contain control files associated with the printer.

5. If the printer is local, the lpd server sends the optional header-identification page (specified in the control file) and the data file(s) to the printing device.

6. If the printer is remote, the server establishes a network connection with its peer lpd server on the remote host and sends the control and data files to the peer. The peer lpd server now processes the files in the same way the local lpd server would have.

There are at least two versions of lpr and lpd. Red Hat 6.0 and Slackware 4.0 use the older BSD-version; Debian 2.1 and OpenLinux 2.2 use a newer LPRng package written by Patrick Powell. LPRng is backwardly compatible with the BSD version.

Configuring the Printer with printtool and YaST

Red Hat provides a print system manager called printtool (see Figure 4.1). SuSE also provides printer configuration with the YaST program (see Figure 4.2). The printtool program is a GUI utility; yast runs as an ASCII-based program with cursor control.

The Red Hat printtool program provides a series of pop-up menus that prompt the system administrator for the various printcap parameters. The

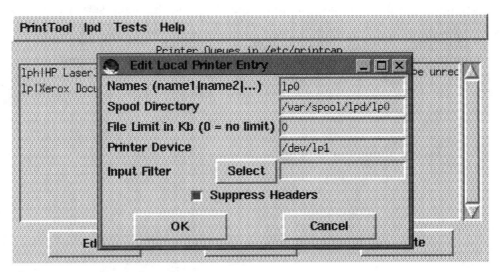

Figure 4.1 Red Hat printtool.

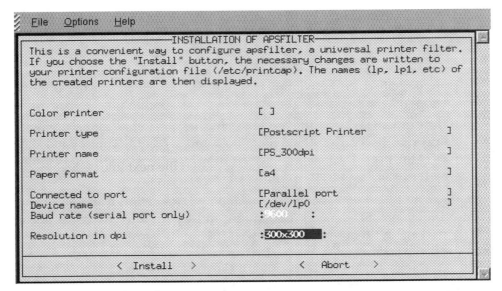

Figure 4.2 YaST printtool.

`printtool` offers to suppress job control headers but fails to notice that this option will not work on entries for remote print servers. Both utilities prompt for the type of printer and options required by presenting a requestor box with empty fields. It is up to the administrator to fill in the correct values.

The Printcap File

As noted in the previous section, the behavior of the client and server provider programs is controlled almost exclusively by the `/etc/printcap` configuration file. The file usually comes unconfigured with a new distribution, and as a result, system administrators often carry old printcap files to new systems so that they do not have to configure the new printcap files from scratch (that is, they will have a template to use). Here are some typical entries in the `/etc/printcap file`:

```
lp1|Dot Matrix:\
    sd=/var/spool/lpd/lp1:mx#0:sh:lp=/dev/lp1:tr=\f:\
    if=/usr/lib/lpf:af=/var/spool/lpd/lp0/acct:\
     lf=/var/log/lpd-errors:

lp2|OMNILab Dot Matrix Printer:\
    rm=cy.olemiss.edu:sd=/var/spool/lpd/omni:\
    lf=/var/log/lpd-        errors:

lp|lj|lj4|HP LaserJet 4 Plus (Just ASCII mode):\
    rp=text:rm=lj4:sd=/var/spool/lpd/lp:\
```

```
        lf=/var/log/lpd-errors:

ljps|HP LaserJet 4 Plus (PostScript mode):\
        rp=raw:rm=192.168.1.20:sd=/var/spool/lpd/lj4raw:\
        lf=/var/log/lpd-errors:
```

The `printcap` file describes the set of printers that can be reached from the current host. Each line describes a printer capability. The line begins with one or more labels for the printer. For example, the third printer in this display can be called `lp`, `lj`, or `lj4`. Each field is delimited with the ":" character; the "\" character followed by a newline indicates that the next line is to be joined with the previous line when the `printcap` file is read by `lpd`.

The lp1 entry. The first line of our example `printcap` file describes `lp1` as an ASCII printer. Its spool directory (`sd`) is: `/var/spool/lpd/lp1`; it has no maximum paper quota (`mx#0`); the job control header page will be suppressed (`sh`); the printer is directly connected to the parallel printer port (`lp=/dev/lp1`); the printer needs a trailer (`tr`) string, which is a form-feed character in this case, so that paper can be ripped off the printer. The (`if`) field says invoke the input filter program `lpf` to paginate the output; the accounting filter (`af`) keeps track of who is printing how much; and the (`lf`) field says put error messages into the file `/var/log/lpd-errors`.

The lp2 entry. The second `printcap` entry describes lp2 as a printer connected to a remote machine with the name cy.olemiss.edu (`rm`). The spool directory is named after the printer as `/var/spool/lpd/lp` (`sd`), and error messages are to be place in the log file `/var/log/lpd-errors` (`lf`).

The lp entry. The third `printcap` entry describes lp, lj, or lj4 as a standalone printer directly connected to the network, and the name of the remote machine (`rm`) is lj4 (this could be an IP address). The spool directory is also lj4, and error messages are to be placed in the file `/var/log/lpd-errors` (`lf`). The name `lp` is special in that if no printer is named in the `lpr` command, then the name `lp` is assumed.

Server chaining. The remote machine field (`rm`) on one server may refer to a similar (`rm`) entry on another machine. In this way, servers may be chained to one another, allowing the print job to be passed from host to host through various gateways. Server chaining also requires that the local machine be allowed into the remote printer. Each remote Linux box, therefore, requires that a file called `/etc/hosts.lpd` be set up to allow others to print on its printers or to pass print jobs onto another host.

The ljps entry. The fourth `printcap` entry is the same as the third, except that it specifies the remote printer (`rp`) name `raw` instead of `text`. Use of this printer name is a signal to the standalone printer that the file contents are to be treated as PostScript and not as ASCII data. The HP LaserJet automatically detects most PostScript files, but some versions of Post-Script require the explicit reference to the raw printer before they will print properly.

As an aside, some `printcap` entries, such as the suppress header (`sh`) command, work only for directly attached printers. If the print daemon is contained within the printer, such as an HP LaserJet, then this option will not work.

Filters in the printcap File

A filter reads from the standard input, transforms the input based on an internal algorithm, and places the result on the standard output.

Printers usually require that ASCII or graphic information be converted to a printer-specific format before accepting print data. Hence, the role of Linux print filters is to: a) convert standard OS formats, b) format unformatted text, or c) convert OS, industry, or printer formats into a target printer-specific format. Example print filters include:

- The `/usr/lib/lpf filter`—Designed for ASCII text reformatting. For example, it converts the \n Unix EOL into the two-character \r\n MS-DOS EOL for a printer.

- The `/usr/bin/nenscript filter`—Reads ASCII files and converts the information to PostScript (which does not seem like much since most PostScript printers accept ASCII text directly). But `nenscript` will also reformat the ASCII text with a smaller font and with multiple columns that will fit two or more ASCII pages on to one PostScript page.

- The `Ghostscript` filter—Converts ASCII to PostScript and also provides parameters that adapt to printer limitations. For example, if the RAM cannot be increased in your printer, the option '-r150' may be added to the invocation of `Ghostscript` to set the resolution from the default 300dpi to 150dpi.

- The so-called magic filters—Converts format based upon file content. One example is automatic detection of DVI format and subsequent conversion to PostScript. Other magic filters can convert DVI, or PostScript, to the printer's native graphic mode instructions, such as HP's PCL format.

The following example shows a printcap entry for the magic filter:

```
lp|lj|hplj4l|HP Laserjet 4L:\
        :lp=/dev/lp0:sd=/var/spool/lpd/hplj4l:\
        :sh:pw#80:pl#66:px#1440:mx#0:\
        :if=/etc/magicfilter/ljet4-filter:\
        :af=/var/log/lp-acct:lf=/var/log/lp-errs:
```

As you can see from these examples, there are two types of filters: input filters (if) and output filters (of). For single file print requests, there is no difference between an if and an of. If there are multiple print jobs requested, the if is applied to each job but the of is applied only once to the first print job. If the if is not specified, of is used instead. Thus, an input filter is better suited to performing accounting. Printer accounting and quotas will be covered in more detail in the system administration study guide.

Printer Use

Linux users have three basic services for printing: the lineprinter request or lpr program, the lineprinter queue request or lpq program, and the lineprinter queue remove request or lprm program. A fourth interactive program, for the superuser, is called the lineprinter control or lpc program.

Lineprinter Request—lpr

To print a file, issue the lpr command with several arguments. A typical command is:

```
lpr -P laser -h -s filename.ps
```

In this example, the lpr program is directed to the printer laser as opposed to the default printer lp. The -h switch suppresses the job page containing the account and host name. The -s switch allows the passing of files greater than one-or-more megabytes to the printer (which is usually the case for PostScript files). The BSD lpr program would refuse to copy these large files into the printer spool area. The -s switch would create a symbolic link back to the user's copy of the file, which removed the need to copy the file into the spool directory. In the newer LPRng program, the -s switch is not necessary.

If typing all those characters seems like too much bother, then maybe this shell script can help. Assume the executable script file is called plj and contains the following line:

```
lpr -h -s -P laser $1
```

Now, the command plj filename.ps passes the file name to the lpr program with the correct arguments.

The lpq, lprm, and lpc Programs

Linux offers several lineprinter utilities that allow both viewing and control of the spooling mechanism. By default, each of these commands, as well as lpr, assume the printer name lp. The -P switch can change the printer name to be viewed or controlled. Moreover, the lpr, lpq, and lprm programs test the shell variable PRINTER to see if it is defined, and if so, automatically switch to that printer. Be sure to export the shell variable with the following command to pass the shell variable PRINTER onto new programs:

```
export PRINTER=laser
```

The lpq *Command*

The command lpq displays the default lp printer queue. For example:

```
Rank      Owner     Job  Files           Total Size
active    lenny     176  calendar         3834 bytes
1st       allison   177  report1         12334 bytes
1st       billy     178  test              38 bytes
```

The lprm *Command*

The command lprm -P laser removes all the queued print tasks for the current user. The command lprm -P laser 177 would remove the specific print task report1.

The lpc *Command*

The command /usr/sbin/lpc status laser reveals both the queue size for all users and the printer daemon status. For example:

```
hostname:~$ /usr/sbin/lpc status laser
  laser:
      queuing is enabled
      printing is enabled
      3 entries in spool area
      waiting for 192.168.1.20 to come up
```

The lpc utility also allows stopping, starting, and cleaning of the printer queues, but only the superuser may issue those system maintenance lpc commands.

Configuring the X Window System

As we noted earlier, Linux is a modular and layered system. Unlike the mono-lith nature of Macintosh and MS-Windows, the X Window System has a series of independent, yet interlocking components that form the GUI. To install and configure an X Window system, you must be familiar with these components. Furthermore, you must know the format of the basic X server configuration file and its location in the file system. Finally, we will review the various system administration tools that offer configuration of the X server.

Five Components of the X Window GUI Architecture

The X Window System is made up of a series of modules that reside outside of the kernel and provide layers of increasing functionality that build into a complete GUI. Recently, there have been additions to the Linux kernel, called frame buffers, that bring some of the X Window routines into the kernel to provide improved performance. The X Window System is equally accessible through the network as well as the system console. One note on terminology—the term X server refers to the device driver module that communicates directly with the video adapter; therefore, the X server in a network configuration will be running on the client machine. Setting up the X Window System is the most demanding aspect of Linux configuration. The reason is that each module represents an independent component and each component has its own configuration parameters.

> **X Server.** The lowest-level component is the X server, which controls the hardware. The X server puts the video adapter into graphics mode (in the same way that a printer is used in graphics mode). The X server accepts logical commands from higher level software (such as: move the mouse cursor) and translates the commands into a series of I/O operations on the video adapter.

> **Display Manager.** The second component is the X Window display manager, or xdm. It configures an environment and sets up a graphical login screen. The screen can be plain, show system log messages, have animated graphics, show system status, etc. Upon successful login, xdm launches the window manager. However, some parameters specified in the xdm initialization file have higher priority than those specified in the window manager initialization file(s). Red Hat 6.0 configures the GNU GNOME display manager (gdm) by default, which allows the selection of window manager before logging into the system.

> **Widgets.** The third component in the X11 system are the widgets, or desktop environments. These library routines build and form the components within a window, such as scroll bars, menu bars, task bars, pop-up menus, requester boxes, etc. Example widget libraries include LessTif (a open source version of the commercial library called MoTif), GTK+ (a GPL

library begun by the GNU image manipulation program, and the Qt library (free to individuals but proprietary to commercial users).

Window Managers. The fourth component is the window manager, or desktop, that provides a graphical look and feel. There are many possible window managers to select from, but most users will accept the default desktop or, perhaps, choose from among a few that are offered in the default installation. The main window managers are Afterstep, KDE, Window Maker, FVWM, Enlightenment, and Blackbox.

Themes. Themes are the highly visible styles of the newer window managers. Style refers to the number of colors supported and the artistic quality of bit-mapped graphics for window frames, title bars, icons, wallpaper, and background. The X11 window managers have a rich set of styles.

Applications. The fifth type of component is made up of the applications that run within the desktop environment. Even though they each have their own configuration (initialization) files, most applications can run under any window manager.

In spite of the effort that has gone into the number of window managers and styles of window managers, there is still room for improvement. The cut-and-paste facilities need to be better developed and more needs to be done with typefaces. Window managers generally offer a change in icon highlight when clicked; however, there is no feedback on program loading progress. Furthermore, typefaces are not anti-aliased against the background in the window managers.

Network Access. The X Window System allows local access and remote access via the network. To permit others access to your workstation, use the `xhost` command to allow the connection from the specified host. Then set the DISPLAY shell variable to the local host address on the remote machine and launch the X11 system on the remote machine with the `startx` command. The X11 system will then connect with the local machine's X server and begin an X Window session on the remote machine.

X servers are also available for MS-Window machines in the form of X32 servers. These MS–Windows-based servers provide an identical look and feel of being directly attached to an X11 console on the remote machine.

Location of X11 Configuration Files

Unfortunately, there has not been a traditional home directory for the X Window System, and directory contents tend to change from installation to installation. Linux distributions have helped to stabilize file positions, and the

Linux effort at creating a file system hierarchy standard (FHS) has also helped. With that caution in mind, the X Window files will probably look like this:

- /etc/X11—The FHS location for X Window configuration programs and symbolic link to the X server named "X."
- /etc/X11/XF86Config—The X server configuration file. In older setups, this file is found at /usr/X11R6/lib/X11/XF86Config.
  - /usr/X11R6/bin—X Window servers, setup utilities, one or more display managers, some window managers, and some common application programs. Here, the X server file, X, is again symbolically linked to one of the X servers having the general name format of XF86_XXX, where XXX is VGA16, SVGA, etc.
- /usr/X11R6/bin/xdm—An X display manager for graphical logins.
- /usr/X11R6/bin/fvwm95—An X window manager.
- /usr/X11R6/bin/afterstep—X desktop manager.
- /usr/X11R6/lib—X Window runtime libraries.
  - /usr/X11R6/lib/X11—X Window configuration files for some window managers and older applications.
- /usr/local/X11R6/—Alternative window managers with configuration files.
  - /var/X11R6/—Alternative window managers with configuration files.
- /opt/X11R6/—Alternative window managers with configuration files.

To discover where other installation-specific X11-related files may be in the file system, use the command locate X11.

X Server Configuration File Format

The X server configuration file, /etc/X11/XF86Config, provides extra details to the X server on how to configure the video adapter, mouse, and keyboard. Even though the X server can obtain many of the parameters by probing the video adapter at runtime, parameters in the configuration file are given precedence since they may have to override one chip feature to obtain a second feature. Variation in system load is another reason for the higher precedence of the configuration file parameters over runtime discovery. In this way, critical timing values can be fixed for the video adapter in spite of system load variations.

Each section of the XF86Config file is delimited with the key words *Section "name"* and *EndSection*. The more common XF86Config sections are:

Section "Files." Contains file names of color values to be used and the location of specified fonts.

Section "ServerFlags." Enables or disables X server runtime flags generated from the keyboard such as "DontZap" (terminate) the X server and "DontZoom."

Section "Keyboard." Enables or disables X server runtime key binding for non-ASCII key binding, such as "LeftAlt" mapping and "AutoRepeat" delay.

Section "Pointer." Lists the mouse protocol (PS/2, MouseSystems, etc), Baud of the serial mouse (if any), and a three-button emulation option for two button mice.

Section "Monitor." Lists the monitor horizontal and vertical frequency ranges and the wave shape for a given dot-clock frequency. These settings require detailed knowledge of the monitor's ability or you will risk causing the raster-scan circuit to fail. But they also control the refresh frequency, which you will, most likely, want to adjust upwards.

Section "Device." Lists the possible dot-clock frequencies for graphic modes and video adapter specific hardware settings. Same caution as preceding section.

Section "Screen." Lists possible graphic modes allowed, virtual display size, and initial viewport into the desktop.

Section "Xinput." Configuration of extended input devices, such as joysticks and graphic tablets.

The X Server Configuration Programs

The X server is responsible for controlling the hardware registers within the video controller chip. Consequently, an X server must be selected for use based upon the type of video adapter present in the machine. Technically, X is symbolically linked to the XF86_VGA16 server that will work with any video card, but it is only for the lowest common denominator, hardware-compatible graphic mode (640X480 pixels with 16 colors). Unfortunately, the results of the XF86_VGA16 server are unacceptable when compared to a custom-configured X server that is designed for the video adapter's advanced features.

The name of the X server is X, and it is most likely located in `/etc/X11/X` or `/usr/X11R6/bin/X`. The first task is to discover which XF86_XXX server needs to be linked to the name X.

1. Use the `/usr/X11R6/bin/SuperProbe` utility to identify the correct server for the video adapter and then link X file name to that server. Or, manually identify the manufacturer and the video controller chip type.

2. Copy the XF86Config.eg example file to XF86Config and build a custom version of the `/usr/X11R6/lib/X11/XF86Config` file. Even after the file has been created by one of the following utilities, it not uncommon to re-edit this ASCII file for fine-tuning. Also, the configuration utilities do not support the extended input devices such as joysticks and graphic tablets, and these items must be entered by directly editing the XF86Config file.

3. Use one of the interactive configuration utilities: xf86config, XF86Setup, Xconfigurator (found in the Red Hat distribution), and SaX (found in the SuSE distribution) to interactively build the XF86Config file.

The xf86config Utility

The `xf86config` utility (note the lowercase xf and c) is the default ASCII command-line utility for configuring the system. It is interactive, prompting the user for responses with detailed screens full of text to be read. Also, this one of the few configuration utilities that reads the `/usr/X11R6/lib/X11/Cards` database, whereas other utilities perform this function with an internal list. Therefore, `xf86config` listing of available X servers may be more up-to-date than the lists displayed in the XF86Setup configuration program.

The xf86config utility also directs the user to read the `/usr/X11R6/lib/X11/Monitors` database file. Upon discovering the proper entries in the `Monitors` file, the user is encouraged to copy them into the XF86Config file. Note that these refresh rates are optimized for a particular monitor and some general classification provided by the other XF86Setup utility.

The xf86config and XF86Setup utilities cover the same configuration topics, so we will discuss these topics using the generally preferred XF86Setup utility. In time, all the configuration utilities will read from the same database to determine the correct adapter and monitor settings.

The XF86Setup Utility

The XF86Setup utility (note the uppercase XF and S) employs the XF86_VGA16 X server to create a minimal graphic interface in order to configure a more sophisticated X server. The utility (as shown in Figure 4.3) begins with an XFree86 splash panel and a menu bar along the top of the screen, containing six options: Mouse, Keyboard, Card, Monitor, Modeselection, and Other. The GUI may be navigated with a mouse or the keyboard. If the mouse has not been properly configured, then use the <Tab> key to move the cursor from button to button. After tabbing into a menu, use the <Arrow> keys to move the highlight among menu items. Pressing the <Enter> key selects the current button or current menu item.

Mouse. Generally, there are two types of mouse protocols: Microsoft two-button protocol and MouseSystems three-button protocol. Furthermore, there are generally two types of mouse interfaces: the IBM PS/2 interface, or /dev/psaux, and the serial port, /dev/ttyS0. If the Microsoft two-button mouse protocol is selected, then you should also choose the Emulate3Buttons option, since the third, or middle, button is used for paste in the X11 copy-and-paste operation.

Some mice can operate either protocol. To switch the mouse protocol, flip the mouse over and look for a switch. It will be labeled MS and PC. MS means Microsoft two-button protocol and PC means MouseSystems three-button protocol. Also, newer Microsoft mice have a third windows scroll button. These mice may have a switch labeled 2 and 3. The 2 refers to the 2 button protocol while the 3 refers to the same protocol but adds a third button. The X server automatically accepts this alternative third button, two-button protocol, and the scroll button becomes the third button.

Keyboard. The X Window System has complete control over the keyboard and the bindings of the keys to functions. The default settings are appropriate for most installations.

Card. When an X server supports multiple families (as with the SVGA server), the chipset menu provides a selection from which to choose. It is not uncommon for probe routines to miss more options than they find. So, if other parameters (such as the amount of video memory) are known about the video adapter, select the values as opposed to selecting "probe."

Monitor. The monitor menu displays 10 types of monitor categories, each with different frequency capabilities. Select the horizontal and vertical frequencies that are less than or equal to your monitor. Do not select frequencies that exceed the monitor specifications.

Modeselection. The XF86Setup utility presents a column of possible graphic modes ranging from 320×240 up to 1600×1200 pixels. There are also four color-depth buttons ranging from one byte-per-pixel to four bytes-per-pixel.

For a 17-inch monitor, typical graphic modes selected are 800×600 and 1024×768 at two bytes-per-pixel. When two or more graphic modes are selected, the XFree86 servers will switch up and down the list of selected graphic modes with the <Ctrl><Alt><Num+> and <Ctrl><Alt><Num-> keys. In this way, the user can select the most comfortable viewing image.

Other. This menu allows the enabling of some of the ServerFlags mentioned in the previous section. The two key flags are: (1) allowing the X server to be terminated with the <Ctrl><Alt><Backspace> keys and (2) allowing graphic mode switching with the <Ctrl><Alt><Num+> and <Ctrl><Alt><Num-> keys.

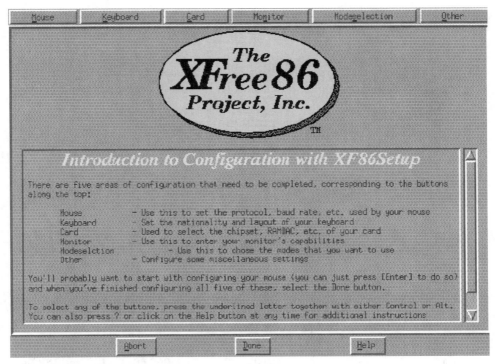

Figure 4.3 XFree86Setup Utility.

To complete the XF86Setup process, activate the Done button at the bottom of the screen. This will overwrite the old XF86Config file with a new version. Again, please note that extended input devices, such as joysticks and graphic tablets, cannot be configured with these utilities and must be entered into the XF86Config file manually.

The Xconfigurator

Since Red Hat Software developed the Xconfigurator and mouseconfig utilities they are generally not found on other non-Red Hat distributions. Unlike the XFree86 GPL utilities described earlier, Xconfigurator does not perform mouse configuration. Instead, it assumes that the mouse is properly configured and uses existing mouse configuration to fill in the Pointer section of the XF86Config file. In other words, if the mouse is changed, the Xconfigurator utility must be run again to reconfigure the Pointer section.

As a note of caution, Xconfigurator does not ask to overwrite the XF86Config file, it just does so. Consequently, if you are just experimenting with other possible configurations, be sure to keep a backup copy of the XF86Config file.

The `Xconfigurator` utility employs the typical color-attributed ASCII screens used by many distributions in the install process, and it has the following steps:

1. The `Xconfigurator` utility begins with a screen announcing that it will edit the XF86Config file and offers to use the existing file as a starting point. This is a plus if other options have already been configured, but not by the `Xconfigurator` program.

2. It lists the `/usr/X11R6/lib/X11/Cards` database and allows a video adapter to be selected.

3. It lists the `/usr/X11R6/lib/X11/Monitors` database and allows a monitor to be selected. There are many more types of monitors than what is available in the database; consequently, there is a good chance that a particular monitor will not be listed. If so, choose the custom monitor entry, which takes you to the same screen as the other X11 configuration utilities.

4. On the custom monitor screen, the basic frequency capabilities of monitors are listed. Again, select the horizontal and vertical frequencies that are less than or equal to the capabilities of the monitor. Do not select frequencies that exceed the monitor specifications.

   `Xconfigurator` will ask to probe the card; once again, it's usually better to select "don't probe" and to select the amount of video memory

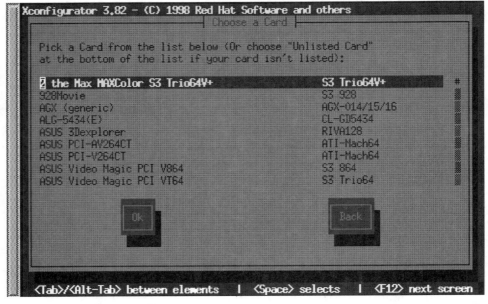

Figure 4.4   Red Hat Xconfigurator.

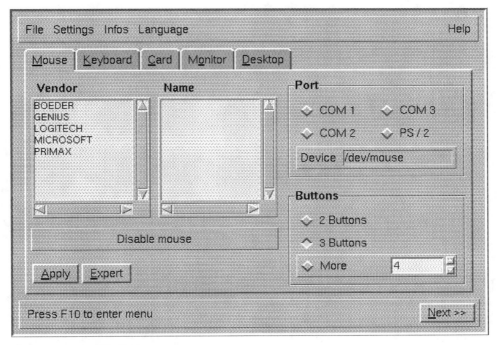

Figure 4.5 SuSE's SaX.

present on the card from the menu. Next, select "no clock chip" and let the X server figure this out at runtime.

5. Finally, select one or more graphic modes to use. Then Xconfigurator will automatically overwrite the XF86Config file. If a mistake was made, copy the backup file made earlier on top of the bad XF86Config file and restart the Xconfigurator utility.

Figure 4.4 is a screen shot of the Xconfigurator utility showing the first screen of adapters from the Cards database.

Version 6.1 SuSE employs its own X Window configuration utility called SaX. SaX wins the praise of those who have used the other configuration utilities. SaX is more user-friendly and less prone to errors than the other X Window configuration utilities. As you can see from the screen shot in Figure 4.5, SaX employs the tab metaphor to navigate among the various configuration options.

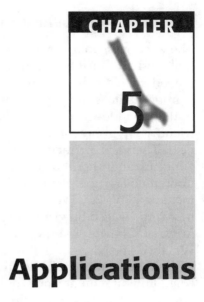

Applications

In this section, we will consider system applications that assist with installation and configuration. An application is a program that uses system services to provide a function that is not part of the kernel or other basic system component. For our purposes, these programs include window managers, various documentation and help functions, as well as traditional applications. But it should also be noted that in the same way the terms "command" and "utility" may overlap, reasonable people may disagree on the exact definition of the term "application."

Window Managers

It may seem surprising to some to consider a window manager an application. However, you must remember that there are many types of X Window managers that are separately installed and added onto X11. Users may select from a set of possible window managers when logging into the system; thus, window manager selection is based upon personal preferences of the user. So, in many ways the window manager is an application, selected by the user that provides a preferred way of interacting with the machine.

Example Window Managers

The window manager runs under X11, and is the program responsible for the look and feel of the windows placed on the screen. Everything that is displayed in an X session is in the form of a window; thus, a window manager is a program that simply manages these windows. Control over the management of these windows allows for the X session to be a unique, pleasant, and user-friendly environment. A subset of available window managers is described next. The window managers are listed alphabetically and they are independent of each other; however, they can also be clustered into families based upon their starting points. The first generation or family of window managers includes TWM, CTWM, FVWM, FVWM2, and FVWM95. These window mangers focused on virtual desktops, simple icons, and limited configuration features. The next family could be called the wharf family and includes Wmaker, The NextLevel, Bowman, and Afterstep. A third family that could be labeled the themes, task bar, and tools family then emerged with members like KDE, Enlightenment, and Gnome. There are other window managers that do not easily fit in these three clusters. Also, there are window managers that run on Linux, such as the common desktop environment (CDE), that require commercial components.

Afterstep

Afterstep evolved from the Bowman Window Manager, which was based on the FVWM window manager. The Afterstep Window Manager was designed to incorporate the look and feel of the NeXTSTEP user interface. The NeXTSTEP interface, to many, is one of the most useful and instinctive GUIs available. Afterstep employs what is known as a "wharf" or a collection of icons that floats upon the desktop and launches programs (see Figure 5.1). Also, the wharf can contain folders of more applications. Furthermore, Afterstep was the first window manager to employ gradient-filled title bars with the NeXTSTEP- style iconize and destroy buttons. The pop-up menus are also gradient-filled and can be configured to accommodate different tastes.

To learn more about Afterstep, visit the team's homepage at www.afterstep .org/.

KDE

The K Desktop Environment, or more simply KDE, with its Qt widget set foundation, is probably the most functional of all the window managers at the time of this writing. The Qt widget set provides a library of graphic functions such as "create a pop-up requester box," "draw a window border," and "draw a scroll bar." The Qt library was developed by Troll Tech AS (//www.troll.no/)

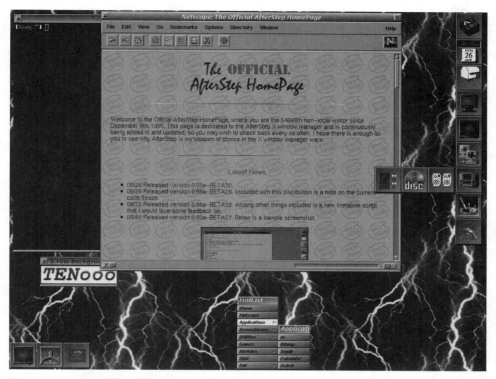

Figure 5.1   Example of Afterstep with animated desktop.

and employs a limited "free" software license controlled by Troll Tech. In other words, Qt is not GPLed.

One key to KDE's success is its default configuration. KDE can be configured to give the look and feel of most any design, but in its default configuration, KDE looks and feels much like MS–Windows (see Figure 5.2). This initial impression gives new users a sense of continuity and the confidence to try other configurations.

KDE is a window manager plus support utilities. KDE utilities include a complete file manager that can access local, remote, and Web-based files. KDE has a sophisticated GUI control panel, a task bar with icons, multiple forms of hierarchical pop-up menus, and help manuals. Other standard applications and utilities are planned for the KDE system. KDE creates a consistent look and feel for applications by specifying a standard GUI toolkit and support libraries that all KDE applications use, and a Style Guide that KDE application authors are strongly encouraged to follow. See www.kde.org for more information.

In spite of these accomplishments, KDE has critics. In reaction to the Qt license issue, a group called Harmony is developing a complete GPLed widget set that is a free replacement of the Qt widget library (http://harmony.ruhr.de/).

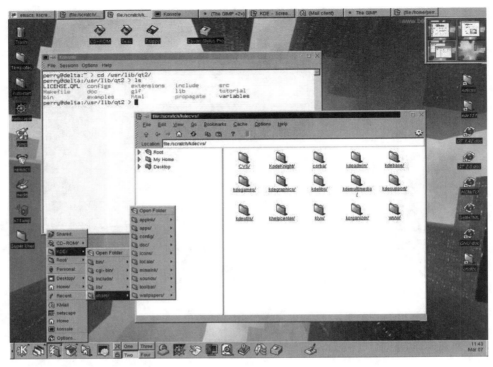

Figure 5.2 KDE desktop.

Another group, called GNOME, is also working on a replacement for KDE (www.gnome.org/). GNOME stands for GNU Network Object Model Environment. The GNOME project intends to build a complete, user-friendly desktop based entirely on GPLed software. The desktop will consist of small utilities and larger applications that share a consistent look and feel. GNOME uses GTK+ as the GUI toolkit for all GNOME-compliant applications. GNOME is being discussed here since it receives a lot of attention in the Linux community, but at the moment, GNOME has not developed into a standalone window manager.

Window Maker

Window Maker bases its look and feel on the NeXT GUI, like that of Afterstep (see Figure 5.3). It is relatively fast compared to other window managers, easy to configure, and easy to use. Furthermore, Window Maker provides integrated support for GNUstep applications.

To learn more about Window Maker, visit the Window Maker Web site at www.windowmaker.org.

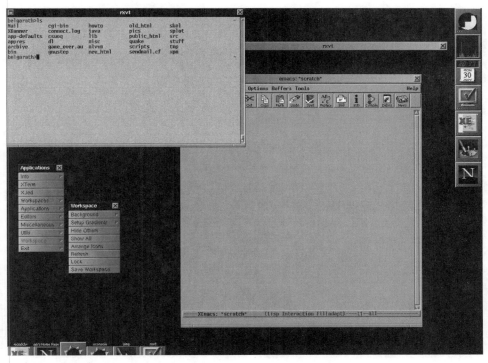

Figure 5.3 Window Maker.

FVWM

FVWM has a long history of development. Also, it is designed to have a small "memory footprint." FVWM comes in two versions: Version 1 (see Figure 5.4), which has been finalized, and Version 2 (see Figure 5.5), with more functions than Version 1. Despite the advantages it offers, FVWM is no longer configured as the default window manager in the distributions, due to a somewhat dated look.

To learn more about FVWM, visit the FVWM Web site at www.fvwm.org.

Enlightenment

The Enlightenment window manager (see Figure 5.6) is based upon the premise that the user should maintain control of the desktop at all times. Enlightenment is designed to embed new low-level features in the window manager by providing an almost infinite number of options via a highly customizable definition language. The definition language allows control of simple backgrounds as well as multiple window border decoration styles. Unlike

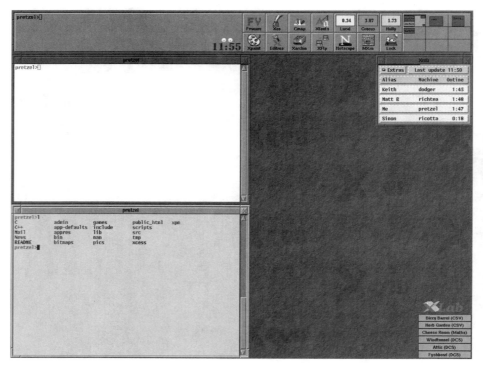

Figure 5.4   FVWM Version 1.

other window managers, Enlightenment's design was not based upon earlier generation window-manager source code. This has given Enlightenment a new freedom to be creative (see Figure 5.7). As a result, other window managers are unable to offer the flexibility of Enlightenment without a significant loss in performance.

To learn more about the Enlightenment window manager, visit the Enlightenment Web site at www.enlightenment.org.

Blackbox

The Blackbox design stands apart from the preceding window managers (see Figure 5.8). Its design goals are simplicity, speed, and elegance. This, in turn, means that it does not support advanced features like multiple image format loading, pixmap decorations, and mouseless operation. To improve performance, Blackbox images are rendered only when they are needed. Once created, the images are also cached, saving CPU time in Blackbox and the X server. Blackbox runs in user space, in less than 1 MB of memory, and is designed to place only a minimal load on the X server, thus making it ideal for network-based X11 displays.

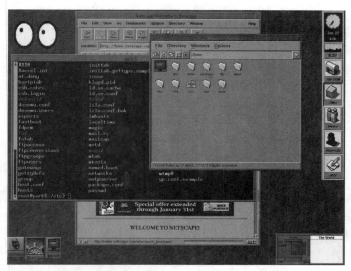

Figure 5.5 FVWM Version 2.

To learn more about the Blackbox window manager, visit the Web site blackbox.wiw.org.

Figure 5.6 Enlightenment.

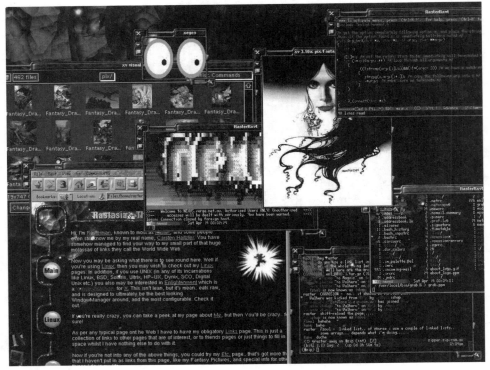

Figure 5.7 Enlightenment shows its wild side.

Finding More Information

Success in the use of Linux rests on the ability to research various types of documentation. Regardless of how many questions or problems you resolve while using Linux, there are ten more questions to replace the one just answered, so mastery of documentation is mastery of Linux. In this section, the use of various programs that assist in finding answers to problems will be described.

Local Documentation

The overall complexity of the Linux and GNU operating system is truly amazing. No one can memorize and keep the vast array of commands, utilities, and applications at their fingertips. Instead, we rely on various forms of online documentation to assist in using unfamiliar or infrequently used commands. The following series of utilities assist with discovering more information about the system. Each will be considered in its own section.

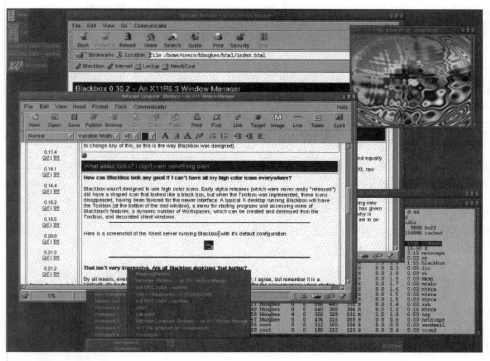

Figure 5.8   Blackbox.

- --help, -h, or -?
- man
- locate
- find
- info
- xman, xinfo, and tkman

Command Line Help Switches

The first step in getting more information is to query the program directly using the switches --help, -h, or -?. In response, the program will display a list of its required arguments, as well as optional arguments enclosed in square brackets []. For example, to find out more about the locate utility type:

```
hostname$ locate  --help
Usage:  locate [-d path] [--database=path]  [--version]  [--help]
pattern...
```

The program will list its acceptable arguments following the usage banner.
Virtually all programs are expected to provide the usage banner in response to
the --help switch or in response to wrong or incomplete arguments. Also, note
that some commands list more than a screen full of options, and therefore, the
output must be directed to a pager, such as less. For example:

```
hostname$ ls --help | less
Usage: ls [OPTION]... [FILE]...

-a, --all               do not hide entries starting with .
-A, --almost-all   do not list implied . and ..
-b, --escape       print octal escapes for nongraphic characters
.
.
```

Some commands, like cd, are internal to the shell. Typing cd --help to
bash will result in the shell saying that --help is an illegal option (or some
other complaint depending on which shell is used).

The --help listings are probably too terse for those who have not used the
command before. So the next step for those users would be to read the man pages.

The man Pages

The man command is the fastest way to get more information on another command or utility, even though it has been demoted by the GNU organization in
favor of their info system. Some of the Linux manual pages are almost exact
copies of the same manual pages that appeared 20 years ago in Version 6 Unix,
and, unfortunately, they only narrowly address the behavior of a given program and not the interaction of the program with the rest of the system. In fact,
it is fair to say that there is no online local documentation that really provides
the big picture with respect to program interactions. For example, the man
pages have sections: (1) User Commands, (2) System Calls, (3) Subroutines, (4)
Devices, (5) File Formats, (6) Games, (7) Misc, (8) System Administration, and
(9) New; yet, there is no man switch that shows the table of contents. (Of
course, you are free to go to the /usr/doc/man? directories to see the file
names of the man pages.)

One way to fish for information is to enter the man command with the keyword argument -k and a keyword that relates to the topic of interest. For
example:

```
hostname$ man -k topic
```

The man command searches each of its sections comparing the keyword to the title of each man page. Unfortunately, the man command does not search the body of each page, and as a result, the search results are usually incomplete.

Using Section Five

One surprising way to get a glimpse of the big picture is to look at the format specification of the various initialization and control files. These specifications are found in section (5) File Formats. Much of this information goes undetected and unused since the man -k topic command only checks the title of the file, and users rarely enter the exact file name as a topic. To see how programs interact with each other, use the name of the control file and explicitly specify the format section of the manual pages with a command like:

```
hostname$ man 5 passwd
```

The resulting man page will describe each field of the password file in detail and list all the programs that use the control file to carry out their various activities.

Two related commands are the apropos command, which is the same as the man -k command, and the whatis command, which displays the title of the manual page.

The File System Name Database

Although the locate program does not provide access to documentation, it is, nevertheless, an extremely helpful command. Locate can be used to reveal the file system layout, the types of configuration files employed in the system, and available programs.

The locate program is fast, easy to use, and is usually among the first steps you would take in trying to discover more information about a file, command, or utility. The locate program searches the complete file system and reports any entry (directory name, file name, or device name) that matches the substring specified as an argument to the locate command. For example, to discover more about the location of the X11 system and its associated programs that have been configured for a particular distribution, enter the command:

```
locate X11 | more
```

The pager more was invoked since there will be many directory entries found that have the substring X11. Scanning the output reveals where all the X11 directories are located as well as the X programs and document files available.

The locate command is fast because it searches a database of directory and file names rather than asking the file manager to step through all the file system inodes sequentially looking for the file name. Thus, the locate utility also prevents loading down Network File System (NFS) configured systems since it avoids the network as well as the remote file manager.

However, one problem with `locate` is that search results may be incomplete or stale if the target file or directory was recently added and the database has not yet been rebuilt. To locate odd files that have been added recently, run the `updatedb` utility before running the locate program.

Exhaustive File System Searching

The `find` program is similar to locate but, unlike `locate`, it is slow. It also differs from `locate` in that it thoroughly searches out every branch of the directory hierarchy. The `find` program also provides additional options. Two of the most used options are (a) the option to find files relative to the creation, access, or modification time of another file, and (b) the option to run additional commands upon discovery of the search target. Because of this flexibility, `find` requires a number of arguments. For example, the command:

```
find / -name "*log*" -print
```

tells the utility to begin searching at the root directory "/" for any file or directory name `-name` containing the string log or having the substring log embedded within the name. The quotation marks are required to pass the wild card * characters onto the `find` program without shell interpretation. Finally, the `-print` argument tells the `find` program to display the results of its search. Newer versions of `find` do not require the `-print` switch and display the results by default.

The info System

The GNU `info` program provides an ASCII-based hierarchical view of revised man pages. Begin at the root of the tree by typing `info`. Programs are arranged by the usage areas Development, Miscellaneous, Administration, Console Utilities, Document Preparation, Games, and General Commands. Individual manual pages are accessed by positioning the cursor on top of the program name and pressing the `<Enter>` key. Subcategories within the command depend upon how the author arranged the material and vary depending upon the type of program being described. In general, info documents tend to be more helpful than the old man pages. They have a more general approach than the man pages and offer information on the ways in which one program interacts with others. On the other hand, the info project is incomplete, and there are more `man` pages than `info` pages. Also, new GPLed software tends to come with a `man` page and not an `info` page.

xman, xinfo, and tkman

xman. There are X versions of both the man and info pages. Generally, the X11 versions work in the same way as the ASCII versions. An exception to this rule is that the xman program builds a table –of contents for each section and allows you to click on the file name to access the manual page.

xinfo. The xinfo utility provides additional menu bar buttons at the top of the window when compared to the ASCII program, but button positions change as the program moves from level to level. This means that you must always look back at the menu bar to see if the desired button has changed position before clicking what might be the wrong button.

tkman. The X11 utility, tkman, offers a true GUI front-end to the man pages. Its main improvement is the use of regular expressions in searches; however, tkman will not search the body of man pages. Also, tkman offers ease-of-use features, such as custom configuration, history list, and hyperlinks among man pages.

Online Information Access

Online information refers to the many Linux information repositories around the world, Linux news, and to the Internet search engines. Well-known examples of Linux repositories follow.

Linux Repository Sites

The Linux Documentation Project (LDP) can be found at www.linuxdoc.org. The LDP is provides links to a wealth of Linux documentation, including HOWTOs, FAQs , and online books (http://www.linuxdoc.org/docs.html).

The main Linux Web pages (http://www.linux.org and http://www .linux.com) are well-organized sites designed for basic information on Linux and for users to keep up on recent Linux news.

There are Linux sites that only link to other sites. Two examples of these sites are Linux Links (www.linuxlinks.com/) and Gary's Linux Encyclopedia (http://members.aa.net/~swear/pedia/).

Linux News Sites

There are many Linux news sites as well as news groups. Here are just a few:

- Linux Today (http://linuxtoday.com/), a listing of newswire reports in the business community concerning Linux events.

- Linux Weekly News (www.lwn.net/), selects and provides a summary of Linux news events for the week.

- Slash Dot (http://slashdot.org/), selects from submissions of Linux-related news stories.

- Fresh Meat (http://freshmeat.net/, accepts submissions of the latest software available for Linux.

- Linux Games (www.linuxgames.com/), accepts submissions of the latest games developed for Linux.

News groups are traditionally accessed via a news reader, but the news reader must be configured to read from a news feed. News feeds are high-volume traffic sites that accept over 3 GB of data per day. If properly configured, your news reader can provide access to the Linux newsgroups. Simply select the entry point "comp.os.linux.x" where x is one of 10 subgroups.

Internet Search Engines

Internet search engines are all helpful in finding Linux-related information. Based upon our experience, the search engines have the following feel:

- Yahoo (http://yahoo.com/), best results with a vague query. Yahoo provides possible categories to follow and refines the search term(s).

- Hotbot (http://hotbot.com/), best results with a set of general unrelated terms. Hotbot is generally thought to reference the largest number of pages.

- Altavista (http://altavista.com/), best results with a specific SQL formatted set of terms. Altavista does a good job of finding specific pages, otherwise it tends to bring up a lot of unrelated material.

- Deja (www.deja.com/), formally DejaNews, exploits the adage about not knowing history ensures that history will be repeated. Deja provides access to old Usenet postings where someone most likely has posted a solution or work-around to your problem. The key to finding the right answer to a problem is to search just as if you were asking a specific question to a coworker who might know the answer to your question.

Deja will also provide access to the Linux news groups. Simply enter one of the following news group names as a search string and click the search button: comp.os.linux.advocacy, comp.os.linux.hardware, comp.os.linux.m68k, comp.os.linux.misc, comp.os.linux.networking, comp.os.linux.powerpc, comp.os.linux.setup, or comp.os.linux.x.

As an aside to using search engines, it should be pointed out that there is evidence that any one search engine probably indexes only about 35 percent of the entire Internet! An exhaustive search, therefore, requires combining the results from at least three search engines regardless of their feel.

Traditional Applications

If you were to shop software catalogs and add up the cost of similar software products that match the functionality of software that comes with Linux, you would discover that the price of proprietary software comes to more than $3500 in individual product licenses. Following is a short description of a few of these traditional applications.

WWW Browser Software

Netscape Communicator is a package of three different communication tools (see Figure 5.9). Each will be considered in turn.

First, its main component is the Netscape Navigator WWW browser. From the start Netscape provided a Linux version of its popular browser. This is the one must-have application if you plan to use the Internet. Netscape's 4.x series browsers are compatible with all of the latest HTML and Java standards, and match up to Microsoft's Internet Explorer very well.

The next component of the Communicator suite of applications is the e-mail management program. Netscape Messenger, as it is termed, is a solidly built

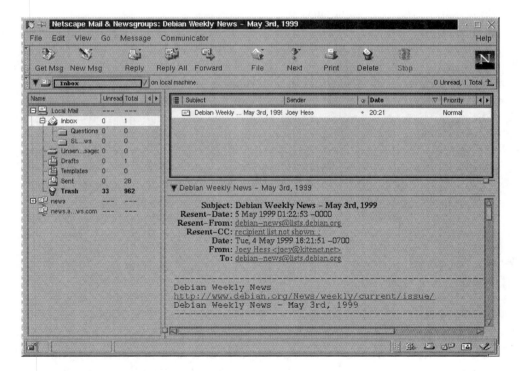

Figure 5.9(a)   Netscape Communicator.

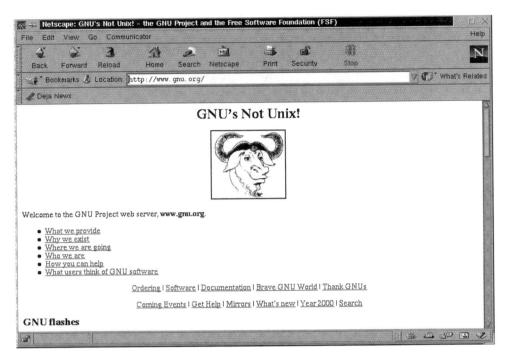

Figure 5.9(b)   Netscape Communicator.

e-mail client. It supports all of the latest HTML encapsulated e-mail, as well as POP 3 and IMAP servers. Messenger also has an immensely useful feature, called filters, for those of us who find our mailboxes swamped. Filters find messages based on certain criteria the user specifies and deletes, moves, or marks them as indicated. This feature can save much time when you receive hundreds of e-mails daily. Along with the Messenger part of Communicator is the Newsgroup reader. Any Linux enthusiast will quickly learn that knowing how to navigate the newsgroups for troubleshooting information is essential. Messenger makes newsgroup navigation an easy task using a tree-structured layout. With this layout, you can look at all of the newsgroups you've subscribed to very easily.

The final component of the Communicator suite is the new Netscape Composer. Composer is an HTML authoring tool that holds its own with other shareware and freeware authoring tools. This tool still leaves many features to be desired, but is a good start for the HTML novice.

FTP Clients

There are many FTP client programs for Linux (see Figure 5.10), ranging from the command-line versions, such as ftp, lftp, and ncftp, to full GUI-versions such as gFTP. Many of them support command completion, recursive file

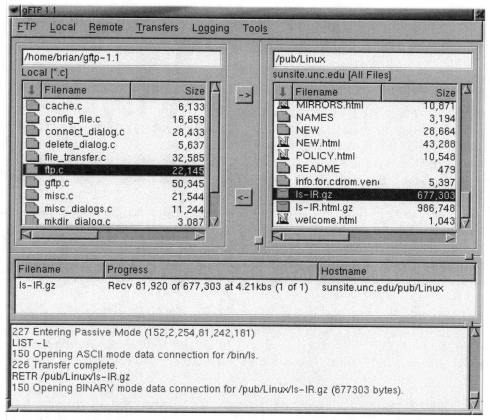

Figure 5.10   FTP client.

retrieval, and simultaneous multiple sessions. As with any of a multitude of X Windows programs, the FTP program you select is based on personal taste.

Telnet

As noted earlier, Linux was designed from the bottom up as a multitasking, multi-user operating system. One key to exploiting Linux is to use the Telnet or other virtual terminal software, such as Xterm or Kterm, to establish a connection with other computers or to establish a connection with the local host through the X Window GUI.

Mail Clients

There are many e-mail clients for Linux, ranging from the command-line type to the X-Window GUI-style. Some of the more common command-line mail programs are elm and pine. pine, developed at Washington University, is more feature-rich than `elm`, and offers many of the features often offered only in GUI-style mail clients. When it comes to GUI-style clients there are a multitude available. As with the FTP clients, selection is based on personal preference.

WordPerfect

Corel has supported Linux beginning with Version 7 of its popular word processor, WordPerfect. In a bold move made last year, Corel released its Version 8 WordPerfect for Linux, free. A personal-use copy can be downloaded from http://linux.corel.com. If you want multi-user versions of the software, or if you want documentation and support, you must buy the full, retail version. Corel has plans to port its entire office suite to Linux. At the time of this writing, Corel announced the pending release of its own Linux distribution featuring a Debian foundation and KDE GUI with custom Corel GUI tools providing access to the Debian base distribution. At the time of this writing, Corel will soon release its own distribution of Linux with Debian as its foundation.

The Linux version of Corel's WordPerfect software is shown in Figure 5.11.

StarOffice Program Suite

StarOffice 5.0 is a fully integrated and Microsoft Office-compatible suite of productivity applications. It provides Web-enabled word processing, spread-

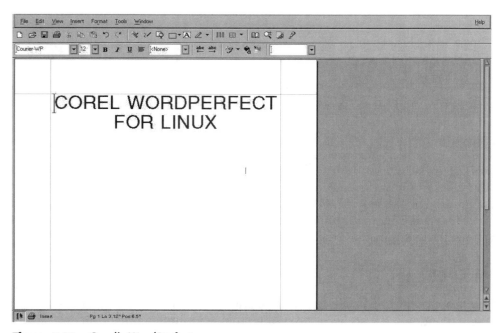

Figure 5.11 Corel's WordPerfect.

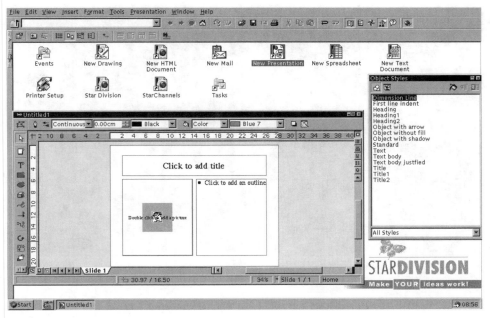

Figure 5.12   StarOffice.

sheet, presentation graphics, e-mail, news, charting, and graphics applications. StarOffice runs native on the Linux Operating Environment on Intel platforms and is also available for other operating systems. Users can access existing Microsoft Office files and data to create spreadsheets, presentations, and word processing documents, and save all data in Microsoft formats or as HTML files to post on the Web or Newsgroup servers. Star Office bridges the gap between Word for Windows and the Linux environment.

Figure 5.12 is an example of the basic StarOffice screen running on a Linux OS.

Ispell

Acceptance of Linux on the Intel X86 family of computers marks a convergence of the older mid-range computer system software and microcomputer software. The Linux design goals of living with other systems is best seen here. Linux has the PC-based WordPerfect and StarOffice products as well as older mark-up systems such as LaTeX. Ispell is one of those old-fashioned programs. Ispell was modeled after the spell program found on the old Digital DEC System 10 computers (see Figure 5.13). The most common usage is `ispell filename`. In this case, `ispell` will display each word that does not appear in the dictionary at the top of the screen and lets you change it. If there are "near misses" in the dictionary (words that differ by only a single letter, a missing or extra letter, a pair of transposed letters, or a missing space or

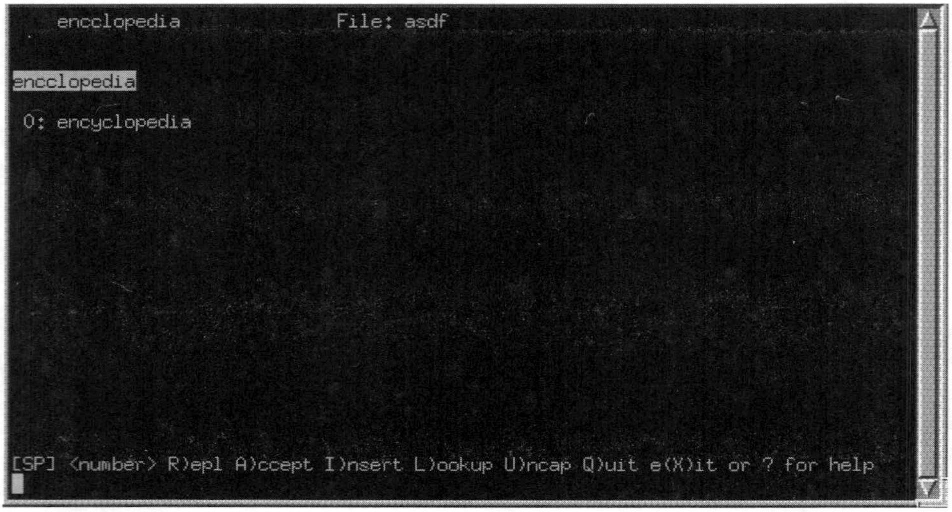

Figure 5.13   Ispell.

hyphen), they are also displayed on following lines. As well as "near misses," `ispell` may display other guesses at ways to make the word from a known root, with each guess preceded by question marks. Finally, the line containing the word and the previous line are printed at the bottom of the screen. If the terminal can display in reverse video, the word itself is highlighted.

WYSIWYG versus Mark-Up Word Processing

As part of its Unix heritage, Linux provides a long line of typesetting, or mark-up languages, (for example, nroff, groff, TeX, LaTeX, and HTML). In these word processing schemes, text creation and display are two separate processes. During the text creation phase, the user writes the information in a plain text file and directs how the text is to be displayed by embedding text-based formatting commands for use by the subsequent display processor. During the text display phase, the display processor interprets the embedded commands in order to know how to lay out the text for display. The typical PC user, on the other hand, usually employs a "What You See Is What You Get" (WYSIWYG) word processor where the text is displayed as it is entered. To accomplish this, the WYSIWYG word processor must embed nonprinting binary information into the text file.

The distinction between WYSIWYG and mark-up reflects a fundamental design issue for Unix (Linux) users, since Unix is predicated on employing all of its utilities (support programs) for processing text files. Embedding binary information into the text file allows only one program, the word processor that created it, to access the text.

A user that moves between the PC and Unix environments must be aware of this distinction and use the various programs accordingly. For example, a user familiar with Microsoft Word (StarOffice) or Corel's WordPerfect may continue to work in the same WYSIWYG environment on Linux. But, if files are to be used elsewhere in the system, they must be exported as "text" files.

Both designs achieve the same end, but a mark-up design offers advantages that a WYSIWYG design does not. Mark-up text can be created with any number of editors; text files can easily be processed by other applications; and mark-up actually provides more control over the display than the set of functions provided inside a given WYSIWYG word processor. This process is similar to the transition that experienced users have when they migrate from mouse-action to keyboard short-cut keys to speed their interaction with the machine. On the other hand, mark-up is difficult to learn and it has a tedious development cycle, requiring editing and testing to ensure that the requested changes were carried out.

GIMP

GIMP is an acronym for GNU Image Manipulation Program and was inspired by the popular MAC- and PC-based programs called Adobe Photoshop. GIMP is a freely distributed piece of software suitable for tasks such as photo retouching, image composition, and image authoring. GIMP can be used as a simple paint program, an expert-quality photo-retouching program, an online batch-processing system, a mass-production image renderer, an image format converter, etc. Furthermore, GIMP is expandable and extensible. It is designed to be augmented with plug-ins and extensions to do just about anything. The advanced scripting interface allows everything from the simplest task to the most complex image manipulation procedures to be easily scripted.

GIMP features include:

- A full suite of painting tools, including Brush, Pencil, Airbrush, Clone, etc.
- Tile-based memory management, so image size is limited only by available disk space
- Subpixel sampling for all paint tools for high quality anti-aliasing
- Full alpha channel support to Layers and channels
- A procedural database for calling internal GIMP functions from external programs, as in Script-fu
- Advanced scripting capabilities
- Multiple Undo/Redo (limited only by disk space)

- Virtually unlimited number of images open at one time
- An extremely powerful gradient-editor and blend tool
- Load and save animations in a convenient frame-as-layer format
- Transformation tools, including rotate, scale, shear, and flip
- Supported file formats: .gif, .jpg, .png, .xpm, .tiff, .tga, .mpeg, .ps, .pdf, .pcx, .bmp, and many others
- The ability to load, display, convert, and save to many file formats
- Selection tools, including rectangle, ellipse, free, fuzzy, Bezier, and intelligent
- Plug-ins, which allow for the easy addition of new file formats and new effects filters
- More than 100 plug-ins, already available
- Support of custom brushes and patterns

For an example of GIMP, see Figure 5.14.

X Fig

xfig is an interactive drawing tool that runs under the X Window System on most Unix-compatible platforms. It is freeware and available via anonymous ftp.

In xfig, users can draw figures using objects such as circles, boxes, lines, spline curves, texts, etc. It is also possible to import images in various formats

Figure 5.14   GIMP.

such as GIF, JPEG, EPSF (PostScript), etc. Objects can be created, deleted, moved, or modified. Attributes, such as colors or line styles, can be selected from various options. For text, various fonts are available.

xfig saves figures in its native format—Fig format—but they may be converted into various formats such as PostScript, GIF, JPEG, HP-GL, etc. xfig has a facility to print figures to a PostScript printer, too.

There are some applications that can produce output in the Fig format (the file format xfig can read). For example, xfig doesn't have a facility to create graphs, but tools such as gnuplot or xgraph can create graphs and output them in Fig format. Even if your favorite application can't generate output for xfig, tools such as pstoedit or hp2xx may allow you to read and edit those figures with xfig. If you want to import images into the figure but you don't need to edit the image itself (like this example), it is also possible to import images in formats such as GIF, JPEG, EPSF (PostScript), etc.

Most operations are performed using the mouse, but some operations may also be performed using keyboard accelerators (shortcuts). Use of a three-button mouse is recommended, but it is also possible to use a two-button mouse (if you have a two-button mouse and your X-server doesn't emulate a three-button mouse, press the Meta-key and right mouse button together to simulate mouse button 3). Normally, mouse buttons 1, 2, and 3 are assigned to the left, middle, and right buttons, respectively.

Figure 5.15 shows an example of an xfig screen.

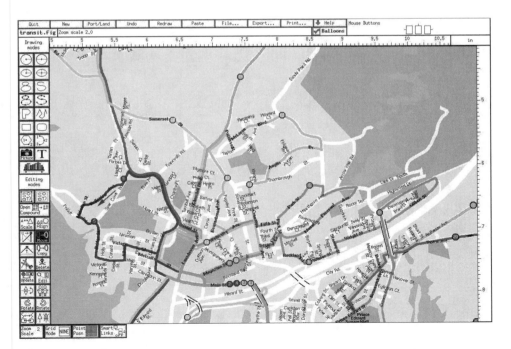

Figure 5.15 xfig.

CHAPTER

6

Troubleshooting

The term *troubleshooting* encompasses an immense landscape of problem analysis that engages several higher order faculties, including the ability to discriminate between concepts and superficial features, the ability to organize concepts in a hierarchical fashion, and the ability to systematically test each concept so that faults may be isolated and repaired.

The evaluation of these skills is beyond the scope of this certificate; however, it is instructive to consider common troubleshooting scenarios so that the candidate may review concepts presented earlier from a new perspective.

General Troubleshooting Strategy

Problem solving goes through two basic phases: the shortcut phase and the analysis and test phase. A good troubleshooter understands these phases and will quickly move into the analysis phase after all the tips and tricks have been tried.

151

Shortcut Phase

The most frustrating aspect of troubleshooting is that there is always a simple answer to solve the problem at hand, and if you could just have access to that bit of helpful information, the problem would be solved and everyone could go back to using their time more productively.

Generally, the shortcut method involves consulting with those around you and using the help tools discussed previously. In other words, reading documentation provides a wealth of shortcut possibilities that can be applied to problem solving. Again, the sequence of documentation reading is (1) use the program help switches (note that some programs, like tar, do not have a man page but they do have an extensive help switch output), (2) use the man pages including any section five applicable file formats, (3) use the info system, and (4) use the Deja news groups and search for a similar problem.

Shortcuts provide an efficient strategy for problem solving, and we all use it to one degree or another; however, once the local experts and documentation has been consulted, and after the news group search engine does not turn up an answer, then we must stop looking for shortcuts.

Analysis Phase

Probably the best advice to give for serious troubleshooting is not to think of the most efficient way to solve a given problem, but instead to think of the most *systematic* way to solve the problem. Complex problems are solved slowly by identifying independent components and testing each component for its correct operation. Moreover, these components must be checked in relationship to how the system is constructed. For example, there is little benefit to checking a failed circuit only to discover that it did not have power applied to the circuit. And there is equally little benefit to checking the power supply or replacing the power supply if the power cord extension has been unplugged in the next room. Unfortunately, the more you know about a system, the better chance that the components will be checked in the wrong sequence. If system components are unknown, then someone must be found who does know the components and they can help you walk through the system checkout procedure.

Common Error Situations

Following is a series of common error or shortcut scenarios found when using Linux. The idea is to provide a perspective in problem solving so that when you see these situations on the job, you will have a reference point to begin the troubleshooting process.

Read Error or File Not Found Error when Installing Linux

Probable causes of Read Errors or File Not Found Errors are poor quality media or wrong media format. An example of poor quality media is to recycle one of those free floppies you received in the mail and use it as the boot floppy. An example of wrong media format is the use of a Macintosh floppy in a PC floppy drive. The solution to both of these problems is to reformat the media, or obtain new media, and recopy installation images.

Archive Errors when Installing Linux

The following error:

```
Tar: read error or gzip: not in gzip format while installing Linux
```

means that the media is OK, but the archive contents have been corrupted. Download a new copy (in binary mode) from a different site.

Device Full Error Message when Installing Linux

Unfortunately, there is no quick solution to this problem. The disk partitions created at the beginning of the installation process are too small for the Linux distribution. You must start over and make new, larger partitions that will hold the software you want.

Read Interrupt Error Message when Installing Linux

A common read interrupt message is:

```
Read_intr: 0x10 error
```

If this occurs with general hard disk access, then the disk drive has bad blocks. Either use the `badblocks` command to search the device for bad blocks or reinstall Linux; regardless, be sure to check the scan-for-bad blocks option.

Another possibility is that this error occurs while formatting a new volume with `mke2fs` or `mkswap`. In these cases, the hard disk stated partition size in blocks is probably smaller than the real partition size.

You may also want to run the `badblocks` program standalone to check the device.

File Not Found or Permission Denied Errors during Installation

This is a rare error message. It means that either there are missing files or the installation software has bugs that set the wrong permissions. Try a different version of the distribution or a different Linux distribution.

Problems with File Transfers

Sometimes it happens that when transferring files via FTP, most of the files are received *except* for the ones with simple file names like README or config. In this case, the problem may be in the way the two FTP commands, `mget *.*` and `mget *`, are viewed. Both commands have the same effect in an MS-DOS environment, but they are different in Linux. In Linux, the first command means get only the files that have a dot character embedded within the name. The `mget *` command means get all of the files.

When LILO Says LI

As LILO performs the boot up procedure, it checks the MBR, finds the target hard disk partition, reads the file system, and locates a secondary loader. The secondary loader reads and uncompresses the Linux kernel image. After the image is loaded, LILO begins executing the kernel.

As a debugging aid, LILO prints a letter of its name as it completes each stage. One of most common breaking points in the boot up sequence occurs at the first attempt to read the file system or after LILO has displayed LI. At this point LILO is attempting to traverse the file system and find the chained loader image `/boot/boot.b`.

The first thing to check for are BIOS incompatibilities. LILO is relying on the BIOS to read disk blocks so here are three possibilities where the BIOS will fail to read disk blocks: 1) The BIOS attempts to read one drive (say, an IDE drive) but the boot image is on another drive (say, a SCSI drive); 2) The hard disk was formatted and the software was installed on another computer but different values for the BIOS disk heads and cylinders were used; 3) The BIOS found the hard disk; however, the old BIOS returns the wrong data because it was not designed to reach beyond 512 Mbs.

A common solution to this third possibility is to make the first hard disk partition a small partition for boot images and mount the partition as `/boot`; this way the BIOS will always be able to reach `/boot/boot.b`.

Make a Linux Boot or Rescue Diskette

At the end of an installation, the install program usually asks if you would like to create a boot floppy disk. Be sure to follow this procedure and keep the floppy in a well-known place for later reference.

This boot floppy will be very important in effecting recovery in situations where the system fails to boot or fails to allow anyone access. If such a situation occurs, the user files become unreachable, and without the boot diskette a new version of Linux would have to be installed, erasing the root partition in the process. (As a last resort, before erasing the root partition some distributions allow an upgrade or expert path through the install program that may reach the section where a boot disk can be created.)

How the Boot Diskette Works

A boot diskette consists of two sections: the compressed kernel image and a RAM disk image called `initrd`. The boot process reads a compressed file system image from the floppy disk and stores the files in memory (not on the hard disk) through a special device driver that makes main memory appear to be a RAM disk. Next, the kernel is read into main memory and started. The kernel, in turn, mounts the RAM disk as the root partition. Thus, from one floppy a complete standalone version of Linux is booted. Once booted, the hard disk can be mounted, examined, and modified as required.

Reasons for Using the Boot Diskette

Following are three common ways to use the boot diskette. (Creating custom versions of boot disks will be covered in a later study guide.)

MBR Corruption

If the `fdisk` program was run improperly or if the first sector (master boot record) of the hard disk is changed, then the system will not boot. The solution is to refresh the MBR with the LILO program, which can be run from the mounted hard disk.

Password File Corruption

Through either a careless or malicious act, the password file can be deleted and, thereby, prevent any login. There are two possible solutions to this dilemma. The first approach depends upon whether a backup copy of the password file exists. (If your system does not make one automatically for you, as Debian 2.0 does, hopefully the system administrator has done so.) Following this approach, the solution is to copy the backup of the password file over the original, now-corrupted password file (called `passwd`). However, if the first approach is not feasible, the second approach is to create a new password file for the root account. This technique can also be used to remove the super-user password if it has been forgotten.

Lost Dynamic Load Module Library

Newer versions of Linux use dynamic load modules that have only the name of one or more library modules in the executable program, or the ELF binary files. If a required library file is corrupted or lost, the ELF binary that needs that library will not execute. In other words, the shell that started the program will continue to run, as will its internal commands (such as cd), but any other external shell command (such as ls) will not be able to find its runtime library module. The solution is to mount the hard disk and copy the backup library file on top of the bad library module and reboot the system.

Alternate Boot Methods

There are many ways to boot up an OS and Linux is no exception. As we review these methods, you should be aware there is no protection from unauthorized access once an experienced user gains physical control of the machine.

Booting the Existing Hard Disk

It may be possible to still boot from the MBR in the latter two cases; if so, use the following arguments to LILO to skip the normal initialization process:

```
boot: vmlinuz init=/bin/bash
```

In this example LILO prompts the user with the boot: message. The user enters the name of the kernel (vmlinuz). The argument root is used to specify the root device, and the argument init is used to specify the starting program. After booting the system, one shell will run as the superuser (UID 0). The superuser then types the following mount command to switch the readonly file system to read/write:

```
mount -n -o remount,rw /
```

In the next command, the superuser edits the password (or the superuser could copy over a new dynamic load module library, etc.). In this case, the old superuser password is deleted by editing the shadow or passwd file.

```
vi /etc/shadow or passwd
```

The command flushes any changes to the disk with the mount command, and the system is rebooted.

```
mount -o remount,ro /
```

Booting Rescue Disks

If the system was not bootable then a standalone (rescue) boot disk is required. Each distribution has its own type of rescue disk. Here is an example technique based upon the Red Hat 6.0 distribution:

1. Boot the install floppy disk or CD-ROM.
2. Type rescue at the boot prompt.
3. Insert the rescue floppy (extended RAM disk) and type <Enter>.

Once the kernel has booted, one shell is run as the superuser. Mount the hard disk into the RAM disk file system with the following command:

```
mount /dev/hda2 /mnt
```

Next, change directory to the /etc directory on the hard disk with the following command:

```
cd /mnt/etc
```

The vi editor is not on the rescue disk, so invoke the vi editor from the hard disk to edit the password file and remove the old superuser password.

```
/mnt/bin/vi passwd
```

After the password has been edited, flush the file to the hard disk with the unmount or synd command.

```
umount /dev/hda2 (or sync)
```

Remove the floppy rescue disk and reboot the system.

The SusSE 6.1 distribution also offers a rescue disk directly off the CD-ROM. To use it, boot up the CD-ROM as if you were going to re-install SuSE. After selecting the "start install" menu, select "start rescue."

If you cannot boot the CD-ROM, a third rescue disk alternative is Tom's root boot (rtbt) floppy disk (www.toms.net/rb/). The rescue floppy was created by Tom Oehser and boots a complete Linux OS. Similar to the other rescue images it loads into memory, but Tom's rtbt creates two RAM disks full of utilities. Tom's rtbt also comes with special tools for checking and repairing file systems.

Boot and L ogin Errors

Following are some of the possible errors, along with suggested solutions, that may occur once the Linux distribution is up and running.

ERROR: Drive not bootable—Please insert system disk.

SOLUTION/EXPLANATION: The MBR has been zapped. Use a rescue disk for the OS you are trying to boot. For example, in MS-DOS, use the command: `FDISK /MBR`.

ERROR: The wrong OS boots.

SOLUTION/EXPLANATION: LILO or another primary boot system is misconfigured. Reconfigure and reinstall LILO.

ERROR: Login incorrect.

SOLUTION/EXPLANATION: Were all the passwords forgotten? Boot Linux in single user mode and run the password program as superuser (see booting the rescue disk, earlier).

ERROR: Either there is no shell or the error Shell-init: permission denied is displayed.

SOLUTION/EXPLANATION: Somehow the password file was erased or else the root permissions are too restrictive. Boot Linux in single-user mode and copy the backup-copy of the password file over the missing or corrupted password file or `chmod` the root directory permissions (see booting the rescue disk, earlier).

Locked Up Programs

When installing Linux, there is usually a colorful ASCII-based, GUI-looking program that guides you through the installation. Sometimes, however, the GUI gets "stuck." In such cases, you have no choice but to give up and begin again. It is in situations like these where the benefits of virtual terminals become apparent.

For example, consider a scenario where the installation GUI is not responding as expected (that is, it's stuck) and there are a number of virtual terminals available, as is the case with Linux. The GUI is on virtual terminal F1; virtual terminal F2 provides a superuser shell prompt; virtual terminal F3 shows the batch commands from the install program being executed; and virtual terminal F4 shows all the kernel diagnostic messages as each subprogram runs.

You can determine where the install process is hanging by using console screens F3 and F4. By switching between these two screens (F3 and F4), you can determine whether the problem is with the floppy drive, the hard disk drive, the CD-ROM drive or the network connections. For example, if the kernel cannot read the floppy, time-out errors from the floppy drive will show up on F4. If the floppy drive does not seem to be the problem, then you must continue systematically down the list of possibilities until the problem is uncovered and isolated. Only then can a solution be prepared.

Some of the newer and less debugged X server or window managers may fail after several weeks of continuous use and lock up the console. In these cases the X Window GUI will not respond and access to the virtual consoles may also lock up. However, you can still log in via a network connection and kill jobs or perform an orderly reboot command.

Troubleshooting an Unresponsive Printer

The following list of steps should be applied in order to troubleshoot an unresponsive printer:

1. Check the `/var/spool/lpd/printer/status` file and the `/var/log/lpd-errs` file for error messages. (The path component name "printer" refers to the name of the printer and its spool directory.)

2. Check for a `/var/spool/lpd/printer/lock` file and remove, if necessary.

3. Check the `/var/spool/lpd/printer/` directory for control and data files. There should be at least one `cf` control file and one `df` data file.

4. Check the `/etc/printcap` entry to ensure it has not been modified.

5. Test the printer directly with the command: `lptest > /dev/lp1`.

6. Check to ensure that the printer can accept the format you are attempting to print with the command: `cat file > /dev/lp1`.

7. If the printer is a serial printer, check to see if UUCP has taken over ownership of the serial port.

8. Finally, check to see if shell environment variables, such as `PRINTER`, are redirecting program output to another logical printer.

The Wrong Time Is Reported

The PC BIOS employs a CMOS clock that Linux reads for the initial date and time. However, CMOS clocks tend to drift. So, to correct the problem of the wrong time being reported, simply update the BIOS time regularly or use a time server to update the system on the fly. One example is to do this with the following command:

```
host$ ntpdate clock.isc.org
```

This command queries a time daemon on the isc.org timeserver for the correct time. Please note that this is just one of many clock servers. If you plan to use ntpdate, please check for a clock near you. This is another situation where you must have a trusted source from which to retrieve the correct time. There are many time servers that are available on the Internet. For more information on time and time servers see: www.eecis.udel.edu/~mills/ntp/.

Adding More Memory Has Made the System Very Slow

In this case, the amount of main memory has exceeded mainboard cache-tag addresses. To correct the problem, you must replace the mainboard. Note that this is not a problem with newer PC-100 DIMM mainboards.

Everything Slows Down when X Is Run

If everything slows down when X is run, this means that there is probably not enough main memory, and the system is spending more time swapping than computing (that is, it's thrashing). Here are both some minimum and typical values for main memory.

APPLICATION	MINIMUM	TYPICAL
Network gateway	4 MB	8 MB
Network server	8 MB	16 MB
Network multi-user	16 MB	32 MB
X workstation	32 MB	64 MB
X with GIMP	64 MB	128 MB

Console Screen Has Weird Characters Instead of Letters

When the console screen is displaying weird characters instead of letters, this means that the terminal emulator has been switched into pseudographics mode and assumes the ASCII characters are commands to display character attributes. Either use the reset command or switch to another console terminal. Use the `reset` command to clear the screen and reset it back to text mode.

Keyboard Repeat Rate Is Too Slow

Some BIOS configure menus do not offer a keyboard repeat rate adjustment. If so, use the `/sbin/kbdrate` utility with the arguments `-r 30` to get a repeat rate of 30 characters per second.

Number Lock Is Not on by Default

Use the `setleds` program to turn on the NUM LOCK function. To do this at boot time for all the virtual consoles, put the following shell script in `/etc/rc.local` or one of the `/etc/rc.d/*` files.

```
for t in 1 2 3 4 5 6
do
    setleds +num < /dev/tty$t >/dev/null
done
```

   The shell script employs a for loop controlled by the shell variable called `t`. It runs the `setleds` utility with the `+num` argument for virtual terminals 1 through 6 `/dev/tty[123456]`, turning on the NUM LOCK key, and redirecting any errors to the bit bucket `/dev/null`.

X Window System Error: Cannot Open Display:0.0

The shell variable DISPLAY must be configured. Use the command: DISPLAY =localhost:0.0

Daemons and System Message Logging

One key to Linux system troubleshooting is knowing where to look for runtime error messages. More often than not, it is forgotten that all background programs (daemons) and many system utilities report general status and error information to a message logging daemon called `syslog`. The `syslog` daemon usually places information into log files found in the directory `/var/log`.

   Because of the rich amount of system information contained within these files, generally only the superuser may access them. Exact file names depend upon how the `/etc/syslog.conf` file was set up by the Linux distribution. Typically, there is a file called `messages` that collects most system status reports. There are also facilities (or types of daemons) that direct specific messages to individual files. For a Debian system, the default `/var/log` files are:

auth.log	daemon.log	debug	faillog
kern.log	lastlog	lp-acct	lp-errs
lpd-errs	lpr.log	mail.err	mail.log
mail.warn	messages	setuid.changes	syslog

For a Red Hat system, the default `/var/log` files are:

cron	maillog	sendmail.st	wtmp

```
dmesg          messages        spoole         xdm-error.log
lastlog        secure          uucp           xferlog
```

The number and names of the /var/log files are controlled by the file
/etc/syslog.conf. Its format looks like this:

```
auth,authpriv.*          /var/log/auth.log
*.*;auth,authpriv.none   /var/log/syslog
#cron.*                  /var/log/cron.log
daemon.*                 /var/log/daemon.log
kern.*                   /var/log/kern.log
lpr.*                    /var/log/lpr.log
mail.*                   /var/log/mail.log
user.*                   /var/log/user.log
uucp.*                   /var/log/uucp.log


*.=info;*.=notice;*.=warn;\
     auth,authpriv.none;\
     cron,daemon.none;\
     mail,news.none          /var/log/messages
```

This example was extracted from a Debian configuration file. The column at
the top left shows the facilities (or types of daemons), both with and without
message priority levels (where facility.level is the format for those facilities with a level indicated, such as news.none or user.notice, and where
facility is the format of those facilities without a level indicated, such as lpr).
All priority levels are included since the wild card character (*) was specified
to the right side of the dot. (For example, considering the user facility, there are
messages with priority levels info, notice, and warn so that the format for each
of the facilities becomes user.info, user.notice, and user.warn and all
of these user messages are collected in the log file /var/log/user.log.)

The user may also insert messages into the message log file with the logger
command. For example, the command:

```
logger "Hi, What's up"
```

places the string "Hi, What's up" in the messages file.

So, if something does not seem right, **remember** to check the most recent
additions to the messages file with the command:

```
tail -300 /var/log/messages | more
```

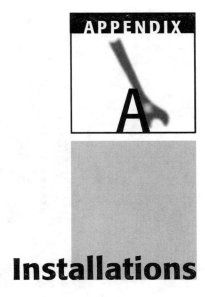

APPENDIX

A

Installations

The walkthrough of the Debian Installation is included on the companion Web site at www.wiley.com/compbooks/maginnis.

Installations

Here are installation walkthroughs of four distributions, Red Hat 6.0, SuSE 6.1, Open-Linux 2.2, and Slackware 4.0. Although the details of each installation are not part of the certificate exams, it is essential that the candidate experience these installations to develop the necessary background for understanding and using Linux.

A.1 Red Hat 6.0

The standard installation first begins by asking you if you would like to install or upgrade an existing Red Hat installation, or enable installation using the expert mode.

The next screen welcomes you to the Red Hat installation and tells you of their site located at www.redhat.com (see Figure A.1.1). Select OK or press Enter. Next, you are asked to choose a language; choose English. Then select OK or press Enter.

Figure A.1.2 shows the keyboard layout screen, choose the generic "us" layout. After doing so select OK or press Enter.

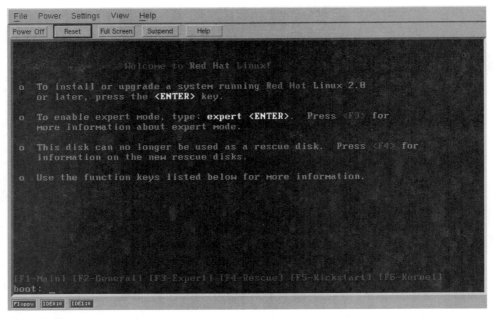

Figure A.1.1 Bootup screen.

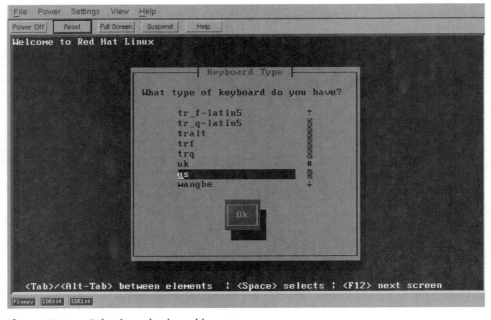

Figure A.1.2 Selecting a keyboard layout.

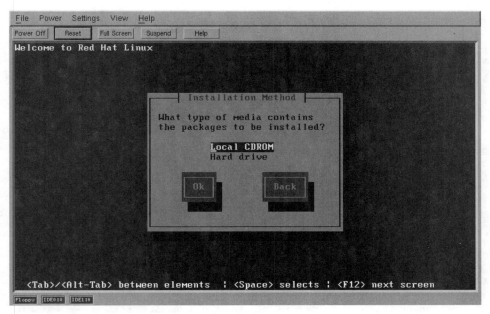

Figure A.1.3 Selecting an installation method.

Installing from a Local CD-ROM

Moving on, you are asked where your source media is located. Since this is a new install and you have the CD-ROM, choose "Local CDROM" (shown in Figure A.1.3.). The installation program will now probe your system and attempt to identify your CD-ROM drive. If it is found the installation will continue; if not, you will be prompted to identify your drive.

If appropriate, choose SCSI; if your CD-ROM is not a SCSI, choose Other. This option is good for proprietary CD-ROMs (that is, connected to a soundcard).

Installing from a Hard Drive

If you have the necessary files stored on a local hard drive partition, you may choose the Hard Drive option as shown in Figure A.1.3. For this option, highlight Hard Drive and select OK.

Installation Method

Next, the installation tool asks if you'd like a workstation, server, or custom installation. You should note that in Figure A.1.4 there is no notice that all your drives would be erased if workstation or server were chosen.

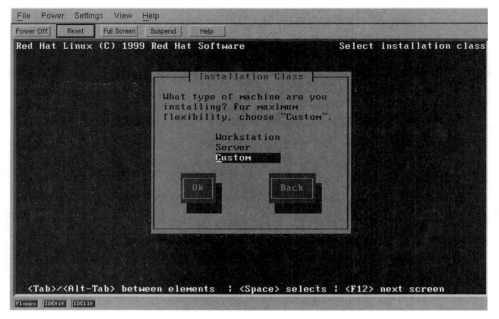

Figure A.1.4   Choosing an installation.

Workstation will erase all existing Linux partitions and attempt to set up a dual boot environment. On the other hand, if you choose server, all data on all drives will be wiped clean. The reason for choosing either of these is the ability to skip some of the manual items that must be set up in a custom installation. For maximum flexibility, you should choose custom according to the installation tool. Also, if you are attempting to set up multiple operating systems or a custom installation, this is definitely the choice. Highlight your choice and press OK or press the Enter key.

SCSI Setup and Installation

Next there will be a SCSI probe for existing adapters. Upon finding an adapter, setup will inquire if there are more. If your card was not found, there will be a list of adapters from which you may choose. If there are none then setup will proceed.

Creating Partitions for Your Red Hat Installation

The next issue involves partitioning your hard drive. The installation tool gives you the choice of using fdisk or Disk Druid (see Figure A.1.5).

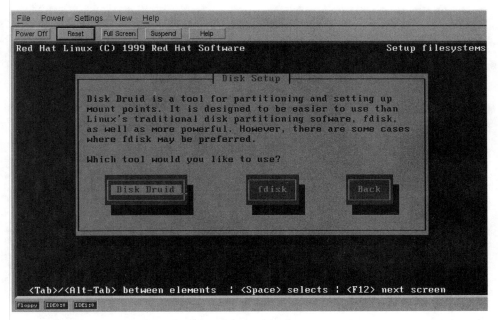

Figure A.1.5 Choosing a method for disk partitioning.

Creating Partitions with Disk Druid

Disk Druid is Red Hat's Linux disk management utility. It manages mount points for each partition, and can create and delete partitions. Figure A.1.6 shows a single 500MB hard disk. To install a partition on this drive, click on Add, which then brings up the screen shown in Figure A.1.7.

It is generally recommended to double the amount of RAM that you have, but it is usually not necessary to exceed 128MB. Click on OK, which will create the desired swap partition. Next you need to make a Linux Native partition, in which your files will be stored. Click on Add as before, and then make the mount point "/", which is usually the standard mount point for a small drive with just one Linux native partition. The size of the partition defaults to 1 MB, so make sure that the desired amount has been placed on this line (this is shown in Figure A.1.8). The allowable drives that you can use are shown in the lower left-hand corner. If this box is checked, then the partition may be created on this drive; if not, diskdruid will not write to the specified drive.

Now click on OK, which brings you to the main screen. After all changes have been made it is time to write the partitions to your hard drive. Click on OK, which takes you to the screen shown in Figure A.1.9, and then choose Yes to write the changes to the partition table.

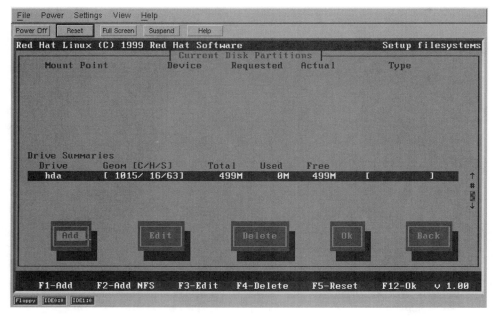

Figure A.1.6   Partitioning the drive.

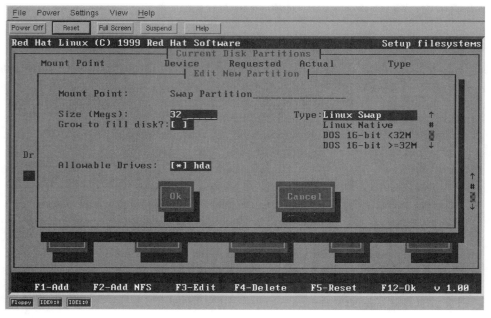

Figure A.1.7   Adding a swap partition.

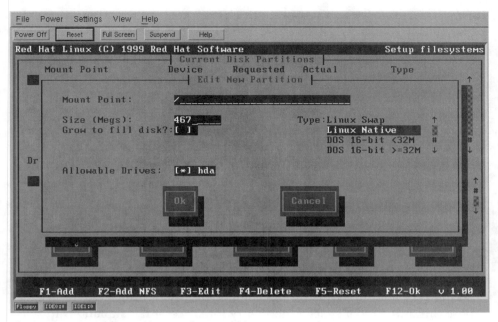

Figure A.1.8   Adding a Linux native partition.

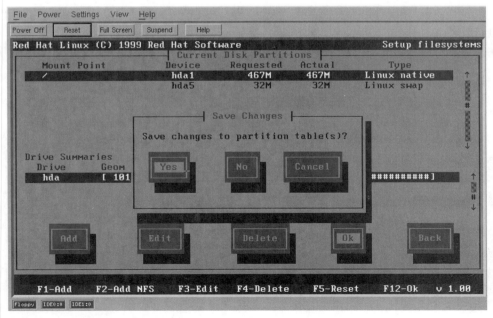

Figure A.1.9   Writing changes to the partition table(s).

Initializing Swap Space and Formatting Partitions

After all changes have been made, you are asked to identify the partition that you will use for your swap space. All swap partitions are shown, and you can choose the desired partition. Then you must decide if you would like to check for bad blocks during formatting. This is usually recommended, but will require a longer period of time to format. After the swap space has been formatted, you are asked for the desired partitions that you would like to format. Again you are asked if you would like to check for bad blocks, as shown in Figure A.1.10.

Selecting Components and Packages

Next, you decide on the components that you will install. Pressing the space bar selects or deselects the components shown in Figure A.1.11. Components group packages together, and you may deselect individual packages even if they are included in a component.

At the very bottom of this list is a component listed as Everything. You can choose this, but a lot of space is necessary for successful installation. To select or deselect individual packages, you only need to check the "Select individual packages" box (shown in Figure A.1.11) at the bottom. Once you select OK, you may deselect or select any items that you might feel necessary. Next, press

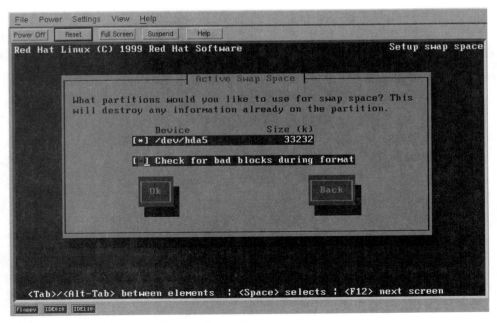

Figure A.1.10   Formatting Linux native partitions.

Figure A.1.11 Selecting components.

the Done button, which will determine if there are any unresolved package dependencies. If there are none you may proceed, but if there are some remember to check the "Install packages to satisfy dependencies" box to ensure that all programs needed by the items that you wish to install are installed. Next press Done and proceed.

Once this has been accomplished, you'll see a screen that tells you that the log of your installation will be kept in /tmp/install.log for future access. Click OK to continue. You will then see a screen that says, "Making ext2 filesystem on . . ." After this, you will see a screen (shown in Figure A.1.12) that will show the status of the installation of the packages that you have chosen.

Finding and Installing a Mouse

Upon completion of package installation, setup will attempt to find a PS/2 mouse (shown in Figure A.1.13). Click OK.

You are then asked to identify the mouse that was found. It is generally recommended to choose the generic mouse (PS/2). You can choose to emulate three buttons by checking the box labeled "Emulate three buttons" shown in Figure A.14.

Click OK; you are ready to proceed.

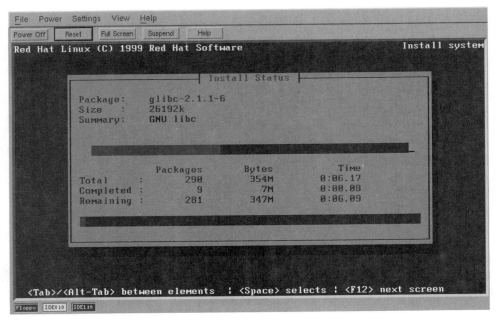

Figure A.1.12 Status of package installation.

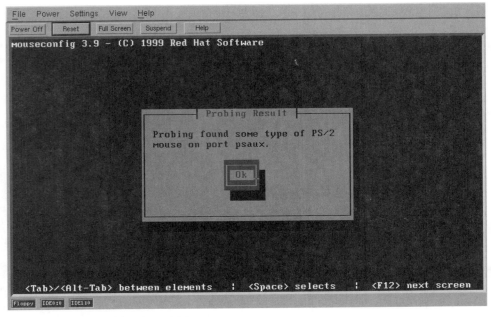

Figure A.1.13 Probing for a PS/2 mouse.

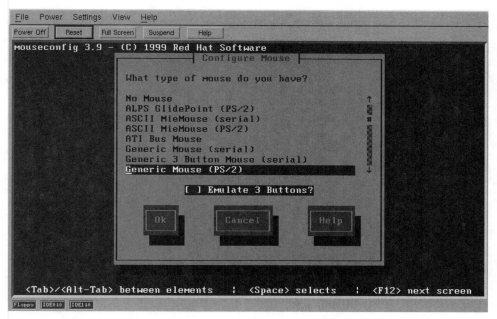

Figure A.1.14   Emulating three buttons and identifying the mouse.

Installing Networking

The next screen, shown in Figure A.1.15, asks if you would like to set up and configure a LAN on the system.

Click on the Yes button to proceed. Setup will now do a probe of your system and will find your network card. If it cannot find a card, setup will ask you to choose a driver that supports your network card, and to specify any options necessary for the driver to locate and recognize it. Once this is done, click OK. The next screen asks for a boot protocol. There are three choices as shown in Figure A.16. With bootp and dhcp, your network configuration will be set automatically and you can skip the rest of this section. Note, though, that in order to choose either of these options, you must have a properly configured bootp or dhcp server.

Choose Static IP address from the menu and click OK. Next, configure TCP/IP for network installation.

Then you are asked to insert your IP address, Netmask, Gateway, and Primary Nameserver. After doing so, click OK. Moving to the next screen (shown in Figure A.1.17), you are asked for the domain name, host name, secondary, and tertiary name servers if they exist. After entering each, you can move to the next line by pressing Enter. After completing the required information, proceed by clicking OK.

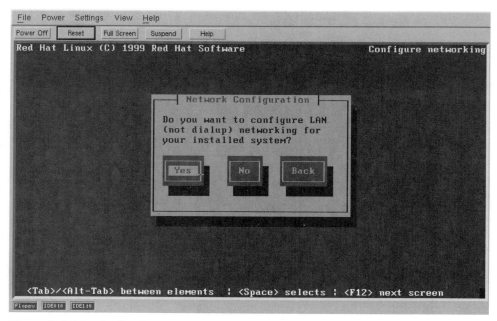

Figure A.1.15   Configuring a LAN.

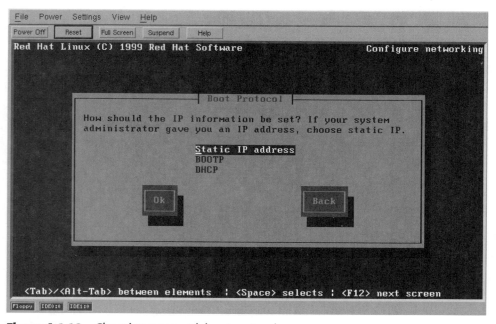

Figure A.1.16   Choosing a network boot protocol.

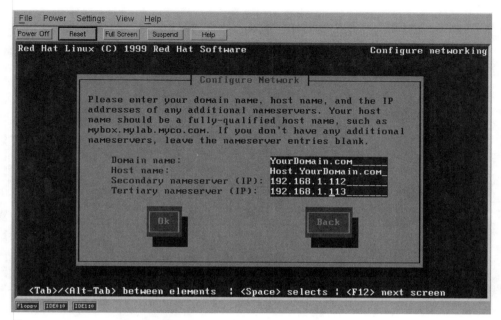

Figure A.1.17 Configuring TCP/IP.

Configuring Your Time Zone

The next screen involves setting up your time zone (see Figure A.1.18). It also has an option for setting your hardware clock to GMT. This will enable your system to properly handle daylight-savings time. However, if you are running another operating system on your machine, choosing this option may cause it to display an incorrect time. After this has been accomplished, select OK or press Enter.

Selecting Services to Run Automatically

This screen lets you configure the different service to start automatically at boot time. If you have done a workstation or server installation, then this has been set for you automatically. You may scroll through the list in Figure A.1.19, and if you're not sure what a particular service is, highlight it and press the F1 key. You will then get a brief description of the service. When you are done, click on OK and press Enter.

NOTE Running services that are not needed presents a security hole in your system. It is wise to turn off any unused service.

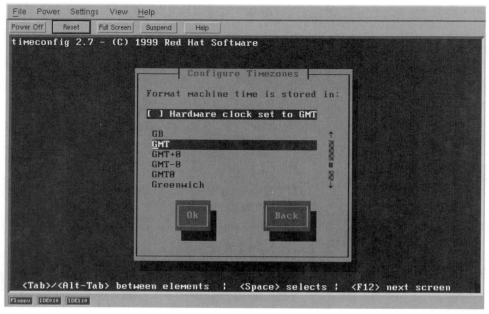

Figure A.1.18   Configuring a time zone.

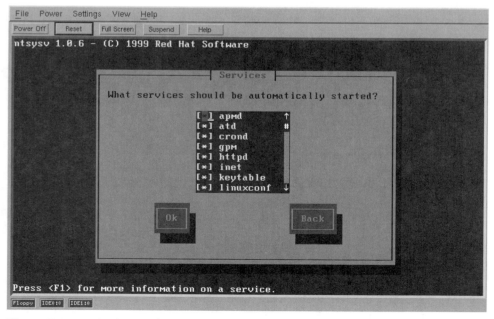

Figure A.1.19   Setting services to start automatically.

Setting up a Printer

Setting up a printer screen presents you with several options:

- Local is defined as a printer connected directly to your computer.
- Remote lpd is a printer connected to your local area network.
- SMB/Windows 95/NT is defined as a printer connected to another printer via SMB networking.
- NetWare is a printer connected to another computer that resides on a Novell Network, and is shared.

After choosing a printer connection, proceed by clicking on OK and press Enter. After filling out all required fields on subsequent screens and clicking on OK, proceed to the next section.

Setting a Root Password and Authentication Configuration

The installation program will now ask you to set a root password as shown in Figure A.1.20. This password will be needed for logging in the first time.

The password must be a least six characters long. It will not be shown on the screen, and you must enter it a second time to confirm that this is the password that you desire. It is recommended that you do not use dictionary words and

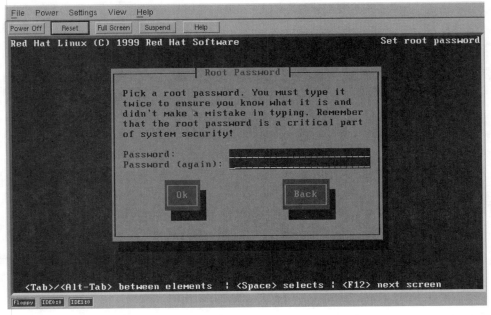

Figure A.1.20 Setting a root password.

that you use numerals mixed with upper- and lowercase letters. Remember that it is case-sensitive and that root has the privilege of complete access to the entire system. Highlight OK and press Enter.

The next screen lets you enable shadow passwords, which will be readable only by root. Also, you can set up MD5 password, which allows long passwords to be used (up to 256 characters). Another option on this screen enables you to use NIS, which is a Network Information Service. Select OK when you are done.

Creating a Boot Disk

Next you are given the option of creating a boot diskette. It is recommended that you create one. This disk maybe used to boot Linux if for some reason LILO doesn't. It can also be used in emergencies along with a rescue disk to recover a crashed system. Selecting OK will prompt you to insert a blank floppy disk; select OK to create the boot diskette.

Installing LILO

You can now install the LILO bootloader. The installation screen is shown in Figure A.1.21. If you are performing a workstation or server installation, then this has been done automatically. The Master Boot Record is the recommended place to install LILO, but if you are using another bootloader, you may install

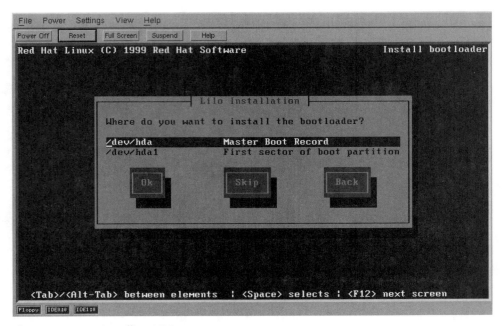

Figure A.1.21   Installing LILO.

it in the First sector of boot partition. Clicking on OK prompts you for special options if there are any. Make any necessary changes, select OK, and press Enter. Pressing Skip skips installation of LILO altogether.

X Windows Setup

You can now set up the X Window System. This is available only if you have chosen to install the X Window package. The installation program prompts you for the proper video card that is installed in your system (shown in Figure A.1.22).

After doing so, highlight OK and press Enter. The installation program will then install the proper package for your video card. Next, you are prompted for the make and model of the monitor, shown in Figure A.1.23.

If your monitor is found, then highlight it and press Enter; if not, select Custom and press Enter. If you do select Custom, you will be prompted for the vertical and horizontal sync ranges of your monitor. These are usually found in the user's manual, and are available from the manufacturers.

After this, you are prompted to probe for default resolution and color depth. If for some reason your card cannot be probed, the Xconfigurator will allow you to enter its properties manually. You are then prompted for clockchip configuration, shown in Figure A.1.24. The recommended choice is No Clockchip Setting. After choosing your desired option press Enter.

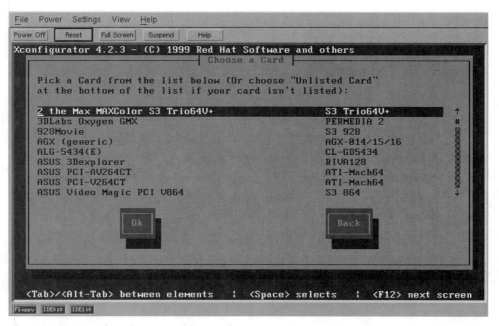

Figure A.1.22 Choosing your video card.

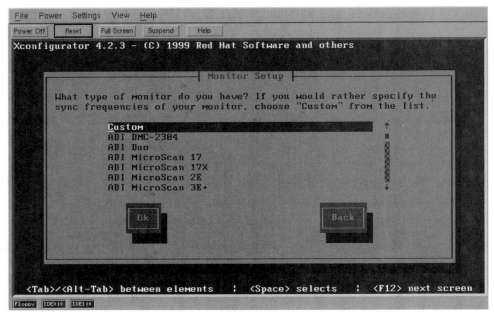

Figure A.1.23 Choosing a monitor.

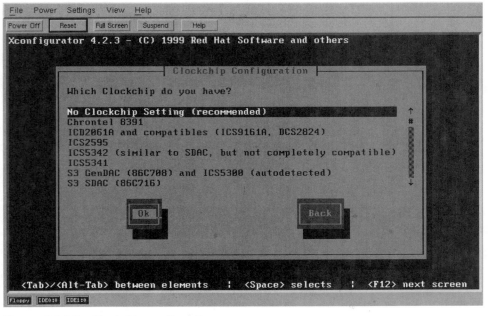

Figure A.1.24 Clockchip configuration.

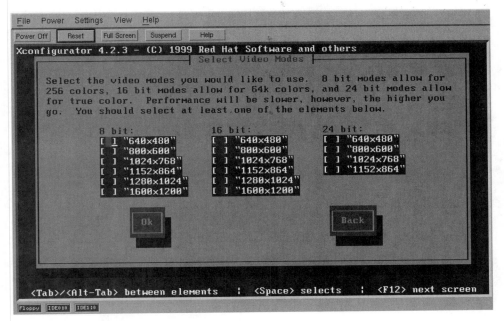

Figure A.1.25 Video modes and color depth.

If your card was not probed as mentioned, you can choose the video modes that you want to use manually by pressing Space on the highlighted selection (as shown in Figure A.1.25).

After identifying all modes and color depths, highlight OK and press Enter. Now Xconfigurator will start X to test your configuration.

Restarting the Computer

Installation is now complete. You are prompted to restart the computer; remove any floppies and CDs, highlight OK, and press Enter.

A.2 SuSE 6.1

SuSE welcomes you to the installation as shown in Figure A.2.1.

After viewing the startup screen, SuSE will wait approximately five seconds before continuing. This can be bypassed by simply pressing Enter. The next screen prompts you for the language of choice. Choose English throughout this sample installation. Highlight OK and press Enter to proceed.

You will now be asked whether you use a color or a monochrome monitor. After highlighting your choice, proceed by pressing Enter. The following screen appears in color if you have previously chosen "color display." You are asked to choose a specific keyboard mapping (shown in Figure A.2.2).

Highlight your choice and press Enter.

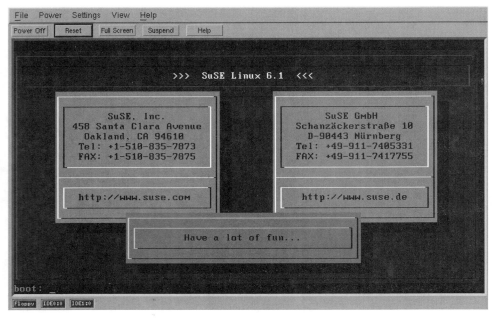

Figure A.2.1　Starting an installation.

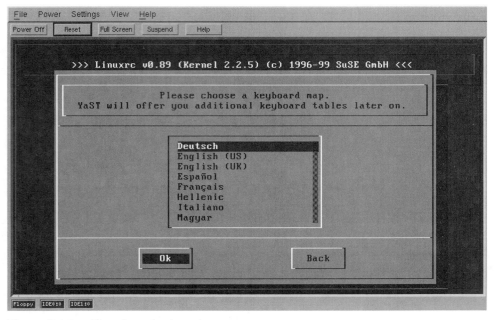

Figure A.2.2　Choosing a keyboard map.

Starting Linuxrc

Linuxrc loads the needed drivers as kernel modules. Figure A.2.3 shows the linuxrc screen, which has several options. The Settings menu contains the several items that you have previously set up including language, display, and keyboard mapping.

The system information, however, shows you the system information of your machine. The next item, Kernel modules, loads modules for your hardware. If you have SCSI hardware or pcmcia adapters click on each submenu and press Enter. However, it is recommended that you use the Autoload submenu shown in Figure A.2.4.

Upon finding a driver, the module loads, and at the end you are given a summary of the devices found along with some hardware information. Press Enter to move to the next screen, which shows that the modules were loaded. Press Enter to return to the Kernel module menu; highlight back and press Enter to return to the main linuxrc menu.

Starting the Installation with Linuxrc and YaST

Moving down the linuxrc Main Menu, highlight Start installation / system and press Enter. A menu appears, with four options as shown in Figure A.2.5.

Figure A.2.3   Linuxrc main menu.

Figure A.2.4 Autoloading modules.

Figure A.2.5 Start installation menu.

From this menu, you can boot a previously installed system and start a rescue of a crashed system. However, since you are installing a new SuSE operating system, highlight Start installation and press OK.

After choosing Start installation, you are prompted for a source media, which is usually from a CD-ROM. After highlighting it, press Enter and the system mounts the CD-ROM and starts YaST (Yet another Setup Tool).

Next you will be asked for the type of installation; there are four options, shown in Figure A.2.6 You can update an existing Linux system, install Linux using the expert mode, or install Linux from scratch. Choose to do the latter: highlight Install Linux from scratch and press Enter to continue.

Selecting "Installing Linux from scratch" lets you choose whether to use the partitioning tools or not. There are two options. The first is "Do not partition," which will immediately move you to the next screen. However, if you do not have a partition on your new hard drive, you will be forced to abort, which sends you back to the screen shown in Figure A.2.6. Choosing "Partitioning" will scan for a drive and ask if you would like to use the "Whole hard disk" or partition it manually with the Partitioning selection. Partitioning the entire disk will effectively erase all data on the specified drive. After selecting the Partitioning option, press Enter.

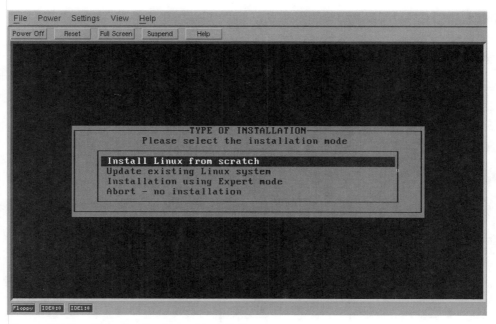

Figure A.2.6 Choosing the type of installation.

Partitioning the Hard Disk

To create a partition, press F5. A window pops up, asking whether you would like a Primary or Extended partition. Note that you are allowed to create only four primary partitions. If you need more partitions, then you must specify one of these as an Extended partition. This will allow you to assign logical partitions inside the extended partition.

If YaST was doing the partitioning, it would create a /boot partition of at least 2 MB so that the kernel could reside here. This would be a good idea if you planned on running multiple distributions of Linux. The reason is that you could update the kernel in one spot rather than in multiple places. Another reason is that in an old BIOS, the kernel might need to be placed on the first 504 MB of your disk so that it can be accessed.

For this installation we will first create a swap space—choose Primary partition and continue by pressing Enter. The next screen (shown in Figure A.2.7) lets you choose the primary partition.

After selecting /dev/hda1 and pressing Enter to continue, you will see a "Starting cylinder" and an "End of partition" input box. Generally, a swap partition is twice the size of the RAM in your machine, but not more than 128 MB. So in the Starting cylinder box, enter 1 (for the first cylinder) followed by +128M in the End of partition box. Highlight Continue and press Enter.

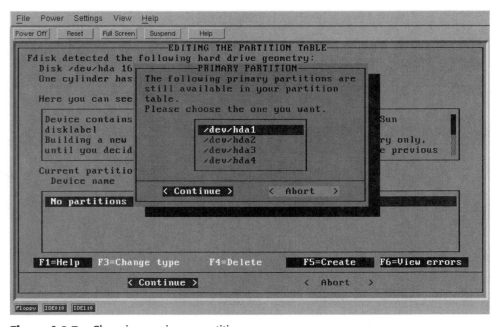

Figure A.2.7 Choosing a primary partition.

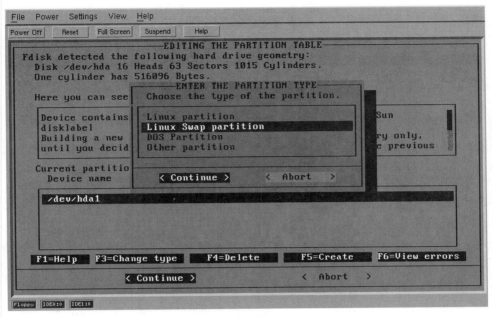

Figure A.2.8 Changing partition type to Linux Swap.

After this, you must change the type of the partition to swap by pressing F3. This asks for the type of partition you want to create (shown in Figure A.2.8). Highlighting Linux Swap partition, press Enter.

Now you must make a Linux native partition. Press F5 to create a new partition. Then choose Primary partition, highlight Continue, and press Enter. Choose /dev/hda2 and press Enter. Since you want the rest of the drive to be used as one partition, leave the default parameters as they appear and highlight Continue. By pressing Enter, you return to the main partition screen. After clicking Continue you are asked if you would like to write the partition table to the hard disk. Click on Yes and press Enter. You will now see the table being written to the hard disk.

To set a mount point on the Linux native partition, highlight the partition and press the F4 key. Choose / and press Enter. You return to the main partition menu. Highlight Continue and press Enter. The next screen tells you that the following file systems will be written to your drive. This is fine; press Enter and the filesystem(s) will be created.

Loading a Configuration

YaST's main menu (shown in Figure A.2.9) appears.

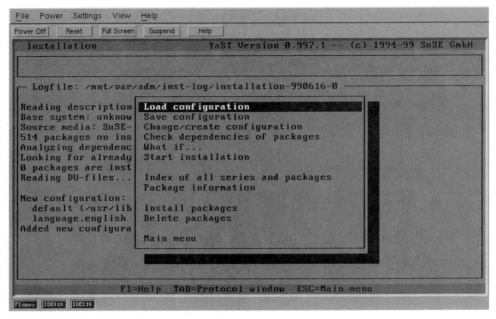

Figure A.2.9   YaST's main menu.

Several predefined configurations are available. Clicking on the "Load con-figuration" presents the options shown in Figure A.2.10. You may load a minimum, development, network, default, or everything configuration.

The space requirements are listed to the right, to prevent you from installing a system that will not fit. You may choose each configuration by highlighting the choice and pressing the space bar. After making all changes click the Add button to load them.

YaST also allows you to select or deselect individual packages that were included in the configuration(s) that you have loaded. By highlighting Change / create configuration you can select a series (shown in Figure A.2.11) by highlighting it and pressing Enter. From there you can select or deselect individual items by pressing the space bar.

After selecting an item, any item with a dependency will pop up a screen telling you the package that is related. Choosing Auto automatically solves these problems by selecting these items for you. To exit from here, must press F10 to proceed. To return to YaST's main menu, press Esc or Enter.

Installing the Configuration

Highlight the "Check dependencies of packages" for YaST's main menu and press Enter. It should read "All package dependencies are satisfied." If not, just click on Auto, and they will be resolved. To return to the main menu, press

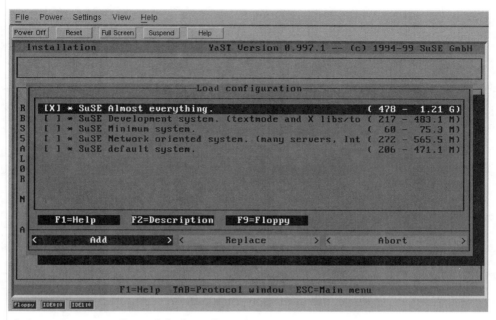

Figure A.2.10   Loading a default configuration.

File   Power   Settings   View   Help

| Power Off | Reset | Full Screen | Suspend | Help |

Series selection   YaST Version 0.997.1 -- (c) 1994-99 SuSE GmbH
┌ Series ──
| a   Linux Base System (You need it!)   [116.6 M]
| ap   Programs that don't need X   [14.3 M]
| beo   Extreme Linux (Beowulf)   [0 B]
| d   Development (C, C++, Lisp, etc.)   [90.8 M]
| doc   Documentation   [29.3 M]
| e   Emacs   [22.7 M]
| emu   Emulators   [0 B]
| fun   Games and more   [33.5 K]
| gra   All about graphics   [17.4 M]
| kde   K Desktop Environment   [52.4 M]
| kpa   KDE alpha applications   [0 B]
| n   Network-Support (TCP/IP, UUCP, Mail, News)   [40.2 M]

┌ <F3>=Zoom ───
| device-name partition   total   used   free   free% mount-point
|
| /dev/hda2   Linux   421.2 M   514.2 M -93.0 M - 22% /

             F1=Help   F4=Resorting   F5=Dependencies   F10=Esc=Exit

| Floppy | IDE0:0 | IDE1:0 |

Figure A.2.11   Selecting a series.

Continue. Next, highlight Start installation and press Enter. You will begin to see the packages being installed (shown in Figure A.2.12). At the top of this screen, you can see how many packages have been installed as well as how many are left. The size of the package currently being installed is also shown.

When the installation is done you are returned to YaST's load configuration menu (Figure A.2.9). From there, highlight Main menu and click Enter.

Choosing a Kernel

Setup prompts you to select a kernel (see Figure A.2.13). Most standard IDE systems will take the first kernel labeled "Standard (E)IDE-Kernel." However, if you are installing to a system that contains SCSI devices, make sure that the kernel supports your adapter. Install the Standard (E)IDE-Kernel by highlighting it and pressing Enter.

A screen appears that asks whether you would like to create a boot disk. If you do not have one, it is definitely recommended. You are prompted to insert a blank floppy disk, and the files will be copied to it. However, if you own a bootable SuSE CD-ROM, then you may click No. Press Enter.

Using LILO

LILO is the Linux bootloader and is installed in the Master Boot Record (MBR). After the MBR is loaded into memory, LILO is started and you may choose what

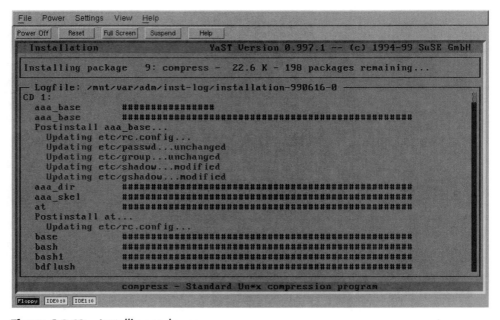

Figure A.2.12   Installing packages.

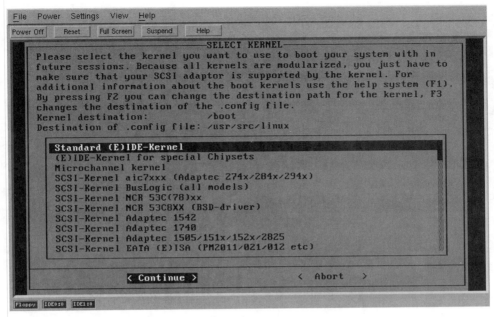

Figure A.2.13   Choosing the correct kernel.

operating system to boot. During setup you are asked if you would like to install LILO. Highlight Yes, and you will see the LILO installation screen in Figure A.2.14. The Append-line shown in the figure allows LILO the capability to pass a command line to the kernel. In this sample installation, leave this line blank.

Pressing F4 lets you create a new configuration. Call this configuration SuSE and place it in the line for Configuration name (shown in Figure A.2.15). The default name is set to Linux, but if you click on it you will see that LILO will also boot DOS/Win and OS/2. Leave it set on Boot Linux and proceed to the next line. You are now prompted for the root partition to boot from. Since you made one large Linux native partition and set the mount point to /, point it to that partition (/dev/hda2). The kernel to be booted by LILO will be set by default to /boot/vmlinuz. Highlight Continue and press Enter.

Now, from LILO's installation main menu, highlight Continue and press Enter. You can see LILO being written out to the MBR. Upon completion, the output is written to a window. The output should read "Added SuSE * ". Highlight Continue and press Enter to proceed.

Time Zone and Configuration

With LILO now set up, you are prompted to set up a time zone. Highlight the desired time zone and press Enter to see the screen shown in Figure A.2.16. Highlight Local time and press Enter.

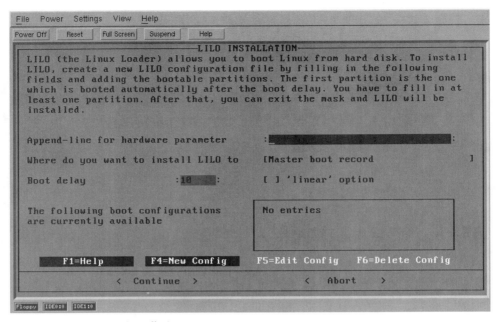

Figure A.2.14 LILO installation.

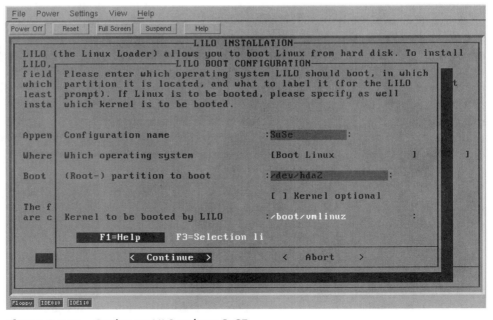

Figure A.2.15 Setting up LILO to boot SuSE.

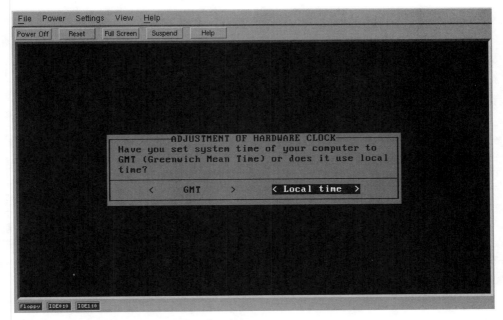

Figure A.2.16   Setting the clock to local time.

Network Configuration

You are now prompted to enter a host name and domain name. Call the machine "Host" and the domain "YourDomain.com" (see Figure A.2.17).

After entering a host name and a domain name, you are asked if you want to be placed on a real or loopback-only network. The latter would be applicable if you intended to develop software for a network, but were not physically connected to one. Choose real network and press Enter.

The next screen prompts you for the "Type of network," defined here as eth0 (shown in Figure A.2.18. Input the IP address, followed by the Netmask, which is usually defined as (255.255.255.0). The default gateway is now installed (usually your IP with a X.X.X.1 and a 1 in the last slot). Highlight Continue and press Enter.

You are then asked if you want to start inetd at bootup, which will start the servers that run Telnet, finger, ftp, etc. Highlight Yes and press Enter.

Immediately following, you are asked if portmap should be turned on at bootup time. Turning this server on could compromise security, so it is recommended that unless you need this sever running, choose No and press Enter.

You are then prompted for a from-address for your new system. Enter a new name or use the default, highlight Continue, and press Enter. Next you are asked if you want to access a nameserver. Choose Yes and press Enter. Figure A.2.19 shows the Name Server Configuration screen. Enter the IP-address of the name server, followed by the Domain list, which is already filled in by default.

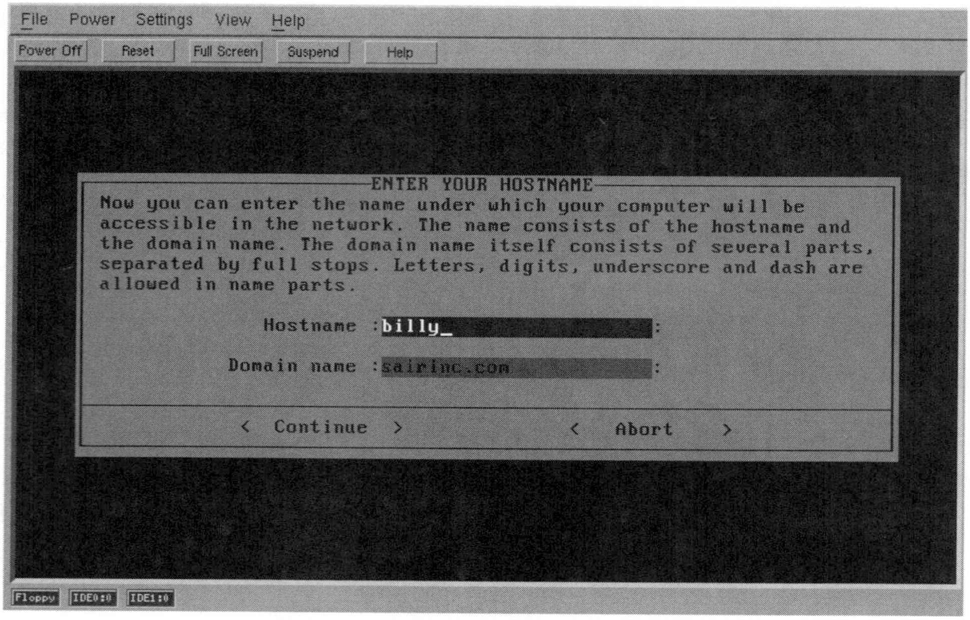

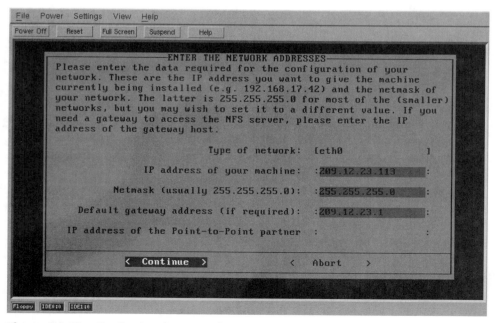

Figure A.2.17   Entering a host name and a domain name.

Figure A.2.18   Configuring the network connection.

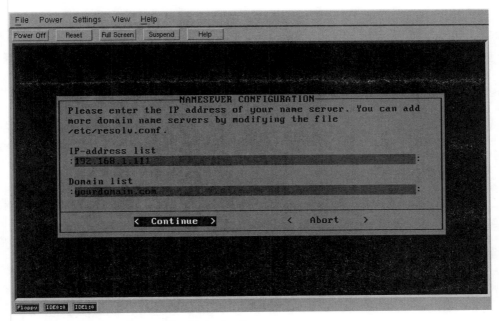

Figure A.2.19   Entering an IP address for the name server.

Highlight Continue and press Enter. You are told that the network software is now configured and will become active after rebooting; press Enter.

Configuring SendMail

To configure SendMail, you are prompted to select a connection; highlight "Host with permanent network connection (SMTP)" and press Enter. The system prompts that SuSE.config is being started. When it stops, choose Continue and press Enter.

Finishing Up

The next screen indicates that the base system has been installed; press Enter. The system will now be rebooted.

Next you are prompted to enter a password for root. The password must be at least five characters long and should be a mix of numeric digits and characters.

Next, if you would like to create an example user, choose Yes and press Enter. The example user screen is shown (see Figure A.2.20); enter a Login name followed by a Password, along with confirmation of the password. Next a description of the user can be entered, or you may use the default name that is supplied.

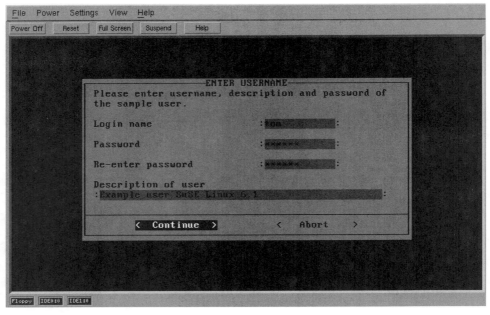

Figure A.2.20   Configuring an example user.

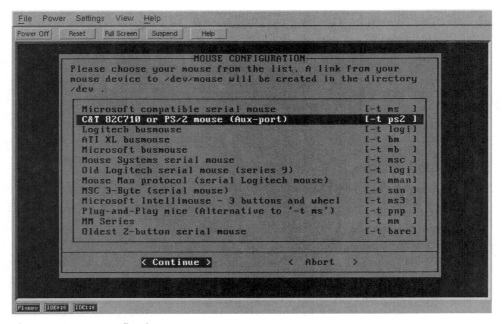

Figure A.2.21   Configuring a mouse.

You are now asked if you want to set up a modem. Since you have installed a network adapter on a LAN, highlight No and press Enter. When asked whether you would like to set up a mouse, choose Yes and press Enter. Then highlight the choice from Figure A.2.21 and press Enter.

You are asked if you want to use Gpm, which lets you exchange text between consoles. Select Yes and press Enter. After testing the Gpm configuration you are told that YaST will now terminate. Select Continue and press Enter. Now you are ready to reboot and start SuSE.

A.3 OpenLinux 2.2

Installation of OpenLinux is among the easiest installations available. The startup screen is shown in Figure A.3.1. The OpenLinux setup program automatically probes for all your hardware and determines the kind of installation. The installation will start by waiting at the boot prompt for input. Just press Enter and the program will start to probe for your hardware. If you are installing from the CD-ROM and have already put the OpenLinux CD-ROM in your drive, it will be detected automatically and installation will continue from there. Note that this requires your CD-ROM to be bootable. After probing for your hardware, wait a few seconds for the OpenLinux Animations to be over to continue.

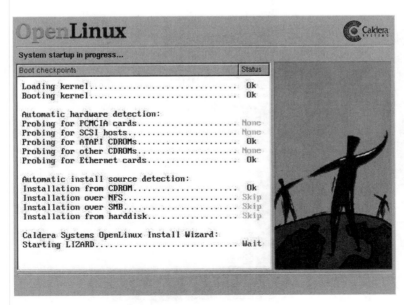

Figure A.3.1   OpenLinux startup screen.

Language Selection

Caldera lets you choose from among four languages—English, German, French, and Italian—for installation. Choose a language by clicking the mouse in the appropriate option box and clicking Next.

Choose and Set up a Mouse

Now you will have to choose and set up your mouse. Generic mice are usually PS/2 mice, so it is recommended that you choose a PS/2 mouse, then choose standard mouse with no wheels from the drop-down menu on the right (see Figure A.3.2). You can test to see if your mouse is working. Move your mouse to the gray area named Test Mouse Here and then press on any of your buttons and see if the corresponding mouse button is lighting up in the mouse illustration on the left. If you have a Microsoft or old Logitech mouse, please choose appropriately. Also, if you have a PS/2 mouse such as Intellimouse or mouseman with gliding wheels, choose the appropriate one from the drop-down box on the right.

Installation Target

Choose the target disk where you want to install your OpenLinux system (see Figure A.3.3). You may use your entire hard disk for OpenLinux or you may want to run it on only one partition. Note that if you choose the entire hard

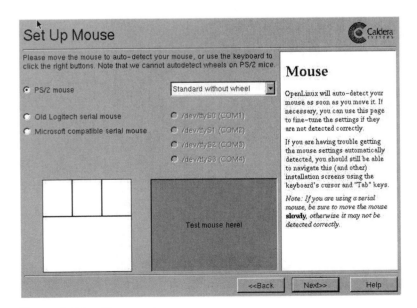

Figure A.3.2   Mouse setup screen.

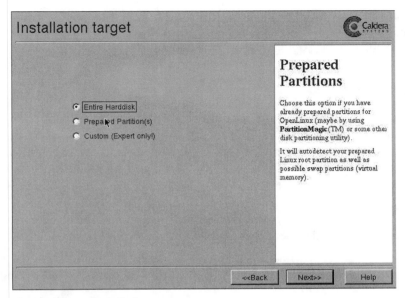

Figure A.3.3   Installation target screen.

disk option, it will wipe your entire hard disk clean. However, if you have an already-partitioned hard disk you might want to use the prepared partition option. This option allows you to install OpenLinux on a specified partition. If you do not want to install it on the entire hard disk and you do not have an already-partitioned hard disk, you will need to go to expert mode to partition your hard disk and then you will be able to install OpenLinux. Choose the appropriate option and press Next.

WARNING **Remember that partitioning a hard disk will delete all data on it.**

Custom (Expert) Mode

If you chose Custom mode from the previous menu, you will get to a screen where you can view the existing partitions. If there are no available partitions, you can partition your hard disk now.

Creating a Boot Partition

Choose the hard disk you want to partition and then double-click on it. Four subtrees appear. Click on /dev/hda1 and then click on Edit. Set the start and end cylinders to the size that you want your partition to be. As you put in the ending value, you will see the actual size of the hard disk in Megabytes to the right. Then, set the system type to Linux from the drop-down box and set mount point to / . Also, check the bootable option. This will be the boot partition.

Creating a Swap Partition

You will now need to create a swap partition for optimum performance of your system. Click on /dev/hda2 and then click on Edit. Set the swap partition size to be 64MB by selecting the difference in starting and ending values to 32. Set the system type to swap. Then click on Write and click on Next.

Choose a Root Partition

Choose the appropriate hard disk and press Next as shown in Figure A.3.4.

Choose the Entire Hard Disk

Choose /dev/hda, as shown in Figure A.3.5, and press Prepare Selected Hard Drive for Linux, and then wait for the hard disk to be prepared. You will know that the hard disk has been prepared when the Next button is reactivated again; press it to continue.

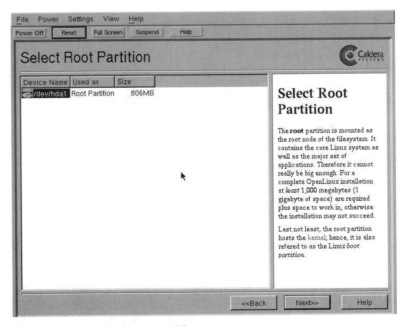

Figure A.3.4   Select root partition screen.

Figure A.3.5 Choose a disk screen.

Partition Information

Click the appropriate hard disk, press Format Chosen Partition, and press Next (see Figure A.3.6).

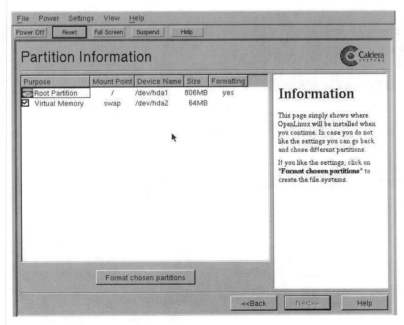

Figure A.3.6 Partition information.

Select Installation

Now you will have to choose the kind of installation you want. You have four options. Minimum set will install all the required minimum files to get Linux running. This kind of installation is most appropriate for machines that will be used as servers and will not be used for development work. This option will install in about 160 MB of space. The second option, All Recommended Packages, is ideal for a minimal workstation and server PC. It will require about 580 MB of space. Recommended + Commercial will install the same base package as the previous option as well as StarOffice 5.0 and WordPerfect Version 8.0. This option requires around 780 MB of space. The last option, All Packages, installs all available software packages that are available at the time of Open-Linux's release. This option requires the largest space, about 1000 MB. Choose the system you want and then press Next.

While choosing other components and configurations for your system, setup will already start to install the packages you chose in the previous screen so that by the time you are done with all configurations, all your software will be very close to being installed.

Select Keyboard Type

Now select the kind of keyboard you have (most common keyboards are Generic 101) and then choose the appropriate layout. Choose U.S. English for this installation and press Next (see Figure A.3.7).

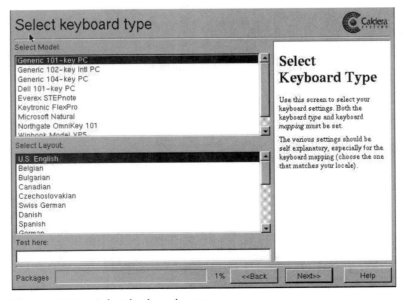

Figure A.3.7 Select keyboard screen.

Select Video Card

Usually, your Video card and Clock speed should be detected automatically by the setup program, but if you find any discrepancies, click on Probe on the lower left hand side of your screen so that OpenLinux will detect automatically your clock speed and your video card type (see Figure A.3.8). Then select the appropriate amount of Video RAM and click Next.

Select Monitor

Now choose the monitor type from the 1700 listed. If you cannot find your monitor from the list, take the manual that comes with the monitor, look for the refresh rates; fill in the appropriate horizontal and vertical rates and then click Next.

Select Video Mode

Select the Video Mode. All of the modes listed are the modes that the setup program has determined to be compatible with the Video Card/Monitor that you have entered previously. 1280×1024, 8–16 bpp is a very common resolution, so select it and click on Test this mode to see how it actually looks. If you don't like the way it looks, just choose another resolution and test it until you get the one you like. Then press Next.

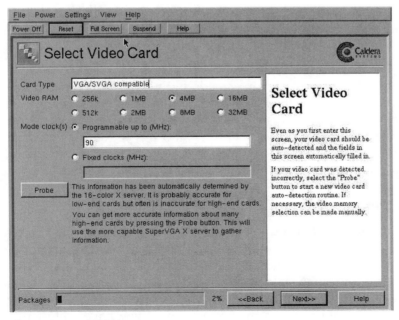

Figure A.3.8   Video screen.

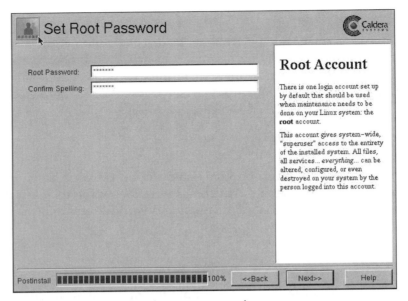

Figure A.3.9 Setting up the root password.

Set the Root Password

Select the root password. Root will be the superuser on your Linux system and will have access to everything. Type a password in the Root Password box and then retype it below to make sure you have typed it correctly (see Figure A.3.9). Then click on Next.

Set Login Names

Now that you have the root setup, you can add individual users on your system. Since Linux is a multi-user system, you can add as many users as you want. To do so, just type in the user's name in the Real Name Box and the Login Name in the appropriate box, then type and retype the password for that user. Choose the shell you want the user to use, and click on Add User. After adding as many users as you wish, click on Next.

Set Up Networking

If a network card is installed in your computer and you want to use it to access the Internet, select Ethernet Configured Statically and then fill in the appropriate data for your IP address, NameServers, and Gateway (see Figure A.3.10). You can obtain this information from your ISP. If your Internet connection dynamically assigns IP addresses, you have to choose Ethernet Configured by DHCP. Then put your Hostname in the bottom box. If you have no Ethernet card, just choose no Ethernet and then click on Next.

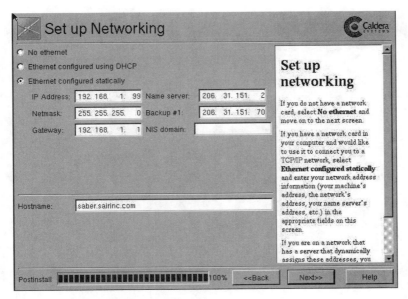

Figure A.3.10 Setting up networking.

Choose the Time Zone

Now choose your time zone. Click on the map on the geographical region near you, and the setup program will set the time for you for that particular region. Also be sure to indicate with the radio buttons at the bottom of the screen whether your system clock uses GMT or Local time.

Entertain Yourself

Now that the configuration is done, as the software is being installed you can play a game of Tetris while you are waiting for the installation to finish (see Figure A.3.11). Just click on New Game to start. To move the objects left and right, use the left and right arrow keys; to rotate the objects, use the up or down arrow keys.

A.4 Slackware Installation

When booting your computer with the Slackware CD-ROM, you will get the screen shown in Figure A.4.1, and the system will wait for you to enter something at the boot prompt. At the boot prompt, you have the option to enter your own hardware parameters or just let Slackware automatically detect them for you by pressing Enter at the prompt. By pressing Enter, Slackware automatically probes for your hardware, detects the hardware, and goes to the installation screen.

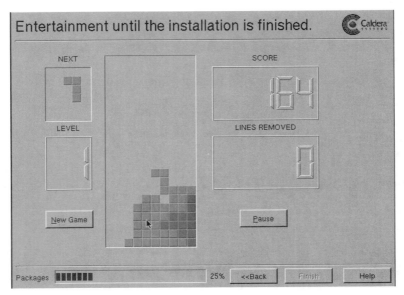

Figure A.3.11 Let the fun begin with Tetris.

But, if you want to specify your specific hardware parameters for Slackware to boot on, you can do so by entering them at the prompt. For example,

```
boot:vmlinuz root=/dev/hda1 load_ramdisk=0 init rd=
```

will boot your system with the vmlinuz kernel.

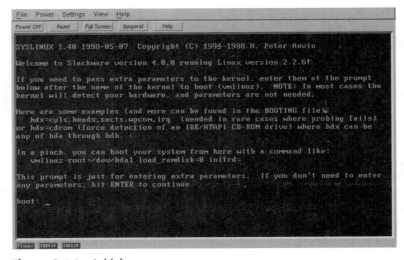

Figure A.4.1 Initial screen.

For an easy start, just press Enter and Slackware should automatically detect your hardware and go on to the actual installation

Slackware will minimally boot up for installation, and you'll have the screen shown in Figure A.4.2.

At this screen, type "root" at the Slackware login prompt and press Enter.

After logging in as root, you can actually start the installation if you have already partitioned your hard disk in Linux native format. If you have not yet done so, you may do so by typing either `fdisk` or `cfdisk` at the # prompt.

fdisk to Partition the Hard Disk

To use the fdisk program, just type `fdisk` at the # prompt. If you don't specify any parameters after the `fdisk`, it will take /dev/hda, which is the first IDE drive, as the default drive. However, if you want to partition the first SCSI disk on your system, you might want to specify that parameter when you start fdisk by using the following command:

```
fdisk /dev/sda
```

Or, if you plan to partition a different IDE hard drive other than the first one, you can specify it as:

```
fdisk /dev/hdb
```

Once in fdisk, the program will wait for your command at the following prompt:

```
Command (m for help) :
```

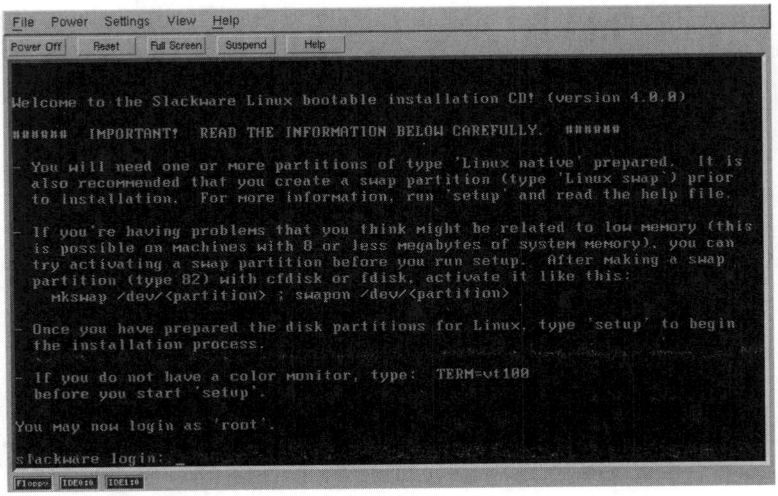

Figure A.4.2   Install the login screen.

You can type m for a list of available commands:

```
Command (m for help) : p
```

First of all, type p to get the partition table information and make note of the current partitions available. If there are not any, just ignore it and go to the next step.

```
Command (m for help) : n
Command Action
   e extended
   p primary partition (1-4)
```

Then, type n to create a new partition on the hard disk and choose p for a primary partition. fdisk will now ask you the number of the partition to create. If you did not have any prior partition, choose 1 or else choose the next available number from the partition table information you noted before.

```
Partition Number (1-4) : 1
First Cylinder (1-761 default 1) :
Last Cylinder or +size or sizeM or +sizeK (1-761 default 761) :
```

By pressing Enter on the First Cylinder, it will take the first available cylinder. Now depending on how big you want this first partition to be, you specify the last cylinder. For this exercise, you want a 1800MB partition. Type +1800M at the last cylinder prompt. Press the n command again and create another primary partition of 128 MB.

The 128 MB partition will be the swap drive. Usually, it is recommended to double the amount of RAM you have on your computer, not exceeding 128 MB. To change it to a swap drive, type t to change the partition type.

Choose the second partition to make our swap drive. Then choose the Hex Code type to make the disk a Linux Swap Partition. The code for swap partition is 82.

```
Command (m for help) : t
Partition number (1-4) : 2
Hex Code (type L to list codes) : 82
```

Now you can type w to write the partition information you just modified to the disk:

```
Command (m for help) : w
#
```

Once you issue the w command, all the changes you have specified will take effect. Remember that you can always quit fdisk by using the q command at any time if you don't want to save your partition information.

Setup

Once you are done with the partitioning and swapping, you can type:

```
#setup
```

and you will get a screen like the one shown in Figure A.4.3.

Choosing a Keyboard Type

You can read the help files by pressing H. The default keyboard map is set to the U.S. standard. If you are not in the United States, press K to get a dialog box to choose the appropriate keyboard map out of the 37 available.

Set up a Swap Partition

If you have made a partition to be used as a swap space during your hard disk partitioning, you will need to set it up and make it active. Press A to set up the swap partition. If you had previously made a swap partition, setup will automatically detect it and display it on the screen. Please see Figure A.4.4.

Choose Yes and press Enter to install the chosen partitions as the swap partition. Press Enter on the next screen.

Now, press Yes to let setup make the swap partition active with mkswap and swapon. It will format your specified partition as a Linux Swap Partition. After formatting your swap partition, setup will add the new information to the fstab. Note that if you had already made any of your swap partitions active using the mkswap command, then you should press No; otherwise, if you let setup use mkswap again, some memory pages may get corrupted.

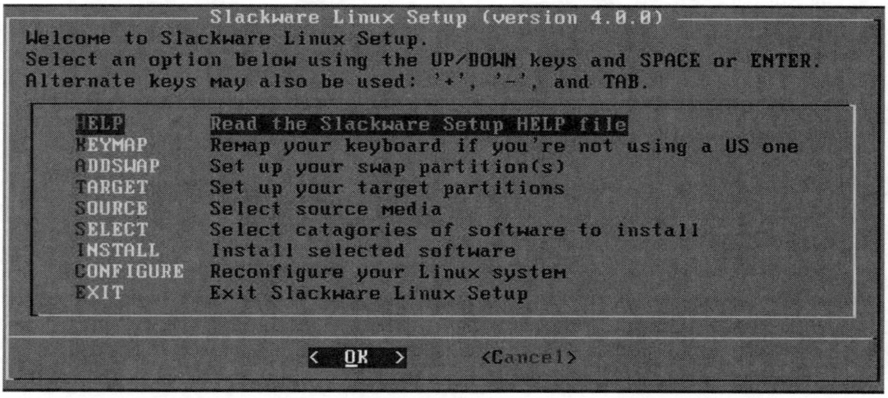

Figure A.4.3 Slackware setup screen.

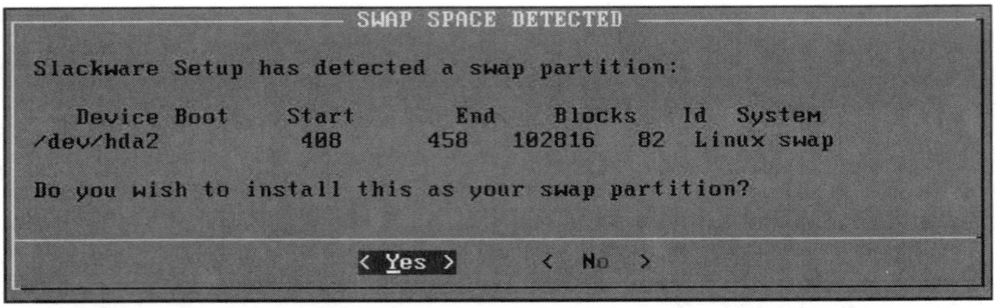

Figure A.4.4   Swap space detection.

Your swap partition will be configured and added to the /etc/fstab. Choose Exit and press Enter to continue. On the next screen, choose Yes and press Enter to go to the next step of the installation or choose No to go back to the main menu. The next step of the installation is Choosing Target Partition.

Set up a Target Partition

Now that you have chosen and set up your swap partition, you can select the main hard disk where you actually want to install Slackware. Press Yes to choose your target dive.

Select the appropriate partition where you want to install the Slackware and press OK (see Figure A.4.5).

Now that you have chosen the hard disk partition, you need to format it in Linux native format before proceeding to the installation as shown in Figure A.4.6. You can choose F for a quick format for the hard disk, or C, which will check for bad blocks on the hard disk as well as formatting it. If you had already formatted your hard disk before, choose No and press Enter. Press F for format and then press Enter to continue.

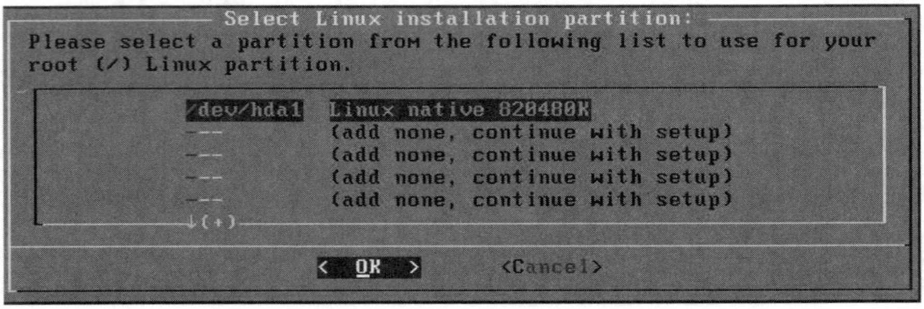

Figure A.4.5   Selecting partition.

Figure A 4.6 Format partition.

Select Inode Density

The Linux native format uses a default value of 4096 bytes per inode. You might want to change this depending on your usage of the system. If you plan to have lots of small files, then choose inodes with less bytes.

For this example, choose the default. Click and Choose 4096 as your Inode size and press Enter to continue. The setup program will then format your hard disk to ext2 format. It might take a few minutes to format your hard drive. Then, press Enter on the next screen where it will indicate the new information added to the /etc/fstab. On the next screen, choose Yes and press Enter to continue with the next step of installation, the selection of source media.

Select Source Media

Now that your destination hard disk has been formatted and is ready for installation, you need to choose the source from where the installation will proceed.

Choose the source medium from where you plan to install Slackware: Choose 1 if you have the Slackware CD-ROM, 2 if you plan to install from a hard drive partition where you have the installation files, 3 if you plan to install from NFS, 4 if you plan to install from a premounted directory, or 5 if you plan to install from a floppy. Use CD-ROM install here, so choose 1 and press Enter.

Choose Installation Type

Now, you have to specify the kind of installation you want. Three methods exist. If you are low on hard disk space, you might want to choose Slaktest to run Slackware from the CD-ROM. For common installation to the hard disk, choose Slakware. For more control over the installation, you can choose Custom, in which you can specify more parameters for the installation. Choose the easiest method, Slakware, and press Enter. Now, you need to select the packages you want to install. Choose Yes and press Enter on the next screen.

Select Package Category

Next, you will choose the individual packages that you want to install (see Figure A.4.7). Make sure that you select at least Base Linux System for the system to work. The rest of the categories are optional. To choose a category, move to it with the up and down arrow keys and press the space bar to choose that category. After you choose all the software you want on your system, choose OK and press Enter. If you have been following all the steps so far, you should be ready for actual installation now. Choose Yes and press Enter on the next screen.

Select Prompting Mode

Now you need to choose the type of prompts you want to have during the installation. Choose the one you'd like and the installation will begin. Full mode will install everything. Newbie mode presents each package one by one and prompts you to accept it or not. Expert and Custom modes are for those who have had Linux experience before and know what they really want. Here, choose Full Installation and press Enter.

Setup will now install all the packages you have chosen to your Target drive from your chosen Media. The installation will take a few minutes; just bear with it for some time because you are not quite done.

```
┌─────────────── PACKAGE SERIES SELECTION ───────────────┐
│ Now it's time to select which general catagories of software to install │
│ on your system. Use the spacebar to select or unselect the software you │
│ wish to install. You can use the up and down arrows to see all the       │
│ possible choices. Recommended choices have been preselected. Press the   │
│ ENTER key when you are finished.                                         │
│                                                                          │
│    [X] A    Base Linux system                                            │
│    [X] AP   Various Applications that do not need X                      │
│    [X] D    Program Development (C, C++, Lisp, Perl, etc.)               │
│    [X] E    GNU Emacs                                                     │
│    [X] F    FAQ lists, HOWTO documentation                               │
│    [X] K    Linux kernel source                                          │
│    [X] N    Networking (TCP/IP, UUCP, Mail, News)                        │
│    [X] T    TeX typesetting software                                     │
│    [X] TCL  Tcl/Tk script languages                                      │
│        ↓(+)                                                               │
│                                                                          │
│              <  OK  >        <Cancel>                                     │
└──────────────────────────────────────────────────────────┘
```

Figure A.4.7 Package series selection.

Making a Boot Disk

It is recommended that you make a boot disk in case your system crashes. There are two types of boot disks: simple boot disk, which is just an image of the kernel for minimal bootup so that you can troubleshoot your system, and LILO disk, with which you can dual boot your system. That is, when you boot up with that diskette, LILO will start and prompt you for the operating system on which to boot. But first of all, you need to format the diskette. Put your floppy in the drive, choose Format, and press Enter. The setup program formats the floppy and returns to the same menu. From that menu, choose Simple and press Yes to make a boot disk, and it will start to make a copy of the kernel to the formatted disk. After formatting the diskette, it will return to the previous screen. Choose continue and press Enter.

Modem Configuration

If you have a modem, you will have to choose it now. Choose the appropriate port at which your modem is connected. You need to make sure that your modem is not a winmodem if you plan to use it with Linux. If you plan to use a network card to access the net, choose No modem, choose OK, and press Enter.

On the next screen, if you would like to try some custom screen fonts, choose Yes and press Enter. For now, skip this step by choosing No and pressing Enter.

Install and Set up LILO

Now you need to set up LILO, the boot loader, which allows you to boot your computer in different operating systems. For those of you who are familiar with LILO, you can choose Expert and enter the parameters in the lilo.conf file. For now, go with the automatic installation of LILO—choose Simple and press Enter.

LILO can be installed in different places in your computer: the MBR (Master Boot Record), Root, or Floppy. Choose MBR and press Enter. (See Figure A.4.8.)

Network Configuration

Now, setup will try to configure your network and set up your TCP/IP. If setup does not succeed in configuring your network, you might change the settings. Press Enter to continue.

Mouse Configuration

Now you have to choose and set up your mouse. Most common generic mice are usually PS/2, so choose PS/2 and press Enter.

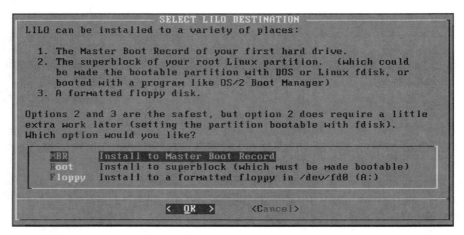

Figure A.4.8   LILO destination.

As shown in Figure A.4.9, GPM is a program that allows you to cut and paste text on virtual consoles using your mouse. If you would like to have this feature, choose Yes and press Enter, and GPM will be started at boot time every time you boot up your system.

Choosing a Root Password

Now that you have set up all components and parameters, you need to specify a root password to be able to log into the system. The root user will be the superuser on your installed system. Root will be able to do any administrative

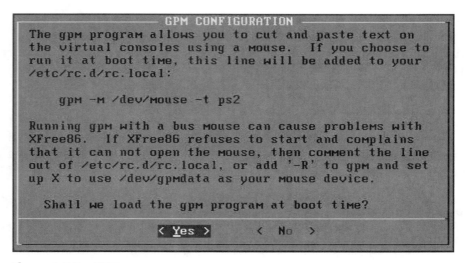

Figure A.4.9   GPM screen.

tasks and kill any processes. Setup will detect that no root password is available, and will set one for you. Choose Yes and press Enter. Then put in a new password. Reenter it again, press Enter, and then Enter again to continue

You return to the initial Slackware setup screen. At this point, you are done with the setup; choose Exit and press Enter. At the # prompt, type exit, and you are given the login prompt again. Login as root and enter the password you had specified before.

Reboot the computer (be sure to remove your CD-ROM from the computer before you reboot the machine).

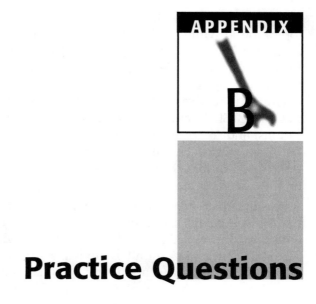

APPENDIX

B

Practice Questions

This Installation and Configuration study guide has been organized into a discussion of the knowledge array proper (Chapters 1–6), a glossary of the main points covered these first chapters, and now a set of practice questions over the concepts, principles, and facts covered in the previous sections.

These practice questions are designed to help you prepare for the Sylvan Prometric Sair Linux and GNU Installation and Configuration exam number 3X0-101. A passing grade for the Installation and Configuration exam is 74% or more correct answers. Fifty questions are randomly selected from an item pool and presented for each test. You have 60 minutes to answer the 50 questions. Most test takers complete the exam in 20–40 minutes. We recommend that you take your time and use the full hour to review questions before answering them. All 50 questions will be asked (it is not an adaptive test format), and you have the opportunity to go back and change an earlier answer if you choose to do so.

About the Practice Questions

This appendix contains just over 100 practice questions, based upon material presented in the earlier sections. Questions presented in the Sylvan Prometric exam and the following exam questions are based upon knowledge matrix topics found within each cell. Therefore, each question is prefaced with three dotted-decimal numbers followed by a letter so that the topic may be located for further study and review. For each question, the left-most number refers to the first knowledge array row, Installation and Configuration. The second dotted-decimal number refers to the knowledge array columns: (1) Theory, (2) Base System, (3) Shells and Commands, (4) System Utilities and Services, (5) Applications, and (6) Troubleshooting. The third dotted-decimal number refers to the topic within that cell. The last letter is simply the Nth question on that topic. For example, the item number 1.3.40.c is the third question with its focus on the cd command.

As stated in the book's introduction, passing the Sair Linux and GNU exams require knowledge and experience. It is our educational philosophy to assess both "book" knowledge and "experience" knowledge by using "naïve-subject-plausible distracters" for alternative answers to questions. Said another way, we use the things that our students would do or say as alternative answers to questions. If you have experience with Linux, then the alternative answers appear to be silly. If, on the other hand, you do not have background experience, then exam questions usually appear to be trick questions.

The Questions

1.2.30.a

Assuming that you have a 12 GB hard drive system with 64 MB of memory, you want to install both Windows 98 and SuSE Linux 6.1 and use LILO loader to load the desired OS. Which ONE of the following steps will achieve the goal?

A. Create two partitions, install Windows 98 on the first partition, SuSE Linux on the second, and boot from first partition using LILO.

B. Create three partitions, install Windows 98 on the first partition, SuSE Linux on the third, a /boot partition on the second, and boot from the second partition using LILO.

C. Create one FAT32 and two Linux partitions (swap and native), install Windows 98 on the FAT32 partition, SuSE Linux on the native partition, and boot either Windows 98 or Linux from the MBR using LILO.

D. Create one FAT32 and two Linux partitions (native and swap), install Windows 98 on the FAT32, SuSE Linux on the swap, boot from the floppy disk using LILO, and swap in either OS.

1.2.70.a

The company wants to attach its intranet through a Linux box to the Internet. Select the command that will ensure that the kernel detects the two required Ethernet adapters, and also select the file to which this command will be appended.

A. append="ether=11,0x280,eth0 ether=5,0x300,eth1", `/etc/lilo.conf`

B. append="ether=11,0x280,eth0 ether=5,0x300,eth1 mem=128M", `lilo .conf`

C. append="eth0:1=11,0x280,SMC eth0:2=5,0x300,3COM", `/etc/network .conf`

D. append="eth0:1=11,0x280,SMC eth0:2=5,0x300,3COM mem=128M", `lilo.conf`

1.4.50.a

You have a Red Hat 5.2 machine and want to configure the X Window System. Which ONE set of the following utilities can be used to set up X11 ?

A. xf86config, xset, SaX

B. xf86config, Xconfigurator

C. xfm, SaX, XF86Setup

D. X, xdm, xf86config

1.2.70.b

The first Ethernet adapter has an address of IRQ=5, I/O=0x280. Now you want to add a second interface adapter in a Linux box, and the Linux kernel can recognize only the first Ethernet adapter. Which LILO argument will solve the problem? (Background: IRQ=10, I/O=0x300 for the second adapter.)

A. append="ether=10,0x280,eth0 ether=5,0x300,eth1"

B. append="ether=5,0x280,eth0 ether=10,0x300,eth1"

C. append="eth0:1=5,0x280,ether eth1:1=10,0x300,ether"

D. append="eth0:1=10,0x300,ether eth1:1=5,0x280,ether"

1.4.10.a

There are two Ethernet adapters in a Debian Linux box. The first card is a 3Com card attaching Ethernet interface 0 (eth0), but the second card cannot be recognized by the kernel. You know the second card uses the Western Digital chip set. Which command line sequence can solve your problem? (Background: Western Digital driver objects are wd.o and 8390.o, and wd.o requires 8390.o to run.)

   A. append="eth0=wd.o,8390.o"

   B. insmod 8390.o; insmod wd.o

   C. insmod wd.o; 8390.o

   D. loadobj="8390.o, wd.o"

1.2.90.a0

Which commands would mount a CD-ROM to the mount point /mnt/cdrom? (Background: the CD-ROM drive is an ATAPI type and the CD-ROM drive is installed as a slave.)

   A. attach /dev/cdrom /mnt/cdrom

   B. mount /dev/cud535 /cdrom

   C. mount /dev/hda /mnt/cdrom

   D. mount /dev/hdb /mnt/cdrom

1.2.90.b

You want to transfer a WordPerfect file (document.wpd) from a Linux box to a Windows 98 machine, but the network has not been set up. Which command line allows you to copy the file onto a floppy disk?

   A. copy document.wpd a:

   B. mv document.wpd a:

   C. cp document.wpd a:

   D. mcopy document.wpd a:

1.4.10.b

A Linux machine is running kernel version 2.0.30. Unfortunately, one of the network device drivers is suspect; it may have been corrupted. There is no source code around to rebuild the driver, but a set of network modules for kernel 2.2.5 are accessible from another machine. These modules will work with the kernel 2.0.30. (Note: The network modules taken from the 2.2.5 kernel have no special modifications.)

   A. True

   B. False

1.2.100.a

John is running two X-term windows in an X Window environment. He is using an emulated 3-button mouse. What are the copy and paste operations to move a string from one virtual terminal to another?

A. <Ctrl-C> to copy and <Ctrl-V> to paste

B. <Ctrl-C> to copy and <Ctrl-P >to paste

C. Highlight the string with the cursor on the first console, click the middle button with the cursor on the second console

D. Highlight the string with the cursor on the first console, click left and right mouse buttons with the cursor on the second console

1.2.30.b

If the computer BIOS cannot boot directly from the CD-ROM and there is not an MS-DOS machine around to create a boot floppy, which of the following command(s) can create the install boot disk from another Linux machine?

A. rawrite vmlinuz a:

B. FIPS vmlinuz a:

C. dd if=vmlinuz of=/dev/fd0 bs=1k count=1024

D. mcopy vmlinuz a:

1.2.90.c

An inexperienced user installed Red Hat 5.1 Linux on a machine and forgot to create and mount a separate file system for the /usr subdirectory. The following is the fstab file on that machine. How can you help this user to solve the problem?

```
# /etc/fstab: static file system information.
# <file system>      <mount point>    <type>  <options>   <dump>    <pass>
   /dev/hda1               /           ext2    defaults      0         1
   /dev/hda2             none          swap      sw          0         0
     proc               /proc         proc     defaults      0         0
```

A. Boot from the original CD-ROM and upgrade the system

B. Run mke2fs to create a file system and add an entry into the fstab file

C. Run mke2fs to create a file system and add an entry into the lilo.conf

D. Run fdisk and mke2fs to create the volume on another drive and add the entry into the fstab file

1.2.50.a

Assuming you are not the superuser, yet you need to turn off a Linux machine safely, which of the following commands would you use?

    A. Type <Ctrl-Alt-Del>

    B. Halt

    C. Shutdown -h now

    D. Reboot

1.2.30.c

You cannot remember a file that was recently created, so you sort file names by creation time, but you also reverse the order of the sort so that the most recently created files will appear at the bottom of the screen. Which of the following commands is the correct one to do this?

    A. ls -lt *

    B. ls -lats

    C. ls -ltr

    D. ls -olt

1.2.100.b

Which of the following commands will let you see who is logged into the system and from where?

    A. w

    B. ps

    C. top

    D. proc

1.2.100.c

Which of the following command(s) start the X server?

    A. X11start

    B. startx

    C. winstart

    D. displayrun

1.3.10.a

As a system administrator, you want to speed up the daily routines and provide some convenience for the users. Can you create a universal shell alias file for all users?

   A. Yes

   B. No

1.4.10.c

Windows 98 is installed on the first hard drive with an ATAPI CD-ROM as a slave drive. A second hard drive is installed on the secondary controller with Linux on it. Which ONE of the following `lilo.conf` stanzas is correct if LILO is to be used as the boot loader?

   A. image=/boot/vmlinz

         root=/dev/hda1

         label=Linux

      other=/dev/hdb1

         label=Windows98

   B. image=/boot/vmlinz

         root=/dev/hdc1

         label= Linux

      other=/dev/hda1

         label=Windows98

   C. image=/boot/vmlinz

         root=/dev/hda2

         label=Linux

      other=/dev/hdc1

         label=Windows98

   D. image=/boot/vmlinz

         root=/dev/hda3

         label=Linux

      other=/dev/hdc1

         label=Windows98

1.1.60.a

A machine has a 2 GB hard drive and 64 MB of memory install. The machine is using the "incorrect" hard disk geometry (size=258/cycl=125/head=64/sectors=63 because of BIOS limitations). It is running fine on the installed machine, but now you would like to move the hard drive to a new machine. After the hard disk is moved and the machine is rebooted, the LI error message appears. Which ONE of the following techniques is the easiest way to solve the problem? (Background: You cannot install a brand new Linux distribution and you do not have the original rescue disk.)

A. Boot the system using another boot disk, recompiled the kernel.

B. Enter the BIOS setup, type in the geometry (size=258/cycl=125/head=64/sectors=63) in the setup file, and reboot the system.

C. Use a program like system commander to boot the system.

D. Remount the hard drive on the original Linux machine, recompiled the kernel.

1.3.10.b

The bash shell has a command completion function. Which of the following key(s) will active the function?

A. <Ctrl> key

B. <Shift>+<Ctrl> keys

C. <Tab> key or <Tab><Tab> key

D. <Tab>+<Page Up> keys

1.1.50.a

It is a common system administration practice to:

A. Always run as root

B. Always run su in a single user mode

C. Always run as a user and su when needed

D. Never run su in a bash shell environment

1.1.50.b

In superuser mode, which ONE of the following commands will lead to a system crash?

A. rm /*.bak

B. rm -rf / home/fred/tmp

C. rm -r f /tmp

D. rm -rf /home/fred/tmp

1.1.60.b

You have a 64 MB of memory system and you are running an X11 desktop GUI with applications. Which number is a good size for the swap partition?

A. 16 MB

B. 32 MB

C. 100 MB

D. 500 MB

1.2.30.d

To avoid the `LI` hang up problem, which ONE of the following approaches is considered to be a reasonable prevention step during installation of the Linux?

A. Make the first hard disk partition a /boot partition for storing kernel image(s).

B. Create several logical extended partitions.

C. Use the MS-DOS-based program System Commander as the OS loader.

D. Use the latest BIOS.

1.1.70.a

Which statement is NOT true about installing Linux over a network?

A. You should get an IP address from the local system administrator.

B. The network mask tells Linux how many hosts can fit in this subnetwork.

C. You need a gateway IP address to send and receive information over the Internet.

D. Most often, Linux installs just as fast from a local area network or from an Internet-based server as it does from the CDROM.

1.2.70.c

Describe the role of the Linux `/etc/rc.d` and `/etc/init.d` initialization scripts. Select all that apply.

A. Some distributions refer to the rc.d directory, which holds the scripts for all run levels.

B. Some distributions refer to init.d directory, which holds the scripts for all run levels.

C. Some distributions refer to the resource.d directory, which holds lists of indirect scripts for all run levels.

D. Some distributions refer to the resource.d directory, which holds lists of scripts for all levels.

1.1.50.c
While you are running the X Window System, you can activate a TTY console by hitting one of the Fx keys.

A. True

B. False

1.2.100.d
One reasonable location for the system-wide initialization files for startx is:

A. ~/xinitrc/

B. /var/X11R6/Xinitrc/

C. /etc/X11/xinit/xinitrc/

D. /usr/RX11/bin/xinitrc/

1.3.10.c
Environment variables are the same as shell variables.

A. True

B. False

1.3.10.d
Which of the following is an invalid shell variable?

A. 34shelltest

B. Shell_Test

C. SHELLTEST

D. Test2Shell

1.4.40.a
You were trying to print an ASCII document to a networked printer. The following error message appeared on the screen: "lpr: cannot create /var/spool/lpd/lp/.seq" Which ONE of the following techniques will solve the problem?

Background: A segment of the printcap file looks like this:

```
lp|xerox|Xerox N40 Printer:lp=:rp=raw:rm=192.168.1.21:\
:sd=/var/spool/lpd/lp:lf=/var/log/lpd-err:ar:bk:mx#0:tr=:cl:sh:
```

A. Add the correct `if` printer filter

B. Add the correct `of` printer filter

C. Use the -s switch in the lpr program

D. Make a new directory `lp` under directory `lpd`

1.2.20.a

There are a lot of compatibility issues that need to be considered before installing Linux. Which ONE of the following answers prevents Linux from working with the hardware?

A. Linux does not have device drivers for larger hard disks.

B. Newer video adapters tend not to have X servers available.

C. Linux drivers work with most of the HP DeskJet printers but not with the PostScript LaserJet printers.

D. All of the above.

1.2.40.a

Which ONE of the following version numbers indicates a stable version of the Linux kernel?

A. 2.3.5

B. 2.3a.5

C. 2.2.5

D. 2.4.5a

1.2.30.e

During installation, the install program will lay down the second-level disk format by using which ONE set of the following utilities?

A. swap, cfdisk

B. mk2fs, swap

C. makeinode, makeswap

D. mkfs, mkswap

1.2.90.d
In addition to the swap and root partition, you decide to configure a third partition. You want mail, log, and printer spool files to go into this separate partition. Which mount point is the one used by convention for storing these files?

   A. /

   B. /usr

   C. /var

   D. /log

1.2.50.b
One of the network protocols did not activate during boot up process. You want to review the boot up messages to see which device failed. Which ONE of the following commands will let you see the messages?

   A. more /usr/log/boot.messages

   B. dmesg

   C. /proc/kmsg

   D. mesg

1.2.100.e
Henry, a new Linux user, is working on a project for his college operating system class, and he would like to know how many processes are running in order to determine system load. Which ONE of the following command(s) can he use?

   A. pwd

   B. ps aux

   C. ls

   D. grep

1.2.30.f
Which of the following statement(s) about the file system is NOT true?

   A. Swap partitions are included in /etc/fstab.

   B. Swap partitions are not mounted.

   C. The fstab file contains a special entry for the /proc file system.

   D. The mount command may be used only by the superuser.

1.4.50.b
Jason, a Linux user, has a problem while running X11. A program goes into an infinite loop locking the X server up; therefore, he types <Ctrl-Alt-Backspace>. What effect does this key combination achieve?

A. Kills the X server (assuming the X server is configured to do so)
B. Restarts the computer
C. Restarts the window manager
D. Instructs the X Server daemon to reread the configuration files

1.4.50.c
If the last command in `.xinitrc` is `exec twm`, then killing the `twm` process will:

A. Delete the X Window server
B. Exit the X Window server
C. Disable the X Window server
D. All of the above

1.1.50.d
To switch between virtual consoles when NOT running the X Window system, you can use:

A. alt-Fn(where n is an integer representing the console number)
B. shift-Fn (where n is an integer representing the console number)
C. ctrl- Fn (where n is an integer representing the console number)
D. The Tab key

1.2.30.g
Suppose you have a single IDE hard drive, with three primary partitions. The first two are set aside for MS-DOS, and the third is an extended partition that contains two logical partitions, both used by Linux. Which ONE of these devices refers to the first Linux partition?

A. /dev/hda1
B. /dev/hda2
C. /dev/hda3
D. /dev/hdc1

1.2.30.h
When partitioning the hard disk, you got a warning that "cylinder > 1024", or you are unable to boot a partition using cylinders number above 1023. Which of the following is NOT a valid reason for this?

A. The BIOS limits the number of cylinders to 1024, and any partition using cylinders numbered above this won't be accessible from the BIOS.

B. The limited number of cylinders effects only the booting process and once the system has booted, you should be able to access any place on the hard disk partition(s).

C. Your options are either to boot the Linux from a boot floppy, or boot from a partition using cylinders numbered below 1024.

D. Partitioning can be done after the system is set up.

1.4.10.d
When booting LILO from the hard drive, you discover that MS-DOS boots by default instead of Linux. Which of the following statements about this situation are TRUE?

A. If you wish to select Linux as the default booting operating system, you have to edit the `/etc/lilo.conf` file and reinstall LILO.

B. While the system is booting, hold <Shift-Ctrl> and press "L" to boot Linux.

C. While the system is booting, hold the <Alt-F7> key to boot Linux.

D. None of the above.

1.2.30.i
Which ONE of the following statements about swap space is NOT true?

A. You may define multiple swap space partitions.

B. You need to execute the appropriate mkswap command before using a swap partition or file.

C. You must set the BIOS swapon setting to enable swap space before booting the operating system software.

D. The command swapon is used to enable swapping to a file as opposed to swapping to a disk partition.

1.3.30.a
Assuming the bash shell is being used, which of the following files in the current working directory will be displayed using the command `ls ?t.c*`?

A. Test.cpp

B. Tt.cpp

C. Test.c

D. TT.c

1.2.50.c

Which ONE of the following statements about shutdown and its options are NOT true?

A. shutdown -k now—do not shutdown but send the shutdown announcement to all users

B. shutdown -h now—halt after shutdown

C. shutdown -c now—cancel a running shutdown

D. shutdown -quick now—do a fast reboot

1.2.100.f

Which of the following are NOT good practices that assist in avoiding unrecoverable system crashes?

A. The superuser should always log in as root, and users should login using their accounts.

B. Make backup files and keep them physically off premise.

C. Prepare and keep emergency boot disks.

D. Copy configuration files to a subdirectory for later reference.

1.4.40.b

Which ONE of the following descriptions about the printer and printing service is correct?

A. The `lpc` command is used by the system administrator to control the operation of the line printer system.

B. `lpd` is the line printer daemon and is normally invoked at boot time.

C. The `lpd` daemon examines a spooling area looking for files to print on the line printer.

D. The `lpq` program reports the status of the specified jobs or all jobs associated with a user.

E. All of the above.

1.3.10.e
Which of the following mtools descriptions is/are INCORRECT? (Select all that apply.)

   A. mdel—delete files from a DOS disk without mounting the disk drive

   B. mdir—list the files on a DOS floppy disk

   C. mgetty—monitor incoming logins to set terminal speed, type, and other parameters.

   D. mesg—run by the user to control the read access others have to the terminal device associated with the standard error output.

1.3.20.a
Ann, a Linux system user and a high school student, needs to write a 750-word report. She creates the report, but doesn't want to spend a lot of time counting the number of words. What utility can she use to perform the counting for her?

   A. wordcount

   B. count

   C. wc

   D. There isn't a word count utility; she must use the `vi` editor to count the words

1.3.20.b
Emily, a Linux system user, types the command `wc` report. The resultant output is:

```
        89        776        5025 report
```

This output means:

   A. 89 lines, 776 words, and 5025 characters

   B. 89 lines, 776 words, and 5025 bits

   C. 89 words, 776 characters, and 5025 bits

   D. 89 pages, 776 paragraphs, and 5025 lines

1.3.90.a
Katey, a Linux system user, needs to erase all the temporary files she has created for a software project. She has five files, named test , test2, test3, test4, and test5. How can she erase these files?

   A. del test?

   B. del test*

   C. rm test?

   D. erase test?

1.3.100.a

Cary, a Linux system user, has completed her software project and needs to erase all the files in the directory `proj`. How can she do this?

   A. del proj/*

   B. erase proj

   C. rm -r proj/*

   D. rmdir proj/*

1.3.80.a

Elizabeth, a Linux system user, needs to create a new directory `newproj` for testing a new software project. Assuming there are no shell aliases, how can she do this?

   A. mkdir newproj

   B. md newproj

   C. pico -d newproj

   D. newdir newproj

1.3.60.a

Lindsay, a Linux system user, needs to copy the `/etc/printcap` file to her home directory /usr/ann. Assuming no shell aliases, and assuming her current working directory is /usr/ann, how can this be accomplished? (Select all that apply.)

   A. copy /etc/printcap /usr/ann/*

   B. cp /etc/printcap ~/printcap

   C. cp /etc/printcap

   D. copy /etc/printcap /usr/ann/printcap

1.3.40.a

Carla, a Linux system user, is currently in the directory /var/spool/lpd/lpj, and needs to change to her home directory, which is /home/clb. What is the fastest way to do this?

   A. chdir /home/clb

   B. cd /clb

   C. cd

   D. cd

1.3.30.b

Julie, a Linux system user, wants to read the contents of file README. Without thinking, she types "README" at the shell prompt. What would most likely be the output from the bash shell?

A. No output, just another bash shell prompt

B. The contents of the file README will be displayed

C. The bash shell will echo the command and output the file README

D. bash: README: command not found

1.4.40.c

A program that converts one file format to another for the purpose of printing is called a:

A. Printer filter

B. Translator

C. Printer driver

D. Printer screen

1.4.50.d

The program to identify installed video hardware is:

A. XF86Config

B. SuperProbe

C. XWindow

D. XF86Setup

1.4.40.d

Tom, a Linux system administrator running as the superuser, needs to take printer lj5 off line so it can be moved. He has checked to see what jobs are waiting to be printed and now he wants to remove them. How can he do this?

A. lpr -Plj5 -

B. lpc -Plj5 -

C. lpq -Plj5 -

D. lprm -Plj5 -

1.4.40.e

The file that controls the behavior of the client and server provider programs for printing is the _____ file.

    A. /etc/printcap

    B. /printcap

    C. /etc/pcontrol

    D. /etc/print.conf

1.3.10.f

Monique, a Linux system user, sometimes has trouble typing the command "more," usually typing it as "mroe." She complains to Janet, a co-worker who also uses Linux, to find out if there is a way to set up her system so that she doesn't have to go back and correct the spelling all the time. Janet tells her:

    A. There is not a way to correct this problem

    B. Use the alias command `alias mroe=more`

    C. Run `ispell` as the last command on the command line

    D. Create a script that runs `ispell` for each word on the command line

1.2.90.e

Which of the following pseudofiles are system abstractions?

    A. /opt/usr/log

    B. /proc/devices

    C. /usr

    D. /tmp/conner2

1.3.50.a

You want to see the report of the disk usage for the current directory. You are going to redirect the output to a file called "status" and place the time and date in front of the disk usage. Which of the following commands should you use? Select all that apply.

    A. du > status

    B. (date; du) > status

    C. date; du > status

    D. date > status; du >> status;

1.3.10.g
What will be printed by the command `echo \*` ?

A. All files in root directory

B. All files in current directory

C. An '*'

D. Empty and waiting for standard input

1.1.50.e
Which ONE of the following statements about the init program is NOT correct?

A. init starts as "the last step of the kernel booting."

B. init is the first program that initializes and configures your system for use.

C. init works by parsing /etc/inittab and running scripts in /etc/rc.d according to either a default or desired runlevel.

D. init is not a daemon.

1.1.50.f
Which ONE of the following statements is NOT true about the structure of Linux?

A. Linux tends to come as a set of building-block components that you may or may not choose to use.

B. Even though the kernel and networking code reside in the kernel memory space, they are largely independent modules.

C. Linux supports preemptive multitasking except when doing disk I/O.

D. Preemptive multitasking supports multiple concurrent user accounts.

1.2.100.g
Based on the GNU utilities, if you want to see a list of the currently logged-in users, which command can you use to accomplish it? Select all that apply.

A. id

B. w

C. users

D. uname

1.3.20.c
To find out the number of user accounts on the system, which ONE of the following commands would you use?

A. more /etc/passwd

B. less /etc/passwd

C. wc /etc/passwd

D. cat /etc/passwd | more | less | pr

1.2.60.a
Which statement is FALSE when describing run levels?

A. Run-level zero is the shutdown level for all distributions.

B. Most distributions agree that run level five will start the KDE GUI.

C. Run-levels one or two are the multi-user levels for most distributions.

D. Run-level six is the reboot run level for all distributions.

1.2.60.b
If only the root account can use the console and no one else can use the system, then it is said that the system is in which ONE of the following states?

A. Remote-file sharing

B. Multiple user

C. Single user

D. User defined

1.2.100.h
You are working in a multitasking state and you want to kill (or renice) a process, so you try to find the PID of that process. Which ONE of the following commands should you use?

A. top

B. free

C. nice

D. ps

1.3.10.h
Which ONE of the following bash shell meta-characters would instruct a command to run in the background?

  A. ;

  B. ()

  C. &

  D. $

1.3.10.i
The commands `setenv` and `umask` are bash shell:

  A. Built-in commands

  B. Variables

  C. Environment variables

  D. File system programs

1.3.10.j
You want to append the contents of the newfile.txt file to the end of the contents of the oldfile.txt. Which ONE of the following operators would you use?

  A. .

  B. >

  C. >>

  D. |

1.3.10.k
You typed the command cat /etc/passwd > /dev/null. What happened?

  A. The contents of the file /etc/passwd are stored in the file /dev/null.

  B. The output is redirected to /dev/null and was discarded.

  C. A new empty file is created, named /dev/null.

  D. The contents of the /etc/passwd were nullified.

1.3.30.c
Which ONE of the following statements is NOT true of the following output of the command ls -l?

```
-rw-rw-rw-  1  david  staff   227  Dec 12 19:33  note
```

  A. The owner of file `note` and any other user accounts cannot execute this file.

B. The owner's user account name of file `note` is `david`.

C. The file note is first created by Dec 12, 1933.

D. The size of the file note is 227 bytes.

1.3.70.a
You are going to rename the file `test` to `sample`. Which ONE of the following is the correct operation?

A. cp test sample

B. mv test sample

C. ln test sample

D. rn test sample

1.3.30.d
For the file permission `rw----r-x`, which ONE of the following numbers is a correct translation from symbolic permissions into numeric?

A. 605

B. 655

C. 755

D. 022

1.3.190.a
The find and locate commands differ in that _____ because _____.

A. locate is slower than find because of database fragmentation.

B. find is slower than locate because of database fragmentation.

C. locate is faster than find because it uses a possibly old database of file names.

D. find is faster than locate because it does not have database overhead.

1.3.10.l
For the bash shell, which of the following are valid shell variable names? Select all that apply.

A. temp

B. 1xyz

C. abc#9

D. efg_1_

1.1.10.a

Assume that a vendor distributes a binary-only program free-of-charge along with an open source program, also free-of-charge. What is the resultant product?

A. All of the software is open source software

B. Just free software

C. A hybrid of free and open source software—with a separate license required

D. It becomes GPL software

1.1.50.g

A process is:

A. The state of a program itself

B. The state of a program as it passes control through itself, libraries, and the kernel

C. The state of all programs in the system, at any point in time

D. A series of steps the typical Linux user must do to load the high moby

1.1.70.b

The format of an IP address is w.x.y.z, where each letter is:

A. A singleton (1 bit)

B. A quad (4 bits)

C. An octet (8 bits)

D. 16 bits

E. 32 bits

F. None of the above

1.2.90.f

A hard disk volume used by Linux:

A. Is given a logical name in the file system that can vary from mount to mount

B. Has a transparent or unknown location (to the typical user) within the directory hierarchy

C. Is always mounted in the same mount point

D. Answers A and B

1.2.90.g
Absolute directory paths are always resolved:

A. With reference to /

B. With reference to the user's home directory

C. With reference to the present working directory

D. With reference to the superuser's home directory

1.2.100.i
Assume that the superuser wishes to set up a user account manually. Which ONE of the following reasons is justification for using the chown command?

A. To change the owner of the account from the previous user

B. By default, the superuser is the owner of each new account's home directory, so to make the user the owner of his own home directory

C. So that the superuser can still monitor each account after users have started using them

D. So that the superuser can turn on shadow passwords for the account

1.2.100.j
Assume Kevin and Jack are two users on one Linux machine and they each have the same GID. This means that (select all that apply):

A. Kevin and Jack have the same access privileges to each other's files regardless of the rwx settings.

B. Kevin and Jack may share access using the same file by setting GID permissions to rw.

C. Kevin and Jack could also have the same access privileges to the files of other users' who also belong to the same group.

D. Kevin and Jack must first disable the "others" permission before being able to share access with the GID permissions.

1.6.30.a
Select from the following situations in which a rescue disk would be helpful (select all that apply).

A. When the system fails to boot

B. After a hard disk failure (for example, head crash)

C. After the root file system was deleted accidentally

D. When no one (including root) can log into the system

E. After the file system has been severely damaged

1.3.50.b

Amanda wanted to read a few files at the same time, yet she does not want to open and close each file individually. Which of the following commands would allow her to do this, and what would be the command syntax?

A. more -n filename1 filename2 filename3

B. less filename1 filename2 filename3

C. more filename1 filename2 filename3

D. Answers B and C

1.1.10.b

The most fundamental aspect of the software system called Linux, that we share, comes from:

A. Linus Trovalds, who forged an Internet community to build the kernel, beginning in 1991

B. Richard Stallman, who invented the GNU general public license, beginning around 1984

C. Robert Scheifler and James Gettys, who codeveloped the X Window system, beginning around 1984

D. Ken Thompson and Dennis Ritchie who co-developed many of the basic ideas used in Linux, beginning around 1974

1.1.10.c

Which of the following statements are TRUE about GNU GPL?

A. Even though Linux is called free software, most everyone pays some fee, direct or indirect, for the software.

B. The word "free" in "free software" is about freedom to use the software and not about the cost of software.

C. If you improve GPL software, and you do not distribute your improvements, then you are not required to show anyone your improvements.

D. If you do share your improvements in GPL software, you must comment your improvements in the source code and write man page documentation describing the improvements.

1.1.10.d

Some use fear, uncertainty, and doubt (FUD) tactics to describe Linux; others describe tradeoffs of using free software versus proprietary software. Which of the following statements are tradeoffs of GPL software?

A. No product warranty, must have in-house support or contract support

B. No patent protection, anyone can claim a patent on the open software

C. No long-term software survivability, all the software may fall into disuse

D. Lack of security, everyone sees the source code

1.4.30.a

Two users are logged in as the superuser, and they are both editing the `/etc/passwd` file to add new user accounts. Which ONE of the following statements is TRUE?

A. Linux ensures `/etc/passwd` file integrity and consistency.

B. The file manager automatically creates a new user's home directory upon completion of editing the `/etc/passwd` file for both instances of the superuser account.

C. There is a problem here, the last superuser to exit the editor will over-write the account just added by the other superuser account.

D. Linux automatically creates the `/etc/shadow` file when done creating a new user.

1.3.110.a

The command `ln test1 test2` will:

A. Count the number of lines in file `test1` and `test2`

B. Count the number of lines in file `test1` and output the results in file `test2`

C. Create a new directory entry so that `test1` and `test2` reference the same file

D. Nothing; there is no such command as `ln`

1.3.110.b

A hard link has been created between the files alpha and beta. This means that:

A. When the file alpha is removed, beta will also be removed.

B. Any changes that occur to file alpha will also appear in file beta.

C. Only a superuser can remove files alpha and beta.

D. When the file alpha is accessed, file beta will automatically be appended to it.

1.4.30.b

Creation of a user account involves which of the following steps?

(i) Edit the /etc/passwd file to add the user

(ii) Create the home directory and set its ownership

(iii) Copy the shell startup files to the home directory

(iv) Create the new group the user must belong to

(v) Edit the /etc/login.defs for the user's default settings

A. i, ii, and v

B. i, ii, iii, and v

C. i, ii, iv, and v

D. i, ii, and iii

1.3.140

The result of the command sequence ps aux | grep "smith" will:

A. List all processes on the display

B. List all processes whose user id contains the name "smith"

C. List all lines of the output containing the substring "smith" including the ps command itself

D. List all processes and output them to the file "smith"

1.1.50.h

A daemon is _____ .

A. A network "sniffer" program

B. A virus that attaches itself to the master boot record of any disk

C. A program that stays resident in memory (or swap space) at all times waiting for requests for service

D. A specialized printer system administration tool for the print system

1.3.190.b

When performing a ls on your home directory, you notice a file named jpgs.tar. Most likely, this file is:

A. A compressed archive of files

B. A compressed archive that automatically decompresses when jpgs.tar is typed

C. The compressed directory listing that the operating system refers to when performing the ls command

D. An archive of files

1.5.10.a
The Deja search engine assists with troubleshooting by indexing, searching, and retrieving detailed technical assistance from past Usenet news group postings.

A. True

B. False

1.5.10.b
You can get all kinds of help from Linux documentation. Which ONE of the following orderings of help programs provides information from the briefest amount of information to the most detailed amount of information?

A. Xman, man, --help, Linux Documentation Project, Deja, locate/find, info

B. locate/find, --help, man, man section 5, Xman, info, Deja, Linux Documentation Project.

C. Deja, Xman, --help, Linux Documentation Project, locate/find, man

D. Linux Documentation Project, --help, Xman, Deja, locate/find, info

1.6.10.a
Which of the following generalizations are TRUE about Linux troubleshooting?

A. Much of Linux's complexity comes from module layering and module integration.

B. Generally, it is more efficient to analyze a problem and solve it step-by-step than it is to query a local expert or use a search engine.

C. Generally, there are only one or two ways you can solve a typical Linux problem and, therefore, the key to successful troubleshooting is to not stop searching until you find that best way to solve the problem.

D. Many Linux problems can be solved by just knowing configuration concepts and configuration alternatives.

1.6.10.b

A Linux installation has hung up with the error message "Device Full." Which ONE of the following statements is the reason for the error and the solution to the error?

    A. The floppy disk has filled with temporary data; insert a new floppy and press <Enter>.

    B. The RAM disk is full; select from the available RAM addresses and select a new address.

    C. The hard disk partition is too small to hold all the selected software; restart the installation process and select a larger partition size.

    D. The aggregate partitions are too small; the hard disk must be upgraded.

Answers to Practice Questions

1.2.30.a - C

1.2.70.a - A

1.4.50.a - B

1.2.70.b - B

1.4.10.a - B

1.2.90.a - D

1.2.90.b - D

1.4.10.b - B

1.2.100.a - D

1.2.30.b - C

1.2.90.c - D

1.2.50.a - A

1.2.30.c - C

1.2.100.b - A

1.2.100.c - B

1.3.10.a - A

1.4.10.c - B

1.1.60.a - B

1.3.10.b - C

1.1.50.a - C

1.1.50.b - B

1.1.60.b - C
1.2.30.d - A
1.1.70.a - D
1.2.70.c - A and B
1.1.50.c - B
1.2.100.d - C
1.3.10.c - B
1.3.10.d - A
1.4.40.a - D
1.2.20.a - B
1.2.40.a - C
1.2.30.e - D
1.2.90.d - C
1.2.50.b - B
1.2.100.e - B
1.2.30.f - D
1.4.50.b - A
1.4.50.c - B
1.1.50.d - A
1.2.30.g - C
1.2.30.h - D
1.4.10.d - A
1.2.30.i - C
1.3.30.a - B
1.2.50.c - D
1.2.100.f - A
1.4.40.b - E
1.3.10.e - C and D
1.3.20.a - C
1.3.20.b - A
1.3.90.a - C
1.3.100.a - C
1.3.80.a - A
1.3.60.a - B and C
1.3.40.a - C

1.3.30.b - D

1.4.40.c - A

1.4.50.d - B

1.4.40.d - D

1.4.40.e - A

1.3.10.f - B

1.2.90.e - B

1.3.50.a - B and D

1.3.10.g - C

1.1.50.e - D

1.1.50.f - C

1.2.100.g - B and C

1.3.20.c - C

1.2.60.a - B

1.2.60.b - C

1.2.100.h - D

1.3.10.h - C

1.3.10.i - A

1.3.10.j - C

1.3.10.k - B

1.3.30.c - C

1.3.70.a   B

1.3.30.d - A

1.3.190.a - C

1.3.10.l - A, C, and D

1.1.10.a - B

1.1.50.g - B

1.1.70.b - C

1.2.90.f - D

1.2.90.g - A

1.2.100.i - B

1.2.100.j - B and C

1.6.30.a - A and D

1.3.50.b - D

1.1.10.b - B

1.1.10.c - A, B, and C

1.1.10.d - A

1.4.30.a - C

1.3.110.a - C

1.3.110.b - B

1.4.30.b - D

1.3.140 - C

1.1.50.h - C

1.3.190.b - D

1.5.10.a - A

1.5.10.b - B

1.6.10.a - A and D

1.6.10.b - C

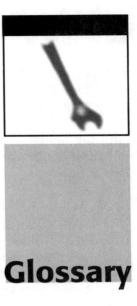

Glossary

$PATH variable. An internal shell variable that contains a list of directories.

$PATH variable, role. The shell searches the list of directories looking for the executable file name specified in the command.

/proc directory. Provides access to routines that provide status information about the kernel.

/ character. Indicates the root directory volume (drive) that is hard-wired or built into the kernel image and is, therefore, known by the kernel at boot time. Also delimits directory names in a path.

access port. To begin the login process, you must find a port that is monitored by the login program (initially the getty program), which is waiting for input from a user. (For purposes of simplicity, we will ignore the role of `telnetd`, which assists with access via the network.)

adapter conflicts. Adapters plugged into the buses may use the same parameter as another adapter. This means that both adapters would respond when the CPU attempted to communicate with one of them.

adduser. Edits the password file, creates the home directory for the account, and copies in the default files from /etc/skel into the new directory.

adduser, augmentation. A small script can be used to duplicate the required arguments to adduser without setting up the configure file /etc/adduser.conf. In this way, adduser can be invoked with just the name of the new user account.

application history file. Applications may save their state information in the initialization files, or other files, so that they may begin execution where they left off earlier.

BIOS. Basic Input and Output System. A ROM-based set of routines that provide diagnostics, read/write services to devices, and are used to boot Linux. Unfortunately, the read and write routines only poll devices and cannot be interrupted during device operation.

BIOS-based adapter configuration. Some vendors include the diagnostic and configuration programs in the ROM on the adapter card and provide access to the programs at boot time by prompting the user to type a special key combination.

buses, PC. The IBM PC architecture employs a memory bus, a high speed input output (I/O) bus called the PCI bus, and an older backward-compatible I/O bus called the ISA bus.

Case sensitivity. All files (including program names) in a Unix-like operating system must be accessed "as is." The command line interpreter (bash or other shell) employs upper- and lowercase characters to differentiate among file and program names.

cd command. Switches the current working directory to the specified directory and uses the new directory to find relative file names.

CD-ROM drives, ATAPI IDE. A new standard for IDE controllers. ATAPI IDE CD-ROM drives are accessed just like any other IDE drive; however, there often are compatibility problems with early ATAPI CD-ROM drives.

CD-ROM drives, SCSI. Accessed through existing SCSI drives, and work well in the Linux environment.

CD-ROM installation. Works great if Linux has the necessary driver for the particular CD-ROM; very fast.

CLI, advantages. Linux shells offer the ability to perform many repetitive tasks with just a few keystrokes. Once the command shortcuts are learned, many users prefer a CLI to a GUI when having to do similar tasks.

client-server printer. Unix-like OSs divide the printing process into two parts. A client program accepts the print request and submits it to a back-end server. The server then takes care of printing the data. In this way, the destination server printer may be local, remote, passed through a gateway, or the server may reside within the printer itself.

configure disk partitions. Administrators most often select the custom install option so that they can best utilize the disk space available.

console switching. Use the `<Ctrl><Alt>Fx` keys to select a new virtual console.

copy and paste. Highlight the text to be copied with the left mouse-button, switch to the "destination" application, and paste with the middle button.

copyleft. Refers to the nontraditional use of copyright to keep software free and to give the right of use and modification to many instead of reserving this right to a few.

data cache. The data cache holds data blocks destined for the hard disk. If the system is abruptly turned off, then file information is lost and the file system becomes inconsistent. To minimize this problem, the daemon `bdlush` moves data cache blocks out to the hard disk every 30 seconds or so.

data viewing, off-screen. Use the `<Shift><Page Up>` key to review things that have scrolled up off of a virtual console terminal.

Debian attributes. It installs in "chunks," has a default configuration with secure Internet servers, and provides robust package installations and upgrades.

default file protection. Creating a file as the superuser means that the file may not be readable or writeable by other user accounts and, therefore, the superuser account will have to be used to manipulate the files created earlier.

Deja. A special type of search engine since it specializes in searching all news group postings, and thus, quickly finding answers to obscure problems.

device conflicts, types. The I/O address of the adapter card, the interrupt request line of the adapter card, the direct memory access channel, and shared memory addresses.

device drivers. Map the physical characteristics of a device into a uniform logical interface that makes the device accessible by all parts of the kernel. Since Linux employs preemptive multitasking, it must provide its own interrupt-driven device drivers and avoid using the BIOS routines.

device section. Tells the X server which parameters to accept and which ones to probe for in the video adapter in the XF86Config file.

disk divisions. Linux requires at least two partitions, one for the swap space and the other for the root file system. If Linux shares the hard disk with another OS(s), more partitions may be required.

disk partitions. Partitions are a means by which the firmware divides up the hard disk and presents partitions to one or more operating systems as disk volumes.

domain name service. A server that translates computer names to IP addresses.

dot debate. Not using the dot character to execute a program in the current directory may lead to a security problem where "pretend" system programs request and save user passwords.

facilities. Messages are directed with the use of a facilities label, indicating the type of daemon message (mail, telnet, lpr, etc.) and the priority of the message (emergency, warning, debug, etc.).

find, design tradeoff. The find command searches the complete directory structure from the specified starting point to each leaf. This requires tens of thousands of file manager queries, and as a result, the program runs slowly. But unlike locate, the find command will perform an up-to-date search.

format documentation. The file format section five of the man pages describes the role of each field in a control or initialization file, and which programs read or write each field. A helpful guide when looking for a bigger picture.

free software. Free software is generally open source and it may be used, modified, copied, redesigned, and shared with others. Free software also carries the built-in cost of requiring expert knowledge with regard to administration of the software package. The term free software refers to how the software is distributed, and not the viewing of the source code. There are forms of free software that are binary-only copies that may not be redistributed.

free software, computer professional use. GPL software allows the computer professional the ability to exploit a highly evolved set of software tools that can greatly improve the productivity of the computer professionals especially when compared to traditional software development environments.

free software, long-term commercial use. GNU GPL software is just as much an attitude as it is an end product. Although it requires thinking "out of the box," commercial users of free software will be able to achieve a much higher level of productivity through implicit cooperation in software development.

free software business model. Businesses do quite well selling GPL software because they have switched their focus from a fee-for-product model to a fee-for-service model. The service can be a product in the form of reconfigured, or improved, software as well as traditional service. The business should expect that just as much, if not more, income can be generated through the world-wide distribution of the lower cost software, which should lead to an extensive audience for future service.

free software product. GPL software takes on a life of its own. It creates a community of programmers that freely share ideas to improve the software, and the software generally evolves into a product of better quality than any one individual or subgroup could have created by themselves.

gateway. Linux distribution term referring to a router, or other host, that has a second network interface connected to the Internet.

global initialization files. Global file settings are found in /etc and affect all users, but they have low-priority default settings.

GNU GPL, advantages. GPL software is open to peer review. As a result, faulty assumptions are usually identified and corrected. Moreover, tens of thousands of developers share the same development environment, allowing quick and easy sharing of ideas and implementations over the Internet.

GNU GPL, limitations. The limitations of the GNU GPL include those who provide new source code but who attempt to make the code unclear. Another limitation of GNU GPL is the question of how much documentation to include with the source code. Finally, there are those that feel that the GNU GPL restricts the use of free software by not allowing it to be embedded into other software products.

GNU GPL, uniqueness. GPL stands out from other software licenses because it keeps software intact, allows it to mature over many years, and prevents any one entity from controlling the software.

GPL. GNU general public license, also called copyleft, is a detailed document describing the freedom to use software.

GPL, keeping software free. The GNU GPL attempts to keep free software free by mandating that all code, including source, must be included in any redistribution of the software, and any new code added to the software must be included in the redistribution.

GPL, response to users. Acting from self-interest, many different developers, over time, contribute to GPL software. This public process leads to code review, bug fixes, and improved features that best meet the needs of all users.

graphic mode. The organization of video memory in the number of X and Y pixels plus the number of colors per pixel.

graphic mode filters. Printer filters may be attached to the printcap file to select PostScript or a graphic-mode format for the printer automatically.

graphic mode printing. In graphic mode printing, the CPU sends over the instructions for printing each pixel of an image.

graphic resolution. The number of X and Y pixels plus the amount of information for each pixel (pixel depth).

GUI, starting. A shell script called `startx` will run the X server and window manger from the command line if `xdm` is not running.

GUI utility, tradeoff. Although convenient, these GUI configuration utilities perform multistep operations without informing the operator, and which may interfere with other configurations.

help information, paging. Sometimes there is more information than will fit on a single screen and information scrolls off the top of the screen. Pipe the output to a pager utility, such as `more` or `less`.

hidden window control. Some window managers allow full screen windows, but the control element may become hidden under another higher priority window. All is not lost—just double-click the title bar, and the whole window will come to the surface allowing access to the window controls.

hierarchical menus. In a hierarchical menu, activating one menu selection causes another menu to pop up. Selecting from the second menu causes a third menu to pop up, and so on.

indirect method. Symbolic file names with implicit start and stop commands that link (point) to the shell scripts in the rc.d directory.

info limitations. The info system depends on contributions from individual program writers or third-party contributors, and as a result, the amount and quality of information varies from subject to subject. Also, some parts of the info system have yet to be completed.

info utility. Designed to provide a broad view of system programs rather than the narrow man page format. Information is arranged hierarchically and a cursor-based user interface allows the selection of topics from various usage areas.

init.d directory. Used by various distributions to hold indirect scripts.

initialization files, X Windows system. The xdm and startx programs use separate initializations files to control the same GUI setup. The xinitrc is used by startx, and xdm uses the Xsession initialization file. The Xsession contents have higher priority than the commands in the startx file.

insmod. Loads device drivers at runtime.

insmod, tradeoff. insmod gives the administrator the flexibility to adapt to many possible configurations by allowing new device drivers to be added at runtime; however, eventually, the drivers should be compiled into the kernel to achieve better performance.

internal commands. Note that some commands appear to be standalone utilities such as the cd command, but they are internal to the shell and do not respond to help requests.

Internet installation. Must set up directories, transfer files, and check directory structure; very slow and error prone.

IP address. An Internet protocol logical address assigned by a central authority that provides a way for others to reach your computer.

kill command. The kill command is really a "send signal" command since it can send any type of signal to the specified program. One signal (#9) cannot be ignored by the program and it causes the program terminate.

kill jobs. By switching to another login port, you can identify and terminate a program that has locked up, without having to reboot the system.

LAN Network installation. Using either FTP, NFS, or SAMBA protocols, read the Linux software from another Linux box or MS-DOS file system; fast install.

LILO. The Linux loader uses the BIOS to read from the floppy, hard disk, or CD-ROM to boot Linux.

LILO append field. The append argument allows the system administrator to provide custom configuration arguments to the kernel.

LILO command. By running the LILO program, the configuration information, along with the boot program, is copied into the MBR for subsequent system boot.

LILO label field. The label argument specifies multiple OS images at boot time from which the user may select.

Linux, booting methods. (1) With LILO from the MBR; (2) From a floppy disk; (3) From another operating system (loadlin, System Commander).

Linux, installation steps. (1) Boot install program; (2) Partition hard disk; (3) Format partitions; (4) Dearchive software; (5) Configure boot-up sequence; (6) Set up X11.

Linux, shutting down. (1) Type `<Ctrl><Alt><Del>` at the console to shut down and reboot the system; (2) become superuser and use the halt, reboot, or shutdown commands; (3) become superuser and switch run levels with the `init 0` command.

Linux, user interfaces. Linux is a layered system; GUI programs depend upon lower level shells to execute commands. Not all shell commands are implemented with a GUI.

Linux in-house warranty service. Millions of people use Linux without warranty service. The key is to develop a staff of qualified individuals who will provide the warranty service in-house through skill and use of Internet resources.

Linux memory requirements. The exact amount of required RAM depends on the mix of applications run and can be as little as 4 MB or as much as the mainboard can hold.

Linux origins. Linux is the result of 20 years of GPL software evolution that recently has been packaged and configured by various vendors.

Linux shells. Serves as the command-line interpreter that provides simple command-line editing, program execution, and flow control in the execution of shell scripts.

Linux subsystems. The major Linux subsystems are kernel, network, init, daemons, login, shells, utilities, and the X Window System.

Linux warranty service. Even though Linux does not come with a warranty, there are many companies that will provide continuing maintenance service for Linux thus, in effect, offering a warranty service.

local initialization files. Local file setting are found in the user's home directory and override global settings.

locate. Interprets its argument either as some part of a file name or as a pathname to a file, and as a result, it displays all pathnames containing the argument.

locate, design tradeoff. Locate provides fast response time by reading a database of path and file names, but the database will not reflect recent changes made to the file system.

logging out. Use the end-of-file character, <Ctrl>D, or the shell commands exit or logout.

lpc command. Queries the print server for status information on one or more printers. The superuser can use lpc to stop and start the server as well as clean the print queue.

lpq command. Queries the local or remote server, depending on the printcap description of the printer location, for pending print requests.

lprm command. Tells the specified print server to remove one or more pending print requests.

ls command. Displays the file names and permissions of files contained within a specified directory.

magic filter. Converts between DVI and PostScript; also converts PostScript format into native graphic format for various types of printers.

man k command. Searches only for keywords found in the title of each documentation page.

man pages. Documentation on acceptable arguments for the program and how the arguments change the programs. However, the program is discussed in isolation with no consideration given to program interaction information.

mark-up. In word processing programs, text display and text creation are two separate processes.

memory size problem. Older SIMM mainboards tend not to have cache addresses that go beyond 64 MB. If this is true, the system will slow to a crawl (to around 12 MHz with 70 ns memory) when memory references go beyond the 64 MB address range.

menu disorientation. Unfortunately many menu items repeat in lower level menus within the menu hierarchy. So, for example, when the linuxconf program menu selections are as follows:

```
Config -> User accounts -> Normal->User accounts,
```

you may become disoriented, and as a result, become confused about where you are "located" within the menu hierarchy.

message direction. Syslog sorts, and if requested, duplicates messages into various files based upon directions in the /etc/syslog.conf file.

modularity, hierarchical. System programs typically provide layers of functionality by placing commonly needed functions in lower level modules (programs) so that higher level programs may use and share the lower level modules when the services of the lower level modules are needed.

modularity, Linux. Linux is made up of many types of programs that are interrelated. Although each program may stand alone as a result of being modular, its true value is not apparent until it is seen interacting with other system programs.

monitor damage. The refresh rate paints the pixels across the CRT at a particular rate per second. Generally, a faster refresh rate is better for viewing comfort, but too fast will break the raster-scan circuit in the monitor.

monitor refresh rates, differences. The XF86Setup utility offers a range of approximate refresh frequencies only where exact and optimal refresh frequencies can be obtained from the "monitor" file.

monitor section. List possible graphic modes and the refresh rate for each graphic mode in the XF86Config file.

mount point. A directory where the file manager switches from the root file system (the hard disk) to another device, such as the CD-ROM or floppy diskette.

mounted CD-ROMs. A mounted CD-ROM cannot be removed from the drive since the eject button is disabled while the CD is mounted. CD-ROMs are mounted as read-only volumes, which means that a permission-refused error is returned (as opposed to device error) to the program that attempts to write on the CD-ROM.

mounted disks. You would want to mount a disk so that another application, such as WordPerfect, can directly access files on the device. Access to an unmounted disk is available through the mtools programs such as mread and mwrite. Accessing the disk with mtools, avoids the need for the mount and umount commands.

mounted volumes. Access to (physical) volumes is controlled by associating a given hard disk or one of its partitions with a (logical) directory name. Switching to that directory provides access to files within that volume.

mouse interfaces. The two common mouse interfaces are the PS/2 (/dev/psaux) and serial port (/dev/ttyS0).

mouse protocols. The two common protocols are Microsoft two-button and MouseSystems three-button.

multitasking. The ability to save the state of a program, select another program to run, restore the state, and run the selected program from the point where it was previously suspended.

multivolumes. Administrators often configure multiple volumes so that in the event of disk overflow, other key system programs are able to continue running.

named and unnamed volumes. Most OSs name each hard disk or hard disk partition and the name must be known by the user to access files. However, on a Unix-like OS there are no names for a given volume.

nenscript filter. Translates ASCII output into multipage PostScript format.

newusers. Adds passwords where the other programs will not, but it also encourages the system administrator to leave a plain-text list of passwords somewhere on the system.

nice command. Lowers the specified program's priority by increasing its priority number from 0 to 20.

odd controllers. Early CD-ROM drives were initially attached to a variety of sound cards. These types of controllers required a driver that can access a particular CD-ROM model through a particular type of sound card.

one-at-a-time configuration. This method of configuration is required because if cards with conflicting values were both installed, the CPU would be unable to communicate with either card. The power should be turned off so as not to damage the cards. Once one adapter is configured to a different parameter, the other may be installed.

online documentation. The Internet provides three types of online documentation. One type is made up of Linux repositories containing HOWTOs, FAQs, and some manuals on Linux components. The second type consists of news outlets for business and individuals as well as news groups. The third type of documentation results from information obtained from search engines such as Altavista, Hotbot, Yahoo, and Deja.

open source. Open source software usually refers to a software package that contains binary and source code that may be used, studied, and modified, but remains under the control of the license holder. Open source software carries the built-in cost of requiring expert knowledge with regard to administration of the software package. This term is used to describe the viewing of the source code, and not the distribution of the software. There are forms of open source software that do not permit code modification and restrict general viewing of the source code.

Open source free software makes some people nervous. Historically, many companies rely upon vendors to support their products. Typically, vendors offer a "no-charge" period of support called a warranty period. Linux has no such warranty period.

P switch. Permits selection of other printers besides the default name `lp`. Many times a remote printer is available, but access to the printer requires use of the `-P` switch.

password. A secret combination of letters and numbers used to verify the account owner.

PC 100 memory. Newer mainboards use high-speed memory (9–10 ns) that runs faster than traditional cache (20 ns) and, therefore, provide high-speed access throughout system memory.

permissions. Each file and its associated directory have access permissions based upon the concept of owner, group, and others. Access permissions are read, write, and execute. If the file is a directory, then the execute permission is interpreted as a search permission for the owner, group, or others.

port switching. This refers to the use of one of the console virtual terminals, the X Window System terminal windows, hardwired TTYs, or the network, to switch among logical terminals so that you can establish multiple login sessions using either the same account or a new account.

PostScript printers. PostScript is a middle-level language that describes the type of graphic images to be displayed on the printer; however, the printer must be able to translate the PostScript descriptions into pixels.

preemptive scheduling. The ability of the kernel to stop one program and lower its priority so that another program may run immediately.

primary and extended partitions. Only four primary partitions are allowed by the BIOS. If more are needed, then one of primary partitions is transformed into an extended partition and it contains the necessary additional logical partitions.

print filters. Print filters translate the content of files between two types of format.

printcap file, four key definitions. At a minimum, each printcap entry should describe the logical name of the printer, its spooling directory, its error report file, and, if required, a print filter.

printcap file, role. The printcap file describes the various printers that are directly connected to the local machine or to the network.

printcap server chaining. The remote machine field (rm) on one server may refer to a similar (rm) entry on another machine, allowing each machine in the chain to pass the print job on to the next link in the chain.

Priorities, message. Syslog messages are directed with the use of a facilities label indicating the type of daemon message (mail, Telnet, lpr, etc.), and the priority of the message (emergency, warning, debug, etc.).

private protocols. Some hardware vendors will not release the private data communication protocols that sit between the CPU and peripheral, thereby preventing others from writing device drivers for those devices. These newer devices tend to have less hardware and require the CPU to perform more detailed operations.

probing tradeoff. Probing is quick and easy; however, all features are usually not caught in the probe. Thus, manual specification in the XF86Config file will override the probe values and enable the extra features.

program assistance. Most Unix-like programs provide help information in response to one or more of three types of queries: "-?," "-h," or "--help."

ps command. Displays the number of processes activated by the user.

pseudo file system. A pseudo file system is an entity that looks like a directory but which really provides access to another kernel routine.

rc.d directory. Used by various distributions to hold the run level scripts.

Red Hat attributes. The most available, has an easy installation procedure, and X window configuration tools.

refresh rate. The higher the resolution, the faster the CRT must be refreshed. However, refresh rates are independent of a particular resolution.

refresh rate, tradeoff. The more graphic information displayed, the slower the monitor refresh rate. Refresh rates of 60 per second or less tend to cause eyestrain when viewing the CRT.

restricted account. The login process usually ends with a copy of the shell waiting for commands, but an account could be configured to run just one program. Termination of the program would also log the user out of the system.

run levels. A group of programs (shell scripts) run by the init program that determines the operating mode of the OS (i.e., single user, multi-user, etc). Two consistent run levels over various distributions are (a) run level 0—system shut down and (b) run level 6—bring up the system.

run levels, types of. (1) single-user (shell) at the console; (2) multi-user with networking; (3) multi-user with networking and GUI.

screen section. Lists which graphic modes the X server should try to support (assuming the video adapter has the capability) and the size of the virtual desktop.

scripts. Made up of one or more shell commands located in a file. Syntax differs among shells, but all scripts have flow control constructs.

shell interactivity. The shell provides command history and command completion. Command history displays and redisplays previous commands. Command-completion completes the directory name, file name, or command name when the <Tab> key is pressed.

shepherding software. The GPL revolutionizes thinking about software by changing it from protectionist to shepherding perspective. Software is distributed without control mechanisms, yet the software creator will watch the news groups to coordinate and otherwise mentor the software while it grows and matures in the hands of many.

spool directory. A spool directory separates the request from the action and allows the user the option to delete a file after the print request has been issued but before the printing has taken place.

Stallman, Richard. Invented the idea of using copyright to protect software from being controlled by any one person, group, or company.

STAT column, ps command. Shows the state of each process. The process could be sleeping, swapped, or running.

superuser. Any user account that has the value of 0 as the UID. If the user account UID is 0, then the file manager does not enforce permissions before performing the requested action.

SuSE attributes. It is the most complete, provides all software on six CDs, and has a robust and easy-to-use configuration tool called YaST and an X11 configuration tool called SaX.

swap drives. Linux uses separate partitions as swap devices to improve the speed at which programs move between the hard disk and main memory (RAM). The disadvantage of swap devices is that once allocated, the swap storage cannot be used for files.

syslog daemon. Since background programs do not have a controlling terminal to report to, they send their status messages to a centralized dispatcher called `syslog`.

tkman utility. Offers a true GUI front-end to the man pages. Offers significant improvement over man by displaying the table of contents for each man section. Also provides for detailed regular expression searches within manual pages.

TTY column, ps command. The TTY column shows which console, direct-connect terminal, or network connection the user is logged into.

UID. When looking up a name for an account, the first matching UID is used. This means that if two users have the same UID, the system programs will show that the first name listed in the `passwd` file is said to own the file.

user account. Defines the files that a user owns and what access the user may have to other files. To use Linux, you must enter through an existing user account that has been set up by the system administrator. When set up by the superuser, the user account associates an ID with file ownership and establishes permissions to access files owned by other accounts.

useradd. Creates new accounts and requires superuser status; `useradd` has a companion program `userdel`, and has a different configuration file from `adduser`.

vendor floppy. Most adapters come with a floppy that has diagnostic and configuration programs. Simply boot the machine with an MS-DOS floppy and run the configuration program directly from the vendor floppy to configure an adapter.

video controller. Reads data from video memory and, based upon its mode, provides a scan rate to the digital-to-analog converter for display on the monitor.

video memory. Accepts data from the CPU and offers access to the video controller. Data is arranged in video memory according to the current graphic mode.

virtual desktop. X11 provides an extra level of control by offering multiple windows on a desktop and multiple virtual desktops that are larger than the screen.

volumes. Partitions seen from the perspective of the OS. A volume could be an entire hard disk, a hard disk partition, or a logical partition within an extended partition.

w command. Provides a summary of the system state, on which terminals users are logged in, and from which network host they logged in. The w command also provides more of an overview of the system performance than the who command.

who command. Displays a list of logged in users and on which terminals they logged in.

WYSIWYG. "What You See Is What You Get." In word processing programs, the text is displayed as it is entered. Files contain binary control characters that allow only the word processor to access the text document.

X file. A symbolic link to an instance of the X server that matches the video adapter.

X server. The video driver for the X11 system. It accepts logical commands from the window manager and transforms these requests into the screen display commands.

X11 architecture, five components. X server, widget library, themes, window manager, GUI applications.

X11 configuration files. Found in /etc/X11 on newer distributions; otherwise found in /usr/local/X11R6.

X11 programs. Usually found in /usr/X11R6/bin.

Xconfigurator. Found only on Red Hat systems, and it does not include mouse configuration. A separate utility, mouseconfig, must be used to set up the mouse.

xdm. Presents a graphic login screen, runs the login program, and starts the X server and window manager.

XF86_VGA16. The "lowest common denominator" video driver. Although it works with all adapters, its low, 640x480 16-color resolution is not acceptable for typical GUI applications.

xf86config, tradeoff. Generally, users do not like this command-line version for X configuration. There are many pages of text, lists of items to read, and items identified by their numbered position within a list. On the other hand, this program reads an external file for the list of available X servers, so it tends to be more up-to-date than many GUI configuration tools.

xf86config.eg file. Provides a template of sections that can be configured for system specific options, including the mouse, video adapter, and monitor.

XF86Setup, tradeoff. GUI setup tool and found on most distributions. Not the easiest configuration utility, but generally available for quick re-configuration.

xinfo utility. X windows version of info; essentially the same program as info. A menu bar was added to `xinfo`, but its buttons change position depending upon which level of the hierarchy the program is visiting.

xman utility. X windows version of man. Offers significant improvement over man by displaying the table of contents for each man section.

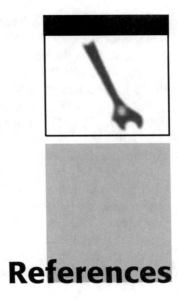

References

Blair, J., Samba, *Integrating UNIX and Windows*, Specialized System Consultants, Inc., 1998, ISBN 1-57831-006-7

Carling, M., S. Degler, & J. Dennis, *Linux System Administration*, New Riders Publishing, 2000, ISBN 0-56205-934-3

Frisch, A., *Essential System Administration*, 2nd ed., O'Reilly & Associates, 1995, ISBN 1-56592-127-5

Garfinkel, S. & G. Spafford, *Practical Unix & Internet Security*, 2nd ed., O'Reilly & Associates, 1976, ISBN 1-56592-148-8

Hunt, C., *TCP/IP Network Administration*, 2nd ed., O'Reilly & Associates, 1997, ISBN 1-56592-322-7

Kiesling, R., ed., *Linux Encyclopedia: The Complete Linux Guide* (Hardcopy HOWTOs), 6th ed., Workgroup Solutions, Inc., 1998, ISBN 0-9644309-2-4

Kirch, O., *Linux Network Administrator's Guide*, O'Reilly and Associates, 1995, ISBN 1-56592-087-2

Kofler, M., *LINUX: Installation, Configuration, and Use*, 2nd., Addison-Wesley Publishing, 1999, ISBN 0-201-59628-8

Martinez, Anne, *Get Certified and Get Ahead: Millenium Edition*, McGraw-Hill, 1999, ISBN 0-07-134781-X

Michael, K., *LINUX: Installation, Configuration, and Use*, 2nd ed., Addison-Wesley Publishing, 1999, ISBN 0-201-59628-8

Mui, L. & E. Pearce, *Volume 8: X Window System Administrator's Guide*, O'Reilly & Associates, 1992, ISBN 0-937175-83-8

Northcut, S., *Network Intrusion Detection: An Analyst's Handbook*, New Riders Publishing, 1999, ISBN 1-7357-0868-1

Peek, J., T. O'Reilly, & M. Loukides, *Unix Power Tools*, 2nd ed., O'Reilly and Associates, 1997, ISBN 1-56592-260-3

Sobell, M. G., *A Practical Guide to Linux*, Addison-Wesley, 1997, ISBN 0-201-89549-8

Volkerding, P., K. Reichard, & E. Foster-Johnson, *Linux Configuration and Installation*, 4th ed., M&T Books, 1998, ISBN 0-7645-7005-6

Wall, L., T. Christiansen, & R Schwartz, *Programming Perl*, 2nd ed., O'Reilly and Associates, 1996, ISBN 1-56592-149-X

Wells, N., D. Taylor, *Star Office for Linux*, Sam's Teach Yourself in 24 Hours Series, 1999, ISBN 0-672-31412-6

Welsh, M., K. Dalheimer, & L. Kaufman, *Running Linux*, 3rd ed., O'Reilly and Associates, 1999, ISBN 1-56592-469-X

Index